MUHAMMAD AND JESUS

MUHAMMAD

AND

JESUS

A Comparison of the Prophets
and Their Teachings

WILLIAM E. PHIPPS

CONTINUUM • NEW YORK

1999

The Continuum Publishing Company
370 Lexington Avenue
New York, NY 10017

Printed in the United States of America

Library of Congress Cataloging-in-Publication Data
Phipps, William E.
Muhammad and Jesus : a comparison of the prophets and their teachings /
William E. Phipps.
p.   cm.
Includes bibliographical references (p.247) and indexes.
ISBN 0-8264-1207-6 (paperback : alk. paper)
1. Muhammad, Prophet, d. 632.   2. Jesus Christ.   3. Islam—
Relations—Christianity.   4. Christianity and other religions—
Islam.   I. Title.
BP75.P45   1999
297;.63—dc20   94-36176
                                                                CIP

ACKNOWLEDGMENTS

Quotations from the Quran have been derived from a number of English "interpretations." Quotations from the Bible are usually my own translation, but indebtedness to a variety of versions can be found.

To Charles Mason Swezey,
Dean of Union Theological Seminary in Virginia
and a steadfast walker in the strenuous way of the prophets. Charley encouraged me
to become a Research Fellow at my alma mater during a sabbatical from Davis
and Elkins College. This study was initiated in the nurturing and
stimulating Richmond environment.

CONTENTS

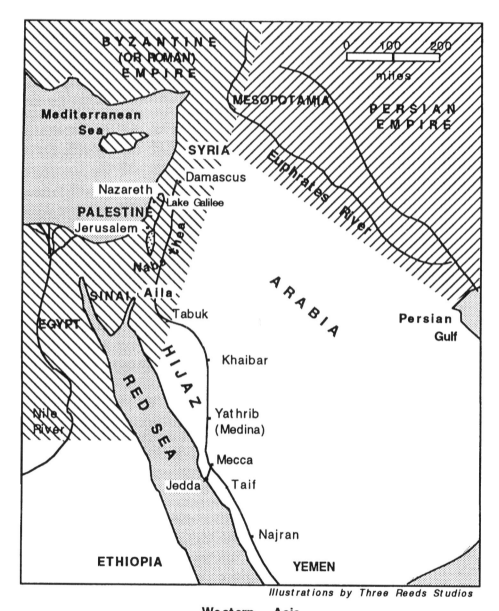

Western Asia

Featuring places of importance for understanding Muhammad and Jesus

Illustrations by Three Reeds Studios

CHAPTER ONE

INTRODUCTION

Jesus and Muhammad have been held in high respect, if not revered, by the billions who have belonged to the religions they founded. Although both men thought of themselves as spokespersons of the same God, little attention has been given to their similarities and differences. A Quranic verse in which Jesus is commended encourages a comparison of the two prophets. God declares: "We have made some messengers to excel over others. To some God spoke directly; others He raised to a lofty status."[1] According to the Quran, Muhammad and Jesus are both revealers and servants of God.

In spite of these similarities, a comparison of the two men is somewhat uneven in the eyes of Muslims and Christians. Muslims regard the Quran as God's inlibraration, that is, as the divine Word becoming a book; Christians regard Jesus as God's incarnation, that is, the divine Word becoming a flesh-and-blood person. Thus, heavy attention will be given to comparing the revelation in the Quran with the life and teachings of Jesus.

This study is an attempt to further frank discussion between branches of a family that have shared the common Semitic culture of western Asia. Muhammad and Jesus belonged to a people who traced their ancestry to Abraham. According to Genesis, that nomadic patriarch is an outstanding Semite, that is, a descendant from Noah's son Shem.[2]

Misunderstandings abound in the religions Abraham sired. The child, Islam, has learned more from its parents, Judaism and Christianity, than the parents have learned from the child. The interaction between family members has been largely a history of polemics, but there are signs that more constructive communication will take place in the next millennium. In accord with the dominant contemporary approach of scholars, I will attempt to give a sympathetic and judicious comparison of the prophets Jesus and Muhammad. The history of the religions that followed in their wake will be a secondary consideration.

Respect for Jesus among Muslims has generally been high because the Quran acknowledges the genuineness of Jesus. The Arabic scripture consistently treats him in a positive manner, ascribing to him not only the high office of prophet (*nabi*)[3] but also the highest human office of messenger or apostle (*rasul*).[4] "Seal of Sanctity" is a title given to Jesus in the Islamic tradition because he is recognized as displaying holiness to a superlative degree. Some sayings attributed to Jesus in that tradition mesh with those in the Gospels.[5] Prince Bandar, ambassador to the United States from Saudi Arabia, sent out a Christmas card on which he quoted from the Quran—in Arabic and in English—this verse: "Behold, the angels said, 'O Mary, God giveth thee glad tidings of a Word from him; his name will be Christ Jesus, the son of Mary.' "[6]

Muhammad Denigrated

Reciprocal generous appreciations of Muhammad by non-Muslims are hard to find. In religion as in politics, vilifying a rival leader is a sleazy but often effective way of promoting one's own favorite. Montgomery Watt, who is both an Episcopalian and a widely respected contemporary biographer of Muhammad, notes:

> None of the great figures of history is so poorly appreciated in the West as Muhammad. Western writers have mostly been prone to believe the worst of Muhammad, and, wherever an objectionable interpretation of an act seemed plausible, have tended to accept it as fact.[7]

Even before the rise of Islam, prejudice was rampant in Judaism and in Christianity against the Arabs. They were recognized as descendants of Abraham by Hagar, one of his concubines from another culture. Rabbis discussed what Abraham must have thought of the children he produced by those slaves. Genesis states that he gave them gifts and sent them to "the east country."[8] The gifts were judged in the Talmud to be sorcery and demonology.[9] According to a rabbinic midrash, the Ishmaelites had nine tenths of all the world's stupidity.[10]

The only New Testament mention of either Hagar or her son Ishmael is by Paul. Displaying his Jewish upbringing, the apostle writes:

> Just as at that time, the child who was born according to the flesh persecuted the one who was born according to the Spirit, so it is now. What does the Scripture say? "Drive out the slave and her child; for the slave's child will not share the inheritance with the freewoman's child."[11]

In this passage, Paul paraphrases those words of jealous Sarah, the wife of Abraham, as though they are God's declaration.

The Arabs were generally unnoticed by the leaders of early Christianity and when mentioned, they were usually treated harshly. Sozomen, a church historian of the fifth century, comments on "Saracens," the common Roman name for the Arabs: "To avoid the charge of bastardy and the low birth of the mother of Ishmael, the Arabs called themselves 'Sara-cens' as if descended from Abraham's wife Sarah."[12]

For more than half of church history, the adversary that Christians have most loved to hate has been Islam. The cultural superiority of Islam during the first millennium after its rise was not appreciated. While Christianity was in its "Dark Age," arts and sciences were flourishing in Muslim states.[13] To compensate for inferiority anxieties, Christians often reveled in spreading crass distortions. Libel toward Muhammad has been common in Eastern Orthodoxy, in Roman Catholicism, and in Protestantism.

A famous Christian monk who lived in the early Muslim culture evaluated the rival religion in a way that has become typical. John of Damascus was aware of Muhammad because his parents were involved in the Muslim government of the Syrian city during the seventh century. John smeared Muhammad in this way:

> A false prophet appeared among them, surnamed Mameth, who, having casually been exposed to the Old and the New Testaments and supposedly encountered an Arian monk,

formed a heresy of his own. And after, by pretense, he man-
aged to make the people think of him as a God-fearing fellow,
he spread rumors that a Scripture was brought down to him
from heaven. Thus, having drafted some pronouncements in
his book, worthy of laughter, he handed it down to them in
order that they might comply with it.[14]

John's view of Muhammad as a hypocritical heretic was widely
accepted by subsequent Christians.

Theophanes, another eighth-century Byzantine monk, wrote:

When he (Muhammad) went to Palestine he lived with both
Jews and Christians, and hunted for certain writings among
them. He had an epileptic seizure, and when his wife noticed
this she became very distressed, for she was noble and had
now been joined to a man who was not only helpless but
epileptic as well.[15]

Theophanes's treatment of Muhammad as a mentally diseased person has been popular in Europe over the centuries.

The medieval Crusades stimulated shrill denigrations of Muhammad in Europe and interrupted centuries of peaceful coexistence among
Jews, Christians, and Muslims in Jerusalem. Crusader values are expressed in the French epic masterpiece, *Song of Roland*. Muhammad is
treated as an idol that the enemy worship:

> *On the loftiest turret they raise Mahound:*
> *Before him the pagans bend and pray.*[16]

The victorious Franks allegedly destroyed images of Muhammad
when they plundered mosques.[17]

Peter the Venerable, a twelfth-century abbot of Cluny, provided
Latin Christianity with the notion of Muhammad as a pseudo-prophet.
After visiting in Moorish Spain, Peter brought back this report to
France:

Muhammad, instructed by the best Jewish and heretical doc-
tors, produced his Quran and wove together, in that barba-
rous fashion of his, a diabolical scripture, put together both
from the Jewish fables and the trifling songs of heretics. Lying

that this collection was brought to him chapter by chapter by Gabriel, whose name he already knew from sacred Scripture, he poisoned with a deadly poison that people that did not know God.[18]

Thomas Aquinas, the magisterial Catholic theologian, relied on Peter of Cluny for much of his knowledge of Islam.[19] Biased by his own vow of celibacy, Aquinas wrote that Muhammad "seduced the people by promises of carnal pleasure to which the concupiscence of the flesh goads us."[20] Aquinas responded to Muhammad's teachings with this diatribe:

> The truths that he taught he mingled with many fables and with doctrine of the greatest falsity. . . . Those who believed in him were brutal men and desert wanderers, utterly ignorant of all divine teaching, through whose numbers Muhammad forced others to become his followers by the violence of his arms.[21]

Dante Alighieri, who lived in the thirteenth century a generation after Aquinas, was heavily influenced by him. The stellar Italian poet tells of Muhammad being convicted of being a *"seminator di scandalo e di scisma"* on Judgment Day. Being destructive to Christian unity as a scandal and schism disseminator, Muhammad is consigned to the ninth level of the *Inferno*. There he receives everlastingly some of the worst punishment that hell has to offer. A gash from throat to anus causes his intestines to hang between his legs. Many of the damned are so horrified by the mutilated Muhammad spectacle that they forget momentarily their own torment.[22] Ironically, much of the form of Dante's poem was inspired by Muslims who wrote imaginatively of Muhammad's visit to realms beyond the earth.[23] Dante probably used a Latin translation that had been made in Italy of that alleged visit.[24]

Muhammad ranked high among the people Martin Luther liked to denounce. No Catholic has ever matched the slander hurled out by that prime Protestant. Luther identified Muhammad with the warring horses of the Book of Revelation that bring great destruction to Christians.[25] Here is a sampling of Luther's invective against Muhammad: "Should you be called a prophet, who are such an uncouth blockhead and ass?"[26]; "When the spirit of lies had taken possession of Mohammed, and the devil had murdered men's souls with his Koran and had destroyed the faith of Christians, he had to go on and take the sword and set about to murder their bodies."[27]; And "We are fighting that the Turk may not put his devilish filth and the blasphemous Muhammad in the place of our dear Lord, Jesus Christ."[28]

Luther's Muhammad is also a voluptuary with the sexual potency of a ram, but he has done less harm to the Church than the Roman pontiff.[29] "The coarse and filthy Muhammad takes all women and therefore has no wife," but the Pope is more immoral because he pretends to be virginal yet is promiscuous.[30]

There has been a widespread legend in Europe that pilgrims are attracted to Muhammad's hometown to gawk at his body suspended in air by lodestone trickery. Stories such as this prompted Ludovico de Varthema, an Italian contemporary of Luther, to visit Arabia. In the first description of Mecca by a European, de Varthema refutes the magnet tale, in part because Muhammad was not buried in the region of Mecca.[31] In spite of countless millions of pilgrims who have visited the place where Muhammad's body was buried at Medina, the nonsense about it hovering "twixt heaven and earth" has continued to entertain Westerners.

In England, there was a widely accepted story that Muhammad had faked divine inspiration by training a white dove to pick grains from his ear while sitting on his shoulder.[32] Through this trick, he is said to have convinced the dumb Arabians that the Holy Spirit was dictating to him. Aware of that story, Shakespeare has a French prince say to Joan of Arc:

> *Was Mahomet inspired by a dove?*
> *Thou with an eagle art inspired then.*[33]

However, a dove is not a Muslim symbol for the Spirit of God, so the story must have originated with someone aware of the story of Jesus' baptism.

For Francis Bacon, another Elizabethan writer, Muhammad was a bungling miraclemonger. A saying attributed to the prophet that has gained proverbial status among English-speaking people may have been inspired by these comments by Bacon:

Mahomet made the people believe that he would call a hill to him, and from the top of it offer up his prayers for the observers of his law. The people assembled. Mahomet called the hill to come to him again and again; and when the hill stood still he was never a whit abashed, but said, "If the hill will not come to Mahomet, Mahomet will go to the hill."[34]

Voltaire, one of the most famous French authors of the eighteenth century, wrote a tragedy about Muhammad. In the conclusion, the dying prophet acknowledges that he has committed crimes. While asking Umar, his associate, to whitewash his record, he confesses, "I have deceived mankind . . . for Mahomet depends on fraud alone."[35] That drama, which church leaders in Paris protested, is primarily a satire on Catholic priests. When Voltaire later made nonfictional comments about Muhammad, he was much more restrained. Responding to the popular misunderstanding of the prophet, he pointed out that the Quran does not say anything about a supernatural "journey into the sky."[36] Also, Voltaire informed those who charged Muhammad's religion with gross sensuality that it involves daytime fasting throughout a month every year, abstaining completely from wine, and giving a significant percentage of one's income to aid the poor.[37]

British missionary Sigismund Koelle expressed a view of Muhammad that was all too typical in the nineteenth century. At the conclusion of his lengthy biography, Koelle writes: "Mohammed was diametrically opposed to Christ, both in his religious teaching and in his practical aims. . . . Islam historically proved itself anti-Christian, because Mohammed personally was an Antichrist."[38]

A sampling from the early twentieth century displays little change in the Christian outlook on Muhammad. Samuel Zwemer, professor of missions at Princeton Seminary, warned his Victorian readers that the subject of Muhammad's relations with women should be "shrouded from decent eyes because of the brutality and coarseness of its character."[39] Duncan Macdonald was a pioneer in interfaith dialogue, and the Macdonald Center for the Study of Islam and Christian-Muslim Relations was named in his honor at Hartford Seminary. Although he aimed at assessing Islam honestly, he evaluated Muhammad in this demeaning way: "He was a pathological case. His revelations came to him in a trance and, like all trance-mediums, he had strangely perverted ideas. . . . He forged the awful machinery of divine inspiration to serve his own ignoble and selfish purposes."[40]

American contempt for Muhammad surfaced again in the late twentieth century, and was intensified by the conflict between the United States and some of the Middle Eastern states. Marius Baar, a fundamentalist Christian missionary to the Muslims, published a diatribe against Muhammad. Not only does Baar allege Muhammad to be "the antichrist" and "a follower of the devil," but he also claims that "Allah is a counterfeit of God."[41] Syndicated columnist Paul Harvey, relying on the bigotry of evangelist John Haggai, stated that "the historic savagery" of Islam is due to its "poison roots."[42] Harvey asserted that Muhammad became personally wealthy by exploiting his enemies and that there is no mention of love anywhere in the Quran.[43]

Salman Rushdie, in spite of his Muslim background, has written an infamous novel that offends many with religious sensitivities.[44] *The Satanic Verses* represents Muhammad as a lecher, and prostitutes are named after his wives. The *Oxford English Dictionary* indicates that Mahound, the name Rushdie gives the prophet, has been used in medieval and modern times to lambaste monsters, false gods, and Muhammad. For example, poet Robert Burns describes Satan in this way: "The De'il cam fiddling thro' the town. . . . Auld Mahoun . . ."[45]

Lack of concern to understand and anxiety over a potential threat are common threads found in most of the judgments by those who have found Muhammad repulsive. Even after understanding, non-Muslims will likely retain points of disagreement with Muhammad. But with the emotional contempt removed, an appreciation can arise and points of agreement may be recognized.

Muhammad Appreciated

To prevent the erroneous idea that no one in Christendom has had a kind word for Muhammad, other voices should be heard. Timothy, a Nestorian Christian and an eighth-century patriarch of the Assyrian Church, stated:

> Muhammad is "worthy of all praise" and "walked in the path of the prophets" because he taught the unity of God. He taught the way of good works; he opposed idolatry and polytheism; he taught about God, his Word, and his Spirit; he showed his zeal by fighting against idolatry with the sword; like Abraham he left his kinfolk rather than worship idols.[46]

George Sale became the earliest Westerner to rise above bigotry toward Muhammad when he translated the Quran into English from Arabic for the first time. That 1734 work, along with his clarifying notes, fulfilled his intention of giving "the original impartial justice."[47] Sale, a Protestant lawyer, writes in his introduction: "Mohammed gave his Arabs the best religion he could, as well as the best laws; preferable, at least, to those of the ancient pagan lawgivers."[48] Responding to Islam-bashers, Sale asserted that they deceive themselves if they imagine this religion was propagated by the sword alone."[49] For two centuries, Sale's work was the best single source in English for the study of Islam.

Later in the eighteenth century, distinguished historian Edward Gibbon gave a balanced treatment of Muhammad's character. Gibbon recognized that Muhammad was "endowed with a pious and contemplative disposition" and that he "despised the pomp of royalty."[50] Gibbon thought that Europeans who stress the prophet's amorous activities have "maliciously exaggerated the frailties of Mohammed."[51]

Thomas Carlyle, another outstanding English writer, became famous for his theory that "the history of the world is but the biography of great men."[52] He discovered Muhammad to have been a sincere leader after approaching him in this positive manner: "I mean to say all the good of him I justly can."[53] Carlyle rejected the characteristic European outlook of the preceding millennium, that Muhammad was "a scheming impostor."[54] While laudatory toward the founder of Islam, Carlyle's appreciation did not carry over to the style of the Quran as he read it in English. He confessed: "It is as toilsome reading as I ever undertook, a wearisome confused jumble."[55]

Writing at the time of Carlyle in the nineteenth century, European historian Johann Doellinger asserted: "No other mortal has ever, from the beginning of the world, exercised such an immeasurable influence upon the religious, moral, and political relations of mankind, as has the Arab Muhammad."[56]

In the twentieth century, non-Muslim scholars have increasingly acknowledged the greatness of Muhammad. For five decades Anglican bishop Kenneth Cragg has been writing books to publicize the admirable qualities of Islam and has translated selections from Arabic religious literature. He states: "Muhammad, as Prophet, was unique, final, irrepeatable. . . . The Quran is the final evidence of the Divine origin of the Prophet's mission. Its Arabic eloquence is indicative of its source in God."[57]

Franciscan missionary Guilio Basetti-Sani offers this positive judgment:

> Mohammad, seen from the perspective of a thorough study of the Quran, emerges as one of the great religious souls of non-Christian mankind. . . . He introduced his people, the sons of Ishmael, to faith in the God of Abraham, thus fulfilling the ancient promise of God to Abraham of a special blessing for the son of the slave girl Agar and her offspring. . . . Though he declared that he was neither a saint nor an intercessor, he was nevertheless a witness, the herald of God's judgments.[58]

Bassetti-Sani is aware that the Bible contains this promise to Abraham: "As for Ishmael, I have heard you; I will bless him . . . and make him a great nation."[59] According to Muslim tradition, Muhammad is a descendant of Hagar's grandson Nebaioth (or Nabit).

Alfred Guillaume, the English translator of the most important Arabic biographical sources on the prophet, writes: "Trustworthy tradition depicts a man of amazing ability in winning men's hearts by persuasion and in coercing and disarming his opponents. . . . He stands out as one of the great figures of history."[60]

Historian Will Durant likewise concludes his treatment of Muhammad with this tribute:

> If we judge greatness by influence, he was one of the giants of history. He undertook to raise the spiritual and moral level of a people harassed into barbarism by heat and foodless wastes, and he succeeded more completely than any other reformer; seldom has any man so fully realized his dream. . . . When he began, Arabia was a desert flotsam of idolatrous tribes; when he died it was a nation.[61]

Michael Hart, a contemporary American scientist, offers a similar estimate of Muhammad's impact. Hart ranks the three most influential persons in history in this order: Muhammad, Isaac Newton, and Jesus. Hart places Muhammad at the top of his list of one hundred humans because he was "the only man in history who was supremely successful on both the religious and secular levels."[62] Within a century, his followers controlled the largest empire in human history.[63]

Reasons for This Study

For international understanding, Christianity and Islam are the most important religions to study. They are, by far, the two largest religions of the world, with adherents numbering approximately half of the global population.[64] Moreover, these religions, now both nonwhite by majority, are showing the greatest growth. Areas in which Islam predominates comprise a wide band of generally arid land above the equator from West Africa to Southeast Asia. In addition, there are many millions of non-Arabic Muslims in the temperate zones of China and Russia. Arabs comprise only 15 percent of the Muslim population.

While western Asia is the birthplace of both Islam and Christianity, the largest concentrations of both religions are far removed from that area. The largest Muslim country is Indonesia, and there are more Christians in the United States than in any other nation. This shows how both religions have been successful in missionary expansion. Both have schisms, but the majority belong to one group: the Muslims are 83 percent Sunnis, and the Christians are 57 percent Roman Catholics.

Muslims were among the earlier arrivals from the Eastern to the Western Hemisphere. They came as Arabic-speaking slaves from Africa, but they were not permitted to practice their religion. The last wave of Muslim immigrants has principally consisted of skilled professionals and students from Asian countries. The Nation of Islam, usually called the Black Muslims, is growing in the United States, due especially to the influence of civil-rights leader Malcolm X. In the twenty-first century, Islam will expand beyond the current several million followers in North America to become the continent's second largest religion, even as it already is in Europe. There are now more Muslims in Europe than there are Jews in the world. Islam is recovering the significance it had in Europe from the ninth to the fifteenth centuries. Ethnic conflicts in the former Soviet Union and Yugoslavia have made Westerners more aware of Muslims in Azerbaijan and Bosnia. What had been thought of as a "third world" religion is rapidly becoming a major force in the "first world."

Studies of history in the West tend to be provincial, giving scant attention to Muhammad and to the sweep of his followers through several continents. Westerners should realize their own vested economic and political interests, if not humanitarian ones, in developing a broader understanding of Islamic culture. Petropolitics, the Iran-Iraq conflict, the Israeli-Palestinian turmoil, and religious-based global terrorism have become sources of a continuing series of crises facing many governments.

Aside from demographics and other secular considerations, important intrinsic reasons for this quest exist. Most of those who have followed the Christian or Muslim religions are convinced that their allegiances have made their lives more worth living. The ideals they have pursued have generally made human civilizations grander, and their caring communities have usually provided individual security and dignity.

Much of the uniqueness of Islam and Christianity is in the character of the founders. I have written this book because I believe that a comparison of Muhammad and Jesus can promote understandings between often warring cultures. For decades my primary interest has been the earliest traditions of Jesus, resulting most recently in my book entitled *The Wisdom and Wit of Rabbi Jesus*. Analyzing now the historical Muhammad seems most appropriate, with the aim of comparing the founders of the two youngest world religions. Although objective records on both of these charismatic leaders are unattainable, it is possible to learn much by weighing biased reports of the prophets' followers. As difficult as it is to ascertain the reliability of biographical information about Jesus in the Gospels, it is even more difficult to discover what is authentic in the lore about Muhammad. The Quran provides very little data for reconstructing his life, and the stories recorded about him are much further removed in time from the original eyewitnesses than what is contained about Jesus in the Gospels.[65] While there are legendary elements in the story of Jesus, the predominant view of recent scholars engaged in research on the historical Jesus maintains that much genuine information about his life and even more about his teachings exists.[66]

In spite of Jesus belonging to the ancient era, there is more historical data for understanding his milieu than for that of Muhammad. Information about his Palestinian culture comes from a variety of sources that are independent of Christian records. In addition to the Dead Sea Scrolls and other archaeological discoveries from the Roman era in Palestine, there are the Jewish histories of Josephus and writings that compose what has been called "The Old Testament Pseudepigrapha." For Muhammad there is some non-Muslim Arabic poetry that provides only a little information about his cultural background.

In my latest pursuit I have been especially assisted by the Center for the Study of Islam in Hartford, Connecticut. Housed there is the earliest and most extensive library in America for probing the relationship between Christianity and Islam. Librarian Edna Madden was most helpful during the period when I engaged in research there. I am also especially appreciative to Professor Emeritus Willem Bijlefeld, the Distinguished Professor of Islamic Studies at Hartford Seminary and former editor of *The Muslim World*. He critically examined a draft of this study and shared with me some of the wisdom he has acquired during his long search for improving interfaith dialogue.

For investigating Islam, as well as Christianity, an abundance of scholarly sources is now readily available for those who work mainly with writings in English. In particular, an English concordance to the Quran and many translations of that scripture have simplified my research.[67] Also, most of the early accounts of Muhammad have now been translated into English.[68] Ishaq (more correctly, Ibn Ishaq), who wrote the earliest biography, has provided historians with the most authoritative non-Quranic source. That eighth-century native of Medina carefully recorded the names of those who provided him with information about Muhammad, so the amount of fabrication is probably slight. Regarding Muhammad's teachings, the most authentic collection (*sahih*) is by Al-Bukhari, who in the ninth century scrupulously collected Muhammad's sayings and actions (*hadith*). He proved their genuineness by citing the chain of transmission over the first two centuries of Islam. Al-Bukhari frequently records several versions of a particular *hadith* as conveyed by different individuals. The *hadith* of al-Bukhari and other authorities are collected in Tabrizi's fourteenth-century *Mishkat Al-Masabih*. I have searched through the thousands of *hadith* that are regarded as authentic in order to gather representative sayings of Muhammad on many topics.

Excellent separate modern studies have been made of Muhammad and Jesus by persons with divergent viewpoints. For example, Fazlur Rahman, a Pakistani Muslim, and Hans Kung, a German Catholic, provide insightful treatments.[69] Karen Armstrong and Marcus Borg have written separate adoring accounts of the two prophets.[70] Surprisingly though, there is a paucity of attempts to compare their lives and teachings. Two generations ago, an Indian Muslim made a comparison that found little merit in the Christian interpretation of Jesus.[71] In the past generation, German scholar Claus Schedl published a monograph on interpretations of Jesus in the Quran.[72]

Spiritual values are less important to French scholar Maxime

Rodinson, who begins an important biography of Muhammad by acknowledging his atheism. Rodinson recognizes that an examination of
legends clustering around either Muhammad and Jesus provides valuable data on charisma. He concludes his study in this way:

> We know very little for certain about this man whose ideas
> and actions have shaken the world, but, as with Jesus, we may
> get, through the unreliable tales and one-sided traditions, a
> glimpse of something that is the echo of a remarkable per-
> sonality which astonished the ordinary men who gathered
> around it.[73]

Philosopher Friedrich Nietzsche, another atheist, provided profound insights into the commitments of Jesus.[74] The outlook on religion
of any scholar colors their interpretations, but those differences provide
a kaleidoscopic delight to the subject being examined.

John Calvin originated the interpretive community to which I
belong. His philosophy of religion has been defined in this way: "Cal-
vinistic thought is a system in which God is made the center of all that is
and happens, God's will pervading human and cosmic events, and upon
whom man is utterly and cheerfully dependent."[75] Along with Presby-
terian children over the past several centuries, I was taught this prime
doctrine: "Man's chief end is to glorify God and to enjoy him forever."[76]
As will become apparent, there is much in common between my religious tradition and Islam. Calvin encouraged openness to traditions
apart from Christianity because he recognized that God's truth cannot
be limited to one religion.[77] That sixteenth-century Protestant reformer
was devoted to the notion that a rational study of human cultures could
dissipate the narrowminded zealots that arise in religions. One of his
legacies is the liberal-arts college he began in Geneva, which became
the forerunner of Harvard, Princeton, Davidson (where I studied), Davis
and Elkins (where I teach), and a host of other academic institutions.

Goethe's aphorism is apropos: "He who is ignorant of foreign
languages, knows little of his own."[78] To paraphrase: Those who know
only their own religion, know little even of that. One of the best results
that can be derived from studying either foreign languages or other
religions is more awareness of the strengths and weaknesses of one's
own. Those who study the religions of other cultures not only broaden
their understanding of what others cherish, but also comprehend their
own faith more fully. One's religion is also like one's language in that, for

most people, neither is a matter of childhood choice. Because people inculcate a particular type of each before they are self-conscious, it is easy to err from childhood onward in presuming that all sensible people speak their tongue and have the same religious views.

Plutarch's study of parallel lives shows that comparisons are instructional and help sharpen one's understanding of both personalities. Also, it is good pedagogy to compare what is relatively better known with what is lesser known. An attempt will be made in this dual biography to follow the historical evidence where it leads, even though a critical examination of some aspects of the two prophets' life stories may be painful.

Those on opposite ends of the religious spectrum may find the historical approach pursued here disturbing. "Modernists" in Christianity and Islam may not like what the early traditions about Jesus and Muhammad contain. For example, the current easy acceptance of impermanent marriages by most Christians prompts some to overlook Jesus' teaching that persons who remarry after divorce are committing adultery.[79] Also, those with ecumenical commitments realize that world peace may not be promoted by writing honestly about the warrior aspects of Muhammad's career. Eager to have respected religious figures from earlier eras conform to contemporary notions of political and social correctness, they tend to discuss only timely features of the lives of Muhammad and Jesus. Historical accuracy is sometimes muted on the false assumption that harmonious interaction among participants in the global community can occur without confronting past antagonisms.

"Fundamentalists" in Christianity and Islam may find the scholarly approach to evoke both disgust and delight. The members of each group examine their different "infallible" scriptures in a selective manner, treating literally those texts that support their glorified image of God's superlative mouthpiece while disregarding or allegorizing those texts that might tarnish that image. Both Fundamentalist types abhor interpretations that do not conform with their inflexible views of "the only true religion" and relish unflattering treatments of other religions.

Having commented negatively about religious groups on the far right, I should acknowledge a common interest. We recognize that secularism is shallow, and we believe that humans need to return to their religious roots to find identity and basic values. The secular humanist does not acknowledge that one of the better ways of defining our species may be this: humans are worshiping animals. However, intolerance need not accompany a conviction that there is a dimension of existence that transcends the physical; religious commitment and freedom can be companions.

There is a reason for naming Muhammad first in the title of this book. Assuming that Western readers have some knowledge of Jesus and his homeland, I direct more attention toward the lesser-known prophet. Most chapters begin with Muhammad, and then germane comparisons are selected from the life, times, and teachings of Jesus. Some facets of the latter are not introduced if parallels are lacking. For example, Jesus' discussion of evangelistic techniques with his disciples are not discussed. Using a kind of "affirmative action," I devote more pages to Muhammad than to Jesus. This might better contribute to overcoming many Christians' appalling ignorance of the earliest history of Islam.

A new era of religious history that I find invigorating is now dawning. Global dialogue is slowly replacing separatism in the area of religion as well as in politics. Among its harbingers is Catholic theologian Paul Knitter, who has written *No Other Name?* to promote open dialogue among religions. Previously, religious spokespersons have been smugly content to deliver monologues to their own constituencies. Knitter observes:

> Christianity, along with all other world religions, is evolving out of the *micro* phase of religious history in which the various traditions grew and consolidated in relative isolation from each other. The direction today is toward a *macro* phase of history in which each religion will be able to grow and understand itself only through interrelating with other religions.[80]

CHAPTER TWO

ANTECEDENTS

The Regional Heritage

Muhammad spent his life in a region known as Hijaz, an arid plateau in western Arabia. Occasional oases, watered by a few annual thunderstorms, distinguish this area from much of the rest of the earth's largest peninsula. Were it not for the slender Red Sea, Arabia would be the eastern part of the desert stretching across North Africa. The Hijaz cash crops were dates, raisins, and aromatic plants, which were traded northward in Damascus and other cities of the Fertile Crescent.

Most of the Arabs were nomadic bedouin who wandered in search of vegetation for their domestic animals. They admired the horse but depended on the less expensive camel for transportation, milk, and meat. In addition, the camel's hair and skin provided clothing and tent material; from its urine came ammonia for washing, and from its dung came fuel for cooking. In contrast to the way the camel is classified in Hebrew scripture, the Arabs regarded it as a clean and holy animal.

Jesus spent his life in an agrarian area located less than a thousand miles northwest of Muhammad's homeland. Olive orchards, grain fields, and freshwater fishing in the Sea of Galilee provided what visitors from a desert area had once called "a land flowing with milk and honey."[1] The trade routes that crossed Galilee gave the people living there access to the cultures of Syria and Egypt. The donkey was the beast of burden most encountered along those commercial roads.

A century before the advent of Christianity, the Romans conquered Galilee along with most of Asia west of the Euphrates River. *Palestinia* was the name they gave to Jesus' province near the eastern extreme of their vast Mediterranean and European empire. Only the Nabataean province on the rim of the Arabian desert was farther removed from the capital at Rome.

The main international difference between the eras of Muhammad and Jesus was the peaceful economy that had been ushered in by Caesar Augustus at the time of Jesus' birth. Although no wars were raging, many people in Palestine had a burning desire to eliminate the Roman army of occupation. Few were enamored by the Herodian dynasty, the Jewish puppet rulers whose actions were directed by the Romans. At Sepphoris, several miles from Jesus' hometown of Nazareth, a revolt against the government had caused the Romans to retaliate by crucifying or enslaving thousands.[2] But a full rebellion against Rome in Palestine did not break out until a generation after Jesus' death.

Arabia was a stateless society governed by numerous contending sheikhs (tribal chiefs). Mecca was a sheikhdom with commerce as its main employment because the valley in which the small city was located was too dry to grow enough food for local needs. It became involved with caravans moving between Mesopotamia and Yemen, in Southern Arabia. Frankincense and myrrh, the resins of certain shrubs in Yemen, were especially valued. This trade is reflected in a biblical story pertaining to Jacob's sons: "They saw an Ishmaelite caravan coming from Gilead on their way to Egypt, with camels carrying gum, balm, and resin."[3] There was also trade between Mecca and Ethiopia (or Abyssinia) via the nearby Red Sea port of Jedda. Some of that trade was in slaves, ivory, and precious metals from Africa. The first biblical mention of Arabia is during the reign of Solomon, who received gold "from all the kings of Arabia."[4] Solomon had a merchant fleet that sailed from Ezion-geber to destinations along the Red Sea and the coast of East Africa.[5] Arab traders were associated with precious stones, as well as with gold and all kinds of spices.[6]

Located about midway between Mesopotamia and Yemen, Mecca was more than a rest stop for caravans originating elsewhere. It was a transportation headquarters, serving as the point of origin and termination for huge caravans that went to the north in the summer and to the south in the winter. The city was also at the crossroad of a trade route from Ethiopia eastward to the Persian Gulf. Sometimes thousands of camels left or returned to Mecca in a single caravan.[7]

Meccan prosperity from trade was in part due to the conflict between the Byzantine (or Roman) and Persian superpowers that had made travel precarious across Mesopotamia to the Orient. The Persian empire included areas east of the Euphrates, principally Iraq, Iran, and Afghanistan. The Byzantine empire included Turkey, Syria, Palestine, Egypt, Ethiopia, and Europe as far north as the Danube. Its capital at Constantinople had survived the fall of Rome in the fifth century. Emperor Justinian requested people living along the Red Sea to purchase silk from India for resale in the West, and thereby deprive the Persians from profiting on the trade.[8]

Arab mobility was not limited to finding pastureland and transporting goods for trade. The scarcity of food in Arabia encouraged many to live as bandits. The Hebrew Bible describes activity that continued unchanged for millennia: bedouin Ishmaelites (or Midianites) became a threat to settled areas shortly after the camel was domesticated.[9] Taming that animal to become the ship of the desert was the most important achievement of the ancient Arabs. The story of Gideon may tell of the first use of camel warfare. At harvest time, the Ishmaelites raided the fertile area of Galilee. "They devastated the land" as they stole grain and livestock.[10] Centuries later, during the last years of the nation of Judah, Arabs were among the invaders who "carried off all the possessions they found in the king's palace, along with his (Joram's) sons and wives."[11]

In the fourth century C.E., Ammianus Marcellinus, a pagan soldier from Syria, compared the Arabs to birds of prey:

> The Saracens . . . in a brief space of time laid waste to whatever they could find, like rapacious kites which, whenever they have caught sight of any prey from on high, seize it with swift swoop. . . . All alike are warriors of equal rank, half nude, clad in dyed cloaks as far as the loins, ranging widely with the help of swift horses and slender camels in times of peace or of disorder. No man ever grasps a plough-handle or cultivates a tree, none seeks a living by tilling the soil, but they rove continually over wide and extensive tracts.[12]

Another source of livelihood at Mecca was the entertainment of pilgrims who visited the city. In western Arabia there were several sacred months annually when marauding bands and tribal feuds were curtailed by a truce. This enabled Arabs to travel safely to certain sanctuaries and participate in festivals.[13] Praying and fasting were prescribed during the sacred month of Ramadan.[14] The focus of the pilgrimage in Mecca was the Ka'ba, so named because the temple was cubical in shape. It was covered with fine cloth, and the area was kept clean by prohibiting "dead bodies or menstruous cloths to come near it."[15] Inside the temple were many images representing local divinities of the tribes who gathered there. Adoration of those objects provided some integration for the Arabian culture. During the holy weeks, worshipers joined in a ritual procession around the Ka'ba, which had as its cornerstone the sacred Black Stone. While circumambulating, the Black Stone was touched and kissed by followers in an effort to inculcate its magical power.

Mircea Eliade includes the Black Stone among the meteorites that were revered in ancient cultures because they fell from heaven.[16] When Elagabalus, a Syrian Arab, became the Roman emperor in 219 C.E., he had a temple constructed in Rome for the black meteorite he brought from Emesa, where he had been a priest.[17] According to Ishaq, litholatry was a Meccan export: "Everyone who left the town took with him a stone from the sacred area to do honor to it. Wherever they settled they set it up and walked round it as they went round the Ka'ba."[18]

Pre-Islamic sacred ceremonies also involved Arafat, a holy hill near Mecca. Pilgrims moved rapidly from Arafat to the valley of Mina, where domestic animals were sacrificed. The camel, sheep, and ox victims were usually cooked and eaten rather than burned whole due to the scarcity of both fuel and meat in the desert.[19] After the sacrificial meat was distributed widely, a head-shaving ritual concluded the pilgrimage.[20]

Among the deities with which the Ka'ba was associated was Allah, a contraction of *al*, the definite article, and *Ilah*, meaning "God." The root for the name of deity in several Semitic cultures is simply the consonant "L," preceded by a smooth breathing. Cuneiform tablets dating back more than four millennia have been excavated in recent years from the Ebla ruin in Syria. '*L* was a prominent masculine god in that ancient city, and later he headed the Ugarit pantheon.[21] He consorted with '*Loah* (or '*Lath*) and produced the many sons and daughters that were local deities in Mesopotamia.[22] The parental deities '*L* and '*Loah*' (-*ah* is a feminine suffix) were honored as remote creators.

Elohim, the name that is used for deity some twenty-five hundred times in the Hebrew Bible, may have developed via the merging of the names of the two primordial deities and the addition of the plural -*im* ending. Walther Eichrodt explains that the plural Elohim was used "to express the higher unity subsuming the individual gods and combining in one concept the whole pantheon."[23] Likewise, Allah became the generic term for deity in Arabia, expressing the unified totality of godness. In Hebrew and Arabic, the plural pronoun was considered proper to refer to the quintessence of divine powers in Elohim or Allah.

Evidence of pre-Islamic honoring of Allah is found in the name of Muhammad's father, Abdullah, which means "servant of Allah." Also, Arab poet Zuhair, writing a generation before Muhammad, warns: "Do not conceal from God (*allah*) whatever is in your breasts, hoping it may be hidden; God knows whatever is concealed."[24] Ar-Rahman, the Compassionate One, was used in Arabia before Muhammad as a synonym for Allah.[25] Rahman echoes Hebrew theology, as this typical affirmation shows: "The Lord was gracious to them and had compassion (*rachum*) on them."[26]

The Quran claims that an Arabian apostle before Muhammad believed Allah to be not only a god, but the only God. Salih proclaimed to his tribe: "My people, worship Allah for there is no other god. It was He who brought you into being from the earth and established you upon it. Beg forgiveness and turn to Him in repentance for my Lord is near and ready to answer."[27] To this plea, his tribe responded: "Salih, we had placed our hopes in you, but you forbid us to worship what our fathers worshiped, and we are suspicious of the faith to which you call us."[28]

The Ka'ba contained hundreds of sacred rocks and statues from many Arabian tribes, but no images of Allah. No special cult was associated with Allah. In the pre-Islamic era, Allah was recognized as the creator of the world and as the giver of rain.[29] He was revered but was considered to be aloof, so popular piety was usually directed elsewhere. Meccans turned to Allah in time of crisis, but after they were delivered, their worship drifted to other deities. For example, when waves enveloped them on shipboard, the Meccans prayed to Allah with fervor, but after safely landing they renewed devotion to other gods and goddesses.[30]

Wilhelm Schmidt used the early Arabic notion of Allah as creator of the world to illustrate his famous high-god thesis.[31] From anthropological data, Schmidt demonstrated that worship of a primal single god has been corrupted in numerous cultures by godlings who represent ancestors or natural objects. Before Muhammad, the high-god at the Ka'ba in Mecca was probably not considered incompatible with tribal symbols, any more than most Americans would regard flag devotion to "Old Glory" incompatible with Christian worship.

Allat, which means *the* Goddess, was prominent in the pagan pantheon of Arabia. Even as Allah was a contraction, so Allat combined *al* and *Ilat*. The mention of "Alilat" by ancient Greek historian Herodotus shows that her cult was established at least a millennium before Islam. The cult was associated with brotherhood pledges made when participants dipped their fingers in blood smeared on sacred stones.[32] Originally, Allat was represented by a white stone.[33] The following inscription was discovered on the edge of the Arabian desert: "The temple . . . built to Goddess Allat."[34] Dated 57 C.E., it was found at Salhad in the Nabataean culture.[35] Epiphanius reports from the fourth century that at Petra, the main Nabataean city, hymns were sung in Arabic to a pagan virgin goddess and to Dhu Shara, her only-begotten son.[36]

At Mecca, Allat was thought of as a daughter rather than as a mother. Pilgrims were attracted to shrines of the three daughters of Allah in the vicinity of Mecca. To the south, Allat was represented as a sun goddess; to the east, Aluzza was represented as the morning-star goddess; and to the north of Mecca, there was a sanctuary to Almanat, the goddess of destiny. Jack Finegan comments on Manat: "The etymology of the name is judged to be connected with the root *mana*, meaning 'to determine' or 'to mete out,' and it is suggested that she was a goddess of fortune or fate."[37]

Both Muhammad and Jesus were more reformers than originators. Muhammad did not attempt to introduce a new deity but urged people to worship only Allah. Likewise, when Jesus quoted a reference to "the God (*Elohim*) of Abraham"[38] from scripture, he was in no way contrasting a previous deity of an earlier religion with his own commitment. The principle of monotheism was a settled matter in his Jewish community; the one God was worshiped in homes, in synagogues, and in the temple at Jerusalem. Only at the temple was there a continuation of the sacrifice of animals prescribed by the Torah. Jesus was oriented primarily toward synagogue Judaism, in which scriptural interpretation by scribes was central.

Adhering to the Mosaic law provided the strongest bond in the Jewish community, but kinship loyalty was more valued among desert peoples. Blood revenge by a victim's family was the basic feature of Arabian justice. The retribution extracted could be less than death; stealing was penalized by cutting off a hand.[39] Regarding the nomad's categorical imperative, Morris Seale writes:

> He had to hate his enemies as steadfastly as he cared for his kin. This unashamed lust for revenge derives from tribal life

where a man had to be his own policeman, judge and executioner. Retaliation was a duty set above all others, serving as a regulatory principle in society.[40]

John Glubb comments on the love for limited warfare at the time of Muhammad:

Arab tribes regarded war as an endemic and natural feature of human life. Perpetual peace would have had for them no conceivable attraction. But one of the reasons why this state of affairs seemed to them not only endurable but desirable, was because they regarded war as a means of gaining honor and plunder, rather than of destroying their enemies.[41]

The religious history of the Arabs and the Christians is rooted in Hebrew culture. Abraham was the first to be called a Hebrew, a name that may have meant "caravanner."[42] He believed that God had established a covenant that gave him both land in western Asia and numerous descendants, through whom he would become a blessing for all people. As a shepherd, Abraham lived in tents and moved in and out of Egypt. He was married to Sarah, who had an Egyptian slave named Hagar. After Sarah presumed she was infertile, she loaned her handmaiden to Abraham to sire an offspring. He hoped that this scheme would enable him to live up to the name God gave him, meaning "the ancestor of many nations."[43] A boy named Ishmael was born, and he was circumcised at puberty as a sign of the Abrahamic covenant.[44]

Sarah and Hagar became rivals, and this friction was especially strong after Sarah gave birth to Abraham's second son. Sarah, unable to tolerate having her son Isaac play with a slave's child, demanded that Hagar and Ishmael be evicted. Also, Sarah wanted to cut Ishmael out of sharing in the family inheritance. Abraham was distressed, but he capitulated to his jealous wife. After supplying Hagar and Ishmael with bread and a skin of water, Abraham sent them off to the wild lands south of where his flocks were pastured. When the water became exhausted and death from dehydration was imminent, the Genesis account states that God showed Hagar a well, and promised that a great nation will come from her son.[45] The story of Ishmael concludes by telling of twelve Ishmaelite tribes who settle to the east of Egypt, which would be known as Arabia.[46]

Ancient sources apart from the Bible associate Hagar with Arabia.

The Assyrians of the eighth-century B.C.E. recorded the submission of the Hagar tribe in Arabia. Greek and Latin writers sometimes designated an Arabian tribal federation as Hagarenes.[47] According to a midrash, Abraham went by camel into the wilderness for an occasional visit with Ishmael and Hagar. To lessen Sarah's anxiety about her husband spending time with Hagar, he agreed not to dismount.[48] That legend of family visitations in Arabia became the basis of subsequent Quranic stories of Abraham at Mecca.

There was a long history of Arabic-speaking Jews living in the midst of the Ishmaelites during pre-Islamic times, and their practices were influential. The first to settle in Arabia may have been some who escaped from Jerusalem before its destruction in the sixth century B.C.E.[49] Arabs abstained from pork and followed some other Hebrew customs as well.[50] The pig prohibition displays the prejudice of nomadic people against a swamp animal that would not be encountered in arid areas.

At the beginning of the Christian era, Josephus told of Ishmaelite boys who were circumcised at puberty, as was Ishmael their founder, and who occupied the desert region "from the Euphrates to the Red Sea."[51] The one mention of Arabs (*Arabes*) in the New Testament pertains to some who visited Jerusalem for a Jewish festival.[52] When Theophilus, a Christian missionary, came to Yemen in the fourth century, there were many Jews living there.[53]

Hartwig Hirschfeld describes the Arabian Jews as generally uninterested in warfare: "They were rather peaceful palm growers, craftsmen and traders who lived in settled habitations round Medina and further north."[54] According to Gordon Newby, "Jews lived in castles and in tents" in the Hijaz and were merchants, bedouin, warriors, sailors, poets, and sculptors.[55] They were especially respected for their linguistic and horticultural abilities. Newby continues:

> The Jews had brought Nabataean techniques of irrigation to the oases of western Arabia, and they employed the techniques of hand pollination of the date flowers to ensure more than a spotty yield. Dates were a major source of nourishment in the Arabian diet, and provided the basis for fermented drink.[56]

Unlike the Jews who were living in Christian areas, religious persecution was not a problem for the Jewish minority in Arabia before the time of Muhammad. Heinrich Graetz writes of their untrammelled condition in the sixth century:

> (Arabian Jews) were allowed to develop their powers in the midst of a free, simple, and talented people, to show their manly courage, to compete for the gifts of fame, and with practiced hand to measure swords with their antagonists. Instead of bearing the yoke, the Jews were not infrequently the leaders of the Arabian tribes. . . . They handled the ploughshare and the lyre, and in the end became the teachers of the Arabian nation. . . . The Jews even succeeded in instructing the Arabs in regard to their historical origin, concerning which their memories were void, and in their credulity the latter accepted this genealogy as the true one. It was of great consequence to the Jews to be regarded and acknowledged by the Arabs as their kinsmen.[57]

In pre-Islamic times, parts of the Jewish scriptures were translated in Arabia.[58] During that era, Al-Bukhari states, "Jews used to read the Torah in Hebrew and interpret it to the people of Islam in Arabic."[59] Some Arabs were intrigued by those in their midst who were devoted to the biblical religion since they knew of its impact in neighboring countries. According to Maxime Rodinson, they honored the "People of the Book" for these reasons:

> Their claims rested on sacred books sent from heaven in ancient times, revered for their antiquity, their worth proven by miracles. They knew the secrets of Allah, they knew how He wished to be worshiped, what prayers and sacrifices, what fasts and processions He required if He was to look kindly on men.[60]

A few years before Muhammad became a prophet, four Meccan youths shared an admiration for Abraham, whom they believed had true faith. Accordingly, they were critical of their idolatrous neighbors because "the Stone they went around was of no account; it could neither hear, nor see, nor hurt, nor help."[61] Because of their search, they were called *hunata*, meaning true religionists, a name that had been given to Abraham and his family. Two of the young men went to Christian countries and converted. One, Waraqa, became Christian but remained in Mecca and gained a mastery of the Bible. The fourth, Zaid ibn Amr, traveled to Syria where he conferred with Jews and Christians. A monk informed him that a prophet was to arise in Arabia. Zaid returned to Mecca, hoping for something better than the prevailing polytheism. At the Ka'ba he prayed: "O God, if I knew how you wished to be worshiped I would choose it, but I do not know."[62]

The Impact of Poetry

Arab poets provide much of the data available on the pre-Islamic era. In this regard, Rodinson writes:

> The poet was a person of importance, and feared, because he was thought to be possessed by a spirit. . . . The poet's chief use was as a propagandist; he was the journalist of the desert. Oratorical contests were held—often at the big fairs—at which each contestant boasted of his own tribe and mocked and reviled those of his opponents.[63]

Audiences were spellbound by soothsayers who chanted oracles in "staccato rhymed phrases" while covering themselves with their cloaks. They would go into trances and forecast in rhythmic prose. Since incantations were alleged to be inspired utterances, soothsayers were consulted about both public and private matters. Muhammad's grandfather urged one to find a way to break a rash vow he had made to sacrifice a son (Muhammad's father) if his wish was fulfilled.[64]

Soothsayers or sorceresses were believed to incarnate *jinn*. They were believed to reside in the atmosphere as invisible spirits, but occasionally they entered humans and animals, causing physical and mental changes. Characterized as crafty, mischievous, capricious, and occasionally destructive, the *jinn* and those who were possessed by them needed to be respected. English readers of the *One Thousand and One Nights* have come to call them "genies."

In pre-Islamic poetry, fate (*dahr*) was believed to be an irresistible force, overwhelming all, and depriving life of meaning.[65] Rodinson notes: "There was no escape from a fundamentally pessimistic view of life except in making haste to enjoy the fierce but fleeting pleasures it

had to offer."[66] This hedonistic philosophy is similar to that of the famous Persian poet Omar Khayyam who lived in the eleventh century.
    About 560 C.E., poet Tarafa celebrated self-indulgence in these lines:

> *If it were not for three things youth loves, I would not care when I died.*
> *Red wine, well mixed and frothy;*
> *A war-horse, when summoned to the fray;*
> *A girl to be closeted with on a wintry day.*
>
> *   *   *   *   *   *   *
>
> *The man of generous spirit satisfies himself during his lifetime. . . .*
> *The grave of the prudent man, the wealth-hoarder, I see not to differ from*
> *   the grave of the . . . spendthrift.*
> *On each stands a mount of earth topped by flat slabs.*[67]

Physical resurrection was considered absurd, but death was not
regarded as annihilation.[68] Pagan Arabs said, according to the Quran:
"There is only our first death; we will not be raised."[69] That outlook is
similar to Job's concept of Sheol, the gloomy abode of the dead: "Those
who go down to Sheol do not come up. . . . They will not awake or be
roused out of their sleep."[70]
    Morris Seale's comments on the life-after-death view of pre-Islamic
Arabs is somewhat more positive:

> They believed that the departed lived a life of their own and
> enjoyed a conscious existence in the grave. . . . Pagan Arabs
> cared for their dead and supplied them with food and
> drink. . . . Coming upon the grave of an acquaintance, they
> would call his name and greet him: the deceased was believed
> to return the greeting. Owls fluttering around were thought to
> be the spirits of the departed, and their screeching was taken
> to be the moaning of the dead.[71]

The recurring bird image in the poetry of pagan Arabians depicts
graphically a basic ingredient of their outlook. Theodor Noeldeke
comments: "The soul of the murdered man was represented as appearing
in the form of an owl, and as continually crying out, 'Give me to drink!'
until vengeance had been executed."[72] That getting-even ethic tended
to stimulate continual feuding in pursuit of justice.
    Toshihiko Izutsu specifies other values championed by the early

Arabs: "That faithfulness or trustworthiness was one of the highest and most characteristic virtues in the desert is known to every reader of pre-Islamic poetry and traditions."[73] Izutsu discusses each of these main virtues: generosity, courage, loyalty, veracity, and patience. Hospitality and helpfulness were also admired by desert people in their struggle for existence. Excessive wine drinking, causing poverty, was a primary vice.[74] Tranquility (al-hilm), combining gentleness and forbearance, was a highly esteemed virtue in pre-Islamic poetry.[75] Thus, the barbarity of the pagan Arab tribes should not be exaggerated.

Jesus was also much influenced by the poetry of his culture. He sometimes appropriated expressions of the Hebrew prophets, whose messages were recorded in poetic form.[76] The psalms, the most significant contribution of the Hebrews to the arts, was a source for some of his sayings. For example, to defend children's loudness in a place of worship, he quotes a psalm that commended what came "out of the mouths of babes and infants."[77] Since the psalms served as Jesus' hymn book, a psalm designated for the Passover festival was probably sung after he ate his last supper with his disciples.[78]

As Jesus was being crucified, he recited prayers from the psalms.[79] One of those prayers was not clearly or fully heard. Jesus probably mumbled the words of a Hebrew who had been tortured by his enemies. This prayer was called the "my-God-why-have-you-forsaken-me" psalm for its opening line. An examination of the devotional poem reveals that the victim does not cry out for revenge in spite of his intense pain. In the latter part of the psalm, the sufferer looks beyond his personal tragedy to the eventual triumph of God's kingdom. Confidence is expressed that all people will accept God's rule.

Women's Place

Jesus belonged to a culture in which some women had been given considerable respect. Among the early Hebrew heroines were Tamar, Miriam, Deborah, Ruth, and Huldah. However, a deterioration of the status of women can be traced in the several centuries before the Christian era.[80] A few generations before Jesus ben Joseph, Jesus ben Sirach charged: "Woman is the origin of sin, and it is through her that we all die. . . . Out of clothes comes the moth, and out of woman comes wickedness. A man's wickedness is better than a woman's goodness; it is woman who brings shame and disgrace."[81] Generally subscribing to Sirach's misogyny in the generation before Jesus, influential Rabbi Hillel commented, "The more women, the more witchcrafts."[82] Pharisee Josephus stated that "woman is in all things inferior to man."[83] Sirach's sentiments had an impact on the Jerusalem Talmud in this way: "The first man was the blood and life of the world . . . and Eve was the cause of his death."[84]

Women were reminded of their lower status in various ways. A father could sell an unwanted daughter into slavery.[85] Women, along with slaves and children, were exempted from reciting the *Shema* creed, which was at the core of Jewish worship.[86] A Jewish menstruant was not accorded as much dignity as a gentile male at the Jerusalem temple for she was excluded from even the outermost of the four courts.[87] The Mishnah echoes a rabbinic debate over whether women should receive religious education. Eliezer associated teaching a daughter the Torah with teaching her promiscuity.[88] Other rabbis believed that it should be taught to both daughters and sons.[89] Judith Wegner explains: "Eliezer fears that the more a woman knows, the more liberated she may become—above all, in her sexual conduct."[90] She concludes her thorough study of the status of women in early Judaism with this judgment: "Woman was never a complete person in mishnaic society, but neither was she always and only a chattel."[91]

According to the Mosaic law, a menstruant was "impure" during her period and for the subsequent week.[92] The rabbis established eleven days as the ordinary duration of this ritual uncleanness.[93] In the division on cleanliness, the longest in the Mishnah, a whole tract is devoted to detecting the menstruant. There the taboo is expressed in this way: "The blood of a menstruant and the flesh of a corpse convey uncleanness."[94] Complete immersion in a ritual bath was required at the end of the taboo period.[95]

Wives accused of infidelity were subjected to a terrifying ordeal, but their sexual partners were not.[96] In order to frighten a confession out of a woman accused of becoming pregnant by someone other than her husband, she was dressed in black and brought to the eastern gate of the Jerusalem temple. There a priest humiliated her by untying her hair and tearing her dress so that her breast was publicly exposed.[97] Then he required her to drink a mixture of holy water, dust from the sanctuary, and ink from the scroll on which the accusation against her was written. Guilt was deemed certain if the potion caused a change in her complexion and a miscarriage.[98]

What can be known about the place of women in pre-Islamic Arabia? Elise Boulding shows that in early nomadic societies, bedouin as well as others, women sometimes were accorded a higher status than they were in more settled societies.[99] Beginning with the Queen of Sheba, there were several illustrious Arab queens, some of whom were sovereigns.[100] Nabia Abbott notes: "In poetry, the major literary passion of pre-Islamic Arabia, the Arab woman figured large."[101] The most popular deities were goddesses, and human females may have benefited from that adoration. On the eve of the coming of Islam, Arab women were occasionally recognized as priestesses and as prophetesses.[102]

"The forerunner of the best side of medieval chivalry,"[103] is the way Stanley Lane-Poole describes pre-Islamic Arabic culture:

> In the old days, says an ancient writer, the true Arab had but one love, and her he loved till death. The Arab of the desert . . . regarded women as divinities to be worshipped, not as chattels to possess. . . . Antar, the Bayard of pagan Arabia, gave his life to guard some helpless women. These verses of Muweylik breathe a tender chivalrous regret for an only love:
>
> *God's love be thine and His mercy, O thou dear lost one! Not meet for thee*
> *   is the place of shadow and loneliness.*
> *And a little one hast thou left behind. . . .*
> *When her crying smites in the night upon my sleepless ears, Straightway*
> *   mine eyes brimful are filled from the well of tears.*[104]

Some basic Semitic marriage customs were found in pre-Islamic Arabia.[105] A bride's guardian was usually given a gift, called *mahr* in Arabic, from the Hebrew *mohar*.[106] In addition to the dowry there was the levirate arrangement whereby a wife could be transferred like property at her husband's death to the nearest male relative.[107]

Although patriarchy seems to have prevailed among the early Arabs, some marital arrangements limited the power of the male. At the time when Muhammad established Islam in Medina, polygyny was probably not the usual pattern of marriage.[108] Geoffrey Parrinder finds evidence of matrilineal structures: "Some of the Arabs before Islam had followed a system of kinship which regulated marriage and descent through the mother."[109] Also, polyandrous marriage of one woman to several men was accepted by some, and wives as well as husbands had the right to divorce.[110] Ammianus Marcellinus describes Arabian culture this way: "The future wife, by way of dower, offers her husband a spear and a tent, with the right to leave him after a stipulated time, if she so elects: and it is unbelievable with what ardor both sexes give themselves up to passion."[111]

Ilse Lichtenstadter concludes a study of pre-Islamic Arabian women in this way:

> On the whole women were esteemed . . . and they occupied a high rank in the community of the tribe. They were honored as wives and mothers, beloved as daughters; it was honorable to fight for them, shameful to abandon them to the enemy.[112]

Also, in Mecca there appears to have been no stigma attached to a woman combining marriage with business operations.

Muslims generally have not acknowledged those aspects of ancient Arabian culture that suggest that many women tended to enjoy a position of dignity. They assume a low state of morality because the Quran frequently refers to the previous era as a time of *jahiliyya.* That term, meaning "ignorance" but interpreted to mean darkness or wildness also, expresses prejudice against anything before Muhammad's revelation.[113] Muhammad's humane contribution looms greater if unlimited polygyny and few female rights are assumed before he arrived, but documentary evidence in support of those assumptions is mixed.

In a monograph showing the evolution of the early Hebrew legends in Arabia, Reuven Firestone demonstrates that there are other important influences from early Arabian culture that carried over into Islam. He concludes:

> Muslim historiographers have regularly claimed that Islam represented an absolute religious break from pre-Islamic times, an assumption that may now be questioned. . . . By assuming a new genesis in the first quarter of the seventh century, this approach tends to ignore the important and lasting influence of pre-Islamic Arabian religious thought (monotheistic as well as pagan) and institutions on nascent and early Islamic civilization.[114]

Christians recognize that Jesus criticized the religious outlook and social institutions that preceded him in significant ways. In general, Christians have not presumed that the separation was as radical as what Muslims have claimed *vis-à-vis* Muhammad. Both Christianity and Islam have been greatly influenced by the theological and ethical viewpoints of the cultures in which they were reared.

CHAPTER THREE

EARLY LIFE

The best source of information about Muhammad is the Quran even though it contains little biographical information. The unconcern of its editors for chronological sequence suggests that it was not composed for historical study. Modern Islamic scholars have generally agreed on where the Quranic revelations were first proclaimed, and knowledge of this assists in biographical reconstruction.

In the following chapters, a critical use will be made of several relatively early biographies of Muhammad, following the standard approach of both Muslim and non-Muslim scholars. None of them was written until more than a century after he lived, but oral tradition can be given considerable weight in cultures that are predominantly preliterate. If no records of Abraham Lincoln's life had been made until the present generation, there would probably be little in a written biography other than larger-than-life stories about the heroic American. Memory training is not an educational emphasis for those who can easily write down data and file it away. Factual forgetfulness is less tolerated in cultures in which literacy is uncommon because that would result in most of the past being lost forever.

There are similar problems pertaining to recovering reliable data on the historical Jesus, who wrote nothing extant. The canonical (church-approved) Gospels are the principal sources for the life of Jesus, but they were not primarily written to give biographical data. In addition, more than a generation had lapsed between his death and their publication. Consider an example of embellishment contained in the Easter accounts of the New Testament. The apostle Paul, who wrote the earliest record of those experiences some twenty years after Jesus' burial, says nothing about his corpse being raised.[1] Decades after that record, accounts alleging Jesus' empty tomb and his physical resurrection are given prominence in the four Gospels.

The legendary biographies of Muhammad and Jesus are compared to reveal parallels and salient points of difference. The many miraculous stories about the two men, which seem to be largely the creations of hagiographers, are discussed in a later chapter.

The Meccan

The story of Muhammad is a tale of two cities, one rather barren and one relatively fertile. This section focuses on Muhammad in Mecca, where he spent fifty years of his life. The last dozen years, when he lived in Medina, are equally important and are treated in the next chapter.

Muhammad belonged to the Quraish tribe, which for generations had been dominant in Mecca. A clan of that tribe, named after Muhammad's great-grandfather Hashim, had high standing as keepers of the Ka'ba sanctuary. Muhammad was a threadbare aristocrat, having both status and poverty. Biographer Sa'd indulges in hyperbole to describe Muhammad's paternal uncles: "Among the Arabs there were no more prominent and stately men, none of more noble profile. Their noses were so large that the nose drank before the lips."[2]

Before Muhammad was born, about the year 570, his father died. Amina, Muhammad's mother, placed her baby with foster parents who were bedouin near Mecca to ensure that he was cared for adequately. After living several years with those shepherds, Muhammad was returned to Amina. He was with her only briefly before she died. After the death of both parents, the boy came under the supervision of his uncle, Abu Talib, the clan head. Muhammad traveled to Syria with a caravan led by his merchant uncle, which exposed him to other religions.[3]

Ishaq tells of Muhammad's encounter with Zaid ibn Amr, an uncle who had abandoned his traditional Meccan religion. As a boy, Muhammad attempted to share meat that he had brought from a shrine for pagan sacrifice. Muhammad later recalled that Zaid, after refusing the offer, "upbraided me for idolatry and spoke disparagingly of those who worship idols and sacrifice to them."[4] Alfred Guillaume calls this "the only authentic story of Muhammad's early years."[5]

Khadija, who may have been the richest merchant of Mecca, heard of Muhammad's trustworthiness and made him her agent for selling caravan goods in Syria. Even though she was some years older than her twenty-five-year-old employee and had been married twice, she asked him to marry her.[6] Sa'd records the following story about Khadija, which may be truthful because it does not glorify Muhammad:

> She called her father to her house, plied him with wine until he was drunk, slaughtered a cow, anointed him with perfume and clothed him in a striped robe; then she sent for the Messenger of God and his uncles and, when they came in her father married him to her. When her father recovered from his intoxication, he said, "What is this meat, this perfume, and this garment?" She replied, "You have married me to Muhammad b. 'Abdallah." "I have not done so," he said. "Would I do this, when the greatest men of Mecca have asked for you and I have not agreed?[7]

The marriage produced several children, but the boys died "in paganism."[8] Zaid, a prisoner or slave ransomed by Khadija and Muhammad, was then adopted as their son. Her wealth relieved her husband of having to work for a living. This new situation helps to explain one of the few biographical references to Muhammad in the Quran. An early record alludes to God making the impoverished orphan prosperous. This question is directed to Muhammad: "Did He not find you destitute and enrich you?"[9] This affluent situation enabled him to devote himself primarily to religious concerns. He and Abu Talib, who remained a pagan throughout life, were intensely involved in the traditional Meccan religion. Ishaq tells of how Muhammad stroked idols and offered sacrifices to them.[10]

At the age of thirty-five, Muhammad helped the Quraish in reconstructing the Ka'ba. Its stone walls were demolished to the foundation and then rebuilt. Controversy arose as to who should have the honor of placing the sacred Black Stone in the rebuilt structure. To settle the dispute, the Quraish called for Trusty (al-Amin), a nickname for Muhammad. Diplomatically, he placed the stone in a cloak and had a representative from each clan take one corner of the cloth in order to lift it together to its appointed place. A carpenter, who was an African Christian, used timbers from the wreck of a Greek ship at Jedda to replace the roof.[11]

Muhammad had developed an antipathy toward polytheism by the age of forty. He was probably influenced by what Zaid ibn Amr had learned from abroad about the anticipation of an Arab prophet, similar to biblical prophets, surfacing. On a mountain near Mecca where Zaid had retreated for meditation a few years earlier, Muhammad and his family spent the month of Ramadan in seclusion each year. There, at a cave called Hira, he became entranced.[12] While asleep during the "night of power,"[13] he experienced an awesome Person: "He stood on the upper horizon. Then, drawing near, He came down within two bow-lengths and revealed to His servant whatever He revealed."[14] The revelation seemed to reverberate through the sky as it ordered Muhammad "to proclaim"[15] (iqra, the Arabic imperative that is the first revealed word, contains the root of what would later become the name of the holy book). Muhammad initially refused to speak out, so the command was repeated again and again. Fearful for his life, he announced: "Proclaim, in the name of your Lord who creates humans from sperm! Proclaim, how the Most Bountiful One teaches by the pen what humans do not know!"[16] Revelations like this would continue intermittently until his death two decades later.

Muhammad's struggle at the beginning of his ministry resembled that of Jeremiah. Far from wanting a religious vocation, that sensitive prophet of ancient Judah resisted his call.[17] Being God's mouthpiece, Jeremiah realized, entailed uttering a message of judgment that his fellow citizens least wanted to hear. He confessed that he was tormented by the ambivalence of his natural desire for popularity and his commission to proclaim the word of God. Jeremiah felt a burning fire within that he could not control in spite of the resulting derision.[18]

After being overwhelmed by his visionary experience, Muhammad agonized over an apparent divine call while in seclusion at Hira. He contrasted his personal hopes with his anticipations of the effects of his new career. The Quran asserts: "You did not expect that the Book would be revealed to you."[19] Muhammad was severely disturbed over the genuineness of the revelation and the nonconformity demands of the prophetic role: "Woe is me, poet or possessed. . . . I will go to the top of the mountain and throw myself down that I may kill myself and gain rest."[20] Muhammad's suicidal anxiety over whether he has had an authentic communication from God displays his sincerity. An impostor consciously making up the message would probably have had no anguish or outcry.

As an Arab who believed the atmosphere was teeming with impish *jinn*, Muhammad asked Khadija if he might have been hoodwinked into seeing a mirage. She responded supportively: "God would not treat you thus since he knows your truthfulness, your great trustworthiness, your fine character, and your kindness. This cannot be, my dear. Perhaps you did see something."[21] She then cleverly devised a test to prove who was possessing her husband. Reasoning that a bad spirit would want to watch sexual relations while a good spirit would modestly leave, she experimented when Muhammad was aware of the presence of a spirit. Khadija had her lover sit in her lap while she removed her clothes. When she exposed her body, Muhammad's mind no longer focused on a troublesome spirit. She then declared triumphantly: "Rejoice and be of good heart, by God he is an angel and not a satan."[22]

Khadija sought advice about her husband from Waraqa, her Christian cousin who had serious religious interests. Upon recognizing the similarity between Muhammad's experience and that of Moses, he judged that Muhammad had had a legitimate prophetic call. Waraqa identified Gabriel, the biblical archangel, with Muhammad's revelation transmitter and warned him to expect persecution in Mecca followed by expulsion.[23]

A revelation at Mecca pertains to the guidance that Muhammad received from Christians or Jews: "If you doubt what We have sent down to you, ask those who have been reading the Book previously."[24] There seems to have been a considerable awareness of the Torah in Mecca because Muhammad was soon to ask his people: "Have you not heard of what is preached in the scriptures of Moses and Abraham?"[25]

It is apparent that Muhammad received psychological reassurance as well as material support from Khadija. She was the first to be convinced of the genuineness of her husband's revelatory experiences, believing in him when he did not believe in himself. As Fatima Mernissi touchingly puts it: "This is the way Islam began, in the arms of a loving woman."[26] Ishaq offers this tribute to Khadija: "He (Muhammad) never met with contradiction and charges of falsehood, which saddened him, but God comforted him by her when he went home. She strengthened him, lightened his burden, proclaimed his truth, and belittled men's opposition."[27] Mutual devotion between Muhammad and Khadija is evident, and he remained a monogamist as long as she lived.

Meccans puzzled over what kind of person Muhammad had

become. Among the opinions expressed was that he was a seer or a poet.
One Meccan called him a sorcerer "who has brought a message by
which he separates a man from his father or from his brother, or from his
wife, or from his family."[28] The Quran's favorite designation for Muhammad is *rasul*, meaning "one who is sent"; "apostle" is a good translation
since it comes from the Greek verb *apostellein*, "to send." Like the biblical
and non-biblical apostles of the Greco-Roman culture, Muhammad
thought of himself as someone commissioned to deliver a message. He
resembled an earlier "prophet crying in the desert," John ben Zechariah,
or the Apostle Peter who spoke out against the Jerusalem establishment.[29]

Muhammad understood his role to be a forceful reciter of what
he heard, not a quiet interpreter of the message. His manner of preaching was similar to that of soothsayers in his culture. In his sermons,
the prophet balanced God's kindly dealings with His harsh judgments.
He invited his people to acknowledge the true and merciful God at the
Ka'ba: "Let the Quraish worship the Lord of this House who has
provided for them against famine and made them secure against peril."[30]
Muhammad told of paradise's delights and contrasted it with the horrors
of hell for idolaters. Muhammad described the Meccans in a disparaging
manner and warned them: "Their worship at the holy House is nothing
more than whistling and clapping of hands. . . . God will separate the
bad from the good, bind the wicked together, and cast them into
Hell."[31]

By the age of forty-three, Muhammad's castigation of idol worshipers had brought hostility from his Quraish tribe for it supervised the
recently reconstructed Ka'ba sanctuary that contained many images. His
unpopular message is evident in this Quranic comment:

> When Our clear revelations are proclaimed to them, those
> who disregard their destiny with Us say, "Proclaim something
> else, or change it." Say, "It is not for me to alter it of my own
> accord. I only follow what is revealed to me. . . . Had God so
> willed, I would never have proclaimed it to you."[32]

Abu Talib, embarrassed over his nephew's persistence, advised him
to spare both of them from tribal contempt. Muhammad responded: "By
God, if they put the sun in my right hand and the moon in my left on
condition that I abandoned this course, until God has made it victorious,
or I perish therein, I would not abandon it."[33] This vow of determina-

tion, accompanied by tears, caused this uncle to assure Muhammad: "Go and say what you please, for by God I will never give you up on any account."[34]

Several of the Meccan revelations conveyed by Muhammad show that he endured much scorn: "The unbelievers look scathingly at you and say, 'He is surely demented!'"[35] Another revelation states, "The unbelievers plot against you to wound you, or to kill you, or to drive you away. . . . They block the way to the sacred mosque and are not fit to be its guardians."[36] Still another states, "When Our revelations are proclaimed to them in plain words, they say: 'This man simply wants to turn you away from the gods your fathers worshiped. This (Quran) is nothing but a fraud.'"[37]

The Quraish leaders viewed Muhammad as their city's leading troublemaker. They based their opinion on these observations: "He had declared their mode of life foolish, insulted their forefathers, reviled their religion, divided the community, and cursed their gods."[38] Ishaq's account continues: "While they were thus discussing him, the Apostle came towards them and kissed the Black Stone."[39] On encircling the Ka'ba several times, he overheard personal denunciation from his tribe. In exasperation, Muhammad shouted: "Will you listen to me, O Quraish? By him who holds my life in His hand I bring you slaughter."[40] When he returned the next day they leapt upon him. Abu Bakr interposed: "Would you kill a man for saying Allah is my Lord?"[41] They then dragged Muhammad's friend around by his beard.[42]

The city leaders promised Muhammad, with questionable sincerity, what he would receive from them if he stopped his judgmental preaching. Ishaq records this tradition:

> If it was money he wanted, they would make him richest of them all; if it was honor, he should be their prince; if it was sovereignty, they would make him king; if it was a spirit that had got possession of him, they would exhaust their means in finding medicine to cure him.[43]

Finding Muhammad had no intention of curtailing his prophecies, the Quraish asked, no doubt tongue in cheek, for a more helpful message:

> If you won't accept any of our propositions, you know that no people are more short of land and water and live a harder life

than we, so ask your Lord who sent you, to remove us from
these mountains which shut us in, and to straighten out our
country for us, and to open up in it rivers like those of Syria
and Iraq, and to resurrect for us our forefathers.[44]

At the beginning of his prophetic work, Muhammad was asked to
prove himself by doing supernatural acts similar to those Abraham and
Ishmael had allegedly done. According to the Quran, the Meccans
challenged Muhammad in these ways: "Let him show us some sign, as
did the apostles of old"[45] and "We will not believe in you until you make
a spring gush forth from the earth for us."[46] But Muhammad regarded
the natural regularities as such a marvelous witness to God that no
unnatural portents were needed. The Quran states:

> It was He who gave the sun its radiance and the moon its
> brightness, ordaining its phases so that you may compute
> seasons and years. . . . In the alternation of night and day, and
> in all that He created in the heavens and the earth, there are
> signs for people who revere Him.[47]

There was a time when Muhammad could easily have claimed to
have had a special sign from God, but he refused to exploit the occasion.
A solar eclipse occurred about the time when one of Muhammad's
children died. Some attributed the eclipse to nature's sympathy, but
Muhammad said regarding the sun or moon: "They are not eclipsed on
account of anyone's death or on account of anyone's birth."[48]

Some taunted Muhammad's lack of success by asking why God had
not given a treasure to His alleged prophet.[49] The scornful asked him to
ascend to heaven and bring back parchment scrolls of the Quran that
they could touch.[50] According to the Quran, its earthly manifestation is
sufficient miraculous proof. To the Meccans' question, "Why has no sign
been given him by his Lord?"[51] came this response: "Is it not enough for
them that We have revealed to you the Book for their instruction?"[52]

Huston Smith's treatment of Muhammad's viewpoint on magical
signs deserves to be quoted at length:

> In an age charged with supernaturalism, when miracles were
> accepted as the stock-in-trade of the most ordinary saint,
> Muhammad refused to pander to human credulity. To miracle-
> hungry idolaters seeking signs and portents, he cut the issue

clean: "God has not sent me to work wonders; He has sent me to preach to you. My Lord, be praised! Am I more than a man sent as an apostle?" From first to last he resisted every impulse to inflate his own image. "I never said that God's treasures are in my hand, that I knew the hidden things, or that I was an angel. I am only a preacher of God's words, the bringer of God's message to mankind." If signs be sought, let them be not of Muhammad's greatness but of God's, and for these one need only open one's eyes. The heavenly bodies holding their swift, silent course in the vault of heaven, the incredible order of the universe, the rain that falls to relieve the parched earth, palms bending with golden fruit, ships that glide across the seas laden with goodness—can these be the handiwork of gods of stone? What fools to cry for signs when creation tokens nothing else! In an age of credulity, Muhammad taught respect for the world's incontrovertible order, a respect that was to bring Muslims to science before it did Christians.[53]

The Meccans whom Muhammad had alienated would probably have killed him soon after he began to proclaim his unpopular message had it not been for the protection of his pagan Hashimite clan. A fatal offense to one clan member would have been interpreted as something the group must avenge. Therefore, the Meccans used reprisals that did not include killing. Persecution against the Muslims consisted of imprisonments, food deprivation, and beatings. A boycott was instituted against them for two years. Those punitive measures caused some to capitulate, but others were strengthened.[54]

Initially, Islam made slow headway, and several years after its beginning there were only a few converts. Muhammad's nephew, Ali, and adopted son Zaid were the first males to accept his message. Waraqa, who encouraged Muhammad during his break with polytheism, remained a Christian. When Muslims invited Abu Talib, Ali's father and Muhammad's uncle, to accept Islam, he said: "I cannot give up the religion of my fathers which they followed."[55] Umar, one of the Meccans who had been determined to rid the world of Muhammad and his companions, became what would prove to be a most important convert.[56] He, like Muhammad, was probably influenced by their uncle, Zaid ibn Amr, who was unsatisfied with the traditional religion of Mecca.

During Muhammad's prophetic years, sick people occasionally

asked him for advice. He expressed confidence in divine healing rather
than in charms, but trust in God was not separated from the use of folk
remedies. He presumed that being bled could improve many illnesses,
whereas applying antimony could clear the sight and make hair grow.[57]
He advocated water for a fever, honey for diarrhea, and cauterization for
a wound.[58]

When Muhammad was forty-five, he sent several dozen Muslims
across the Red Sea for safe haven to Ethiopia, which was ruled by a
Christian, called the Negus. The king gave protection, hospitality, and
full freedom of religion to the refugees, which included Muhammad's
daughter Ruqaiya and her husband. The Quraish, disturbed to learn that
the Muslims had found security in Ethiopia, attempted to bribe the
Negus. They sent him gifts of Meccan leatherwork, which was prized in
Ethiopia, along with a request that he should cease to give sanctuary to
those who professed a false religion.

The Negus then asked a Muslim spokesperson to tell about his
religious leader. Ja'far, a cousin of Muhammad, responded with this
information:

> He summoned us to acknowledge God's unity and to worship
> Him and to renounce the stones and images which we and our
> fathers formerly worshiped. He commanded us to speak the
> truth, be faithful to our engagements, mindful of the ties of
> kinship and kindly hospitality, and to refrain from crimes and
> bloodshed. He forbade us to commit abominations and to
> speak lies, and to devour the property of orphans, to vilify
> chaste women. He commanded us to worship God alone and
> not to associate anything with Him, and he gave us orders
> about prayer, almsgiving, and fasting.[59]

When the Negus requested to hear the Quran, Ja'far recited what is
now entitled "Mary." That chapter tells of Jesus and his virginal mother,
Zechariah and his son John, as well as stories about the Hebrew patriarchs. The Negus and the bishops reportedly wept on hearing the
revelation. The king said: "Of a truth, this and what Jesus brought have
come from the same niche. . . . Go, for you are safe in my country. . . .
Not for a mountain of gold would I allow a man of you to be hurt."[60]

The refugees were soon to hear an unfounded rumor that the
Quraish had accepted Islam. Some returned to Mecca from this first
migration while others remained behind.[61] All had become aware of

Christian doctrines, and some who settled in Ethiopia became Christians.

At forty-nine, Muhammad was grievously struck by the deaths of Khadija and Abu Talib, his two main supporters. Another uncle, Abu Lahab, who became chief of the Hashimite clan, withdrew protection from the Muslims. Even though two of his sons had married Muhammad's daughters, he and Umm Jamil, his wife, became prominent adversaries. Umm Jamil, a poet, composed this taunt:

> *We reject the reprobate.*
> *His words we repudiate.*
> *His religion we loathe and hate.*[62]

Family alienation is also bitterly expressed in this Quranic prophecy: "The power of Abu Lahab will perish, as will he. His wealth and his acquisitions will not save him. He will roast in flames and his wife will carry the wood."[63]

For Muhammad, the traditional patriarchal bonds were now secondary to monotheism. The Quran asserts: "Believers, do not accept your fathers and your brothers for friends if they choose unbelief rather than faith."[64] It also states that children and personal property should not be held with more enthusiasm than obligations to God.[65] Muhammad's tie with the embryonic Muslim community took priority over family friendships.

Bereft now of any influential protector, Muhammad realized that an emigration of all Muslims from Mecca was imperative. He first took refuge in Taif, an oasis sixty miles to the south, but he was treated with ridicule there. When Muhammad asked the people in Taif to accept Islam and help him, one chief scornfully said: "If you are an apostle from God as you say you are, you are far too important for me to reply to, and if you are lying against God it is not right that I should speak to you!"[66]

Muhammad fled to an orchard, where he prayed:

> O God, to Thee I complain of my weakness, little resource, and lowliness before men. O Most Merciful, Thou art the Lord of the weak, and Thou art my Lord. To whom will Thou confide me? To one afar who will misuse me? Or to an enemy to whom Thou hast given power over me? If Thou art not angry with me I care not.[67]

At that time, a young slave named Addas took a platter of grapes to Muhammad, who initiated this conversation:

"From what country do you come, O Addas, and what is your religion?" He (Addas) replied that he was a Christian and came from Ninevah. "From the town of the righteous man Jonah son of Mattal," said the Apostle. "But how did you know about him?" asked Addas. "He is my brother; he was a prophet and I am a prophet."[68]

After escaping from the Taif hecklers, Muhammad returned to Mecca and encountered some men from Yathrib who were there on a pilgrimage. They thought that as a leader from another city, the prophet might be more impartial in settling their feuds and thereby unifying their people. There were two main pagan tribes in Yathrib; allied with them were three Jewish tribes who formed a large part of that community. The ancestors of those Jews were probably the first people to settle in that area.[69] They may have migrated there from Palestine, but their use of the Arabic language and Arabian names suggests that many years earlier some pagan Arabs had converted to Judaism. The pagan tribes of Yathrib had been prepared to be receptive to monotheism by their influential Jewish neighbors. Unlike the Meccans, the pagans of Yathrib were little offended by the prophet's denigration of Arabian polytheism.

Muhammad asked that the Yathribites agree to protect him from his enemies by the force of arms, but the pilgrims had no authority to agree to that request. That first agreement was called the "pledge of women" because it lacked muscle.[70] A year later, a large delegation from Yathrib, now including representatives from both Arab tribes, returned to Mecca and promised to accept him as their sheikh. They agreed to go to war in defending Muhammad in exchange for his promise of rewards in paradise.[71]

The Yathribites who formed this compact hoped that Muhammad's religion might protect them from a messianic prophet whom some expected. Some years earlier, a rabbi from Syria had warned them that a fearsome prophet "will be sent to shed blood and to take captive the women and children of those who oppose him."[72] Not only might Muhammad's monotheism satisfy the Jews in Yathrib, but he had adopted Jerusalem as the direction of prayer after access to the Ka'ba was cut off to Muslims.[73] Also, he encouraged his followers to fast on

Yom Kippur, the most important holy day of the Jewish year. Un-
diplomatically, however, the Jews were not invited to negotiate with
Muhammad before he came to Yathrib.

When Meccan leaders learned of the Muslim plan to establish
themselves in Yathrib and then noticed that some had already taken
refuge there, they gathered to discuss what they should do. Although
Muhammad's diatribes about Judgment Day might have been unpleas-
ant, the thought of Muslims achieving retaliatory power gave them even
more consternation. Perhaps they were foresighted enough to see that
Muhammad might even muster a force to effect an economic blockade
of Meccan caravans traveling in the vicinity of Yathrib. Abu Jahl, the
head of the Quraish tribe, proposed that Muhammad be killed as soon as
possible. The leaders accepted his scheme: A member of each clan,
except the Hashimites, should strike him with a sword simultaneously so
that the responsibility for his blood would be distributed to all Meccans.

Muhammad benefited from the tribal openness with which Meccans regulated their city. He was tipped off regarding the details of the
joint murder plot, and escape plans were made. By the time the assassination party came to the prophet's house, he and Abu Bakr had hidden
in a cave outside of Mecca. An intense search then got underway,
stimulated by a reward of one hundred camels for their capture. After
eluding the Meccans by hiding in the cave for several days, the companions made a breathtaking escape to Yathrib, where they were eagerly
received by the dozens of Muslims who had emigrated earlier.[74]

The Nazarene

The first three decades of Jesus' life, when Nazareth was his hometown,
are examined here. (The remaining months, when his focus was on
Jerusalem, are considered in the next chapter.) According to the Gospel
of Matthew, infant Jesus and his parents spent some time in Egypt as
political refugees.[75] Although the story may not be historical, the
cruelty of the Herodian dynasty during the time of Jesus is amply
documented.[76] Jesus belonged to a Jewish people who had lost their
independence to Roman tyrants and their Jewish surrogates.

According to the Talmud, a Jewish father's duties to his son numbered five: circumcising the child, presenting him in the place of

worship, instructing him in the Torah, training him in a trade, and arranging a marriage for him at pubescence.[77] The Gospels discuss the circumcision of Jesus when he was eight days old as a sign of the covenant made with Abraham.[78] A month later, a presentation ceremony for the infant was held at the Jerusalem temple; Jesus' parents sacrificed doves because they could not afford a lamb.[79] Since Jesus' family is recorded as carefully observing some traditional Israelite practices, it is likely that they also observed other customs that are not mentioned.

A prayer used at mealtime among Jews in Jesus' day might well have been used in his Nazareth home. It expresses a breadth of concern for the whole of creation: "Blessed are You, Lord our God, King of the universe, who sustains the whole world with goodness, kindness, and mercy. You give food to all creatures, for Your mercy endures forever."[80] The benevolence of the divine probably dominated Jesus' outlook throughout his life.

The Gospel accounts suggest that Jesus was much indebted to his parents. Joseph, who is usually represented as the father of Jesus in the only Gospels that refer to his conception,[81] is portrayed as both just and kind in his relations to Mary.[82] Mary's song depicts God as opposed to the arrogant and helpful to the poor.[83] Jesus learned to appreciate much of the theology and ethics of his peasant parents.

Aramaic, a Semitic language closely related to Hebrew, was Jesus' mother tongue. He probably read Hebrew as a result of attending a synagogue school in Nazareth whose only text was the Hebrew Bible. It was called *The House of the Book*, and theology was only one of the subjects considered. History, literature, political relationships, morality, and cultic practices were studied from the scriptural anthology that scribes had recorded over the previous millennium. Comprehension of the archaic Hebrew language was assisted by Aramaic paraphrases, called *targums*.[84]

Both Muhammad and Jesus spent many years in secular employment. In accord with cultural expectations, Jesus was apprenticed in boyhood in his father's carpentry craft. He probably continued in the work for about two decades in Nazareth.

Like Muhammad, Jesus belonged to a town far from the center of civilization. He thought of Jerusalem as the geographic hub of world culture. Prophets had referred to the historical capital of "the holy land"[85] as the earth's "navel".[86] In contrast to Muhammad, for whom Arabia was at the center of world cultures, Jesus referred to Sheba, or Yemen, as "the end of the earth."[87]

The Torah instructs the faithful to make pilgrimages to the central sanctuary of Israel on festive occasions.[88] Rituals associated with such trips resemble those engaged in during pilgrimages to Mecca. Ceremonial washing,[89] shrine circling,[90] and hair cutting[91] were featured events. When Jews from Palestine and the Diaspora arrived, they sang this psalm:

> I was glad when they said to me,
> "Let us go to the house of the Lord!"
> Our feet are standing within your gates, O Jerusalem.
> Jerusalem—built as a city that is bound firmly together.
> To it the tribes go up. . . .
> Pray for the peace of Jerusalem.[92]

The one boyhood story of Jesus in the New Testament tells of his going with his parents to Jerusalem, where he experienced a rite of passage into adulthood. He displayed to the scribal authorities there an in-depth knowledge of his religious heritage. That vignette concludes by affirming a fourfold growth: "Jesus increased in wisdom, in stature, and in divine and human favor."[93]

There was this saying in Jesus' day: "There are four types among them that sit in the presence of the sages: the sponge, the funnel, the strainer, and the sifter."[94] The "sponge" soaks up everything the instructor says and deposits it elsewhere relatively unaltered; it is simply a bit adulterated. The "funnel" receives what is poured in one ear and slowly discharges it out the other ear, retaining nothing. The "strainer" lets out the wine and keeps the worthless sediments. But the commendable student is the "sifter" who separates the coarse particles from the fine flour.[95] Jesus was a "sifter," discriminatingly refining religious traditions for contemporary use.

Just as the historical record does not specify if Joseph fulfilled his duty in teaching Jesus the Torah, no mention is made of his finding a wife for his son after the age of twelve. The New Testament is silent on all of Jesus' early adult activities. As I have argued elsewhere, it is probable that Joseph found a wife for teenage Jesus.[96] Had Jesus not followed custom, criticism of his remaining a bachelor would be expected because this would be viewed as a rejection of what was commanded in the creation stories of his culture.[97] Regarding rabbis, the Mishnah states: "An unmarried man may not be a teacher."[98] Rabbi Jesus was denounced for many things by Jewish leaders, but his marital status was not one of them. The Gospels, like the Quran, take the Semitic obligations of circumcision and marriage for granted, often without mentioning them in individual cases.

John the Baptist was the living prophet who strongly influenced Jesus at the beginning of his ministry. John stimulated a religious awakening among Jews who had thought that Abraham's descendants were insulated from God's judgment. Contemplating privileges rather than responsibilities, they had presumed that there was a most favored nation status in the divine government. To counter the smugness of God's alleged chosen, John thundered:

> Do not fancy that you can get by with saying, "We have Abraham as our ancestor"; for I tell you, God is able to produce descendants for Abraham from these stones. The ax is ready to strike the trees at the root; every tree that fails to bear good fruit is cut down and thrown into the fire.[99]

John considered changed life important, not correct lineage. Becoming baptized was efficacious only if it symbolized the washing away of past bad behavior. Jesus admired that prophet's emphasis on the fruitfulness that results from repentance; a fig tree should be chopped down if it produces nothing after careful nurturing.[100] Neither prophet believed that a people could live on the momentum of godly forbears because the living faith of the dead easily becomes the dead faith of the living.

Jesus' prophetic ministry was launched by an experience that paralleled what happened to Muhammad in a remote area near Mecca. At about the age of thirty, the Galilean came to the Judean desert where his cousin John was preaching. Growing religiously for Isaiah and subsequent prophets meant becoming conscious of the imperfections of their society and of themselves, as well as of a desire for forgiveness.[101] Accordingly, Jesus wanted John to baptize him and to get a fresh start on his life's vocation. While participating in the sacrament at the nearby Jordan River, he experienced a momentous "call" resembling that of some of the Israelite prophets.[102] A vision and voice were revealed to Jesus: "He saw the firmament open and the dovelike Spirit descending on him; and from heaven came this declaration, 'You are my chosen Son.'"[103]

By the time of Jesus' baptism in the Jordan, he was fully aware of being called to a special mission. He then withdrew to the bare hills near the Dead Sea where there was little to distract him from spiritual contemplation. As he attempted to define his new role, Jesus pondered several possibilities for the future. These were: "Should I aim at satisfying material needs?," "Should I choose any effective means for achieving control over others?," and "Will showing off special personal power promote my cause?"

Jesus may have thought of attempting to become a new Moses, delivering his people from latter-day pharaohs while providing physical sustenance. The Exodus story claims that water, manna, and quail miraculously appeared along the way for Israelite consumption. Is the role of a savior, Jesus wondered, inseparable from providing literal food for down-and-out people? He either had the scroll of Deuteronomy with him in the desert or had memorized verses from it because his responses to this and other career possibilities came from that source. Jesus found a principle relevant to his situation in words attributed to Moses: "Bread is not the only human need."[104]

In the second temptation—to follow the order in Luke's Gospel—Jesus is shown, in his mind's eye, all the earth's kingdoms. He is promised authority over all humans if he uses devilish tactics. In the centuries before and after Jesus, conquest by war has been the most common means that leaders have used to gain international power. Although Jesus desired to promote God's transcultural kingdom, he rejected the principle that a good goal justifies any evil means for diminishing nation-states.

Jesus' final wilderness temptation apparently occurred while he was meditating on a theme from the poetic anthology with which he was most familiar. Psalm 1 announces a motif that is occasionally repeated in subsequent poems, that the pious prosper and the wicked wither. The most outspoken expression of that theme is in Psalm 91, in which a poet claims that the person who trusts in God will remain unscathed by surrounding disaster:

> You will not fear the terrors of the night, nor the dangers of the day;
> Neither the plague that stalks in the dark, nor the calamity that spreads
> havoc at midday.
> Though hundreds die at your side and thousands close at hand, the
> pestilence will not harm you.
> You will look about you and see how sinners are punished.[105]

Thus, the religious are promised safety during an epidemic. The righteous can gaze with satisfaction at those who are dying all around them in recompense for their wickedness. A bold declaration is then made regarding the future:

> *God has charged his angels*
> *to guard you wherever you go.*
> *They will carry you in their arms*
> *to keep you from hitting your foot against a stone.*[106]

Presuming that the divine Protector never allows bad things to happen to good persons, the psalmist concludes his encouragement to fearlessness by assuring those who are devoted to God that they will not only be rescued from trouble but will also be rewarded with long physical life.

The Quran and Psalm 91 view angelic rescue missions similarly. When attacking a Meccan army at Bahr with a comparatively small number of troops, the Muslims called for more help. A miraculous response followed:

> When you prayed to your Lord for help, He answered: "I am sending to your aid a thousand angels, rank after rank." . . . Your Lord inspired the angels, saying: "I am with you; strengthen the believers. I will cast terror into the hearts of those who disbelieve. Strike them from head to finger!" Whoever defies God and His Apostle will be sternly punished by God.[107]

While Jesus was apparently reflecting on the sentiments of a psalmist who believed religion could prevent pain and illness, an idea entered Jesus' imagination: could he, as one with strong religious convictions, jump off the highest building he had ever seen and be rescued in midair by guardian angels? Had not John the Baptist called him a mighty man?[108] The temple in Jerusalem rose hundreds of feet above a ravine below. Jesus worked over the perennial problems of special providence. Should a person expect God to counter dependable natural forces and save life and limb in a supernatural manner? Would a person who jumps from the temple be a praiseworthy believer or a stupid exhibitionist?

Out of this contemplation, Jesus rejected the simpleminded belief that the righteous can rest assured that their health and lives will be miraculously preserved by divine intervention. He recognized that God did not save the devout person whose prayer is recorded as Psalm 22 from torture and premature death. To the contrary, Manasseh, the most wicked of all kings of Judah, had the longest reign while his grandson Josiah, the most righteous of those kings, was killed at the age of thirty-nine.[109] Also, the depraved monarch who began the Herodian dynasty died at a ripe old age possessing enormous wealth and power.[110] Jesus did not endorse the Psalm 91 fantasy of God's agents hovering over the righteous to make emergency rescues that contravene the natural order.

Whereas Jesus found the wiles of Satan in Psalm 91, he discerned the will of God in this proclamation attributed to Moses: "You shall not put God to the test as you did at Massah."[111] During the exodus from Egypt, some Israelites withheld their trust in God until receiving water at Massah in a spectacular manner.[112] While in another wilderness, Jesus decided that he should not attempt to test God as the Israelites had done. He appears to have associated the testimony in Psalm 91 with the evil inclination in humans that mistakes fanatical foolhardiness for religious courage.

Jesus' scriptural interpretations were like those of the resourceful scribe whom he commended as being able to "bring out of his treasure what is new and what is old."[113] The Nazarene thought of his gospel as "new wine" that would explode the hardened forms of ceremonial Judaism.[114] Like his prophetic antecedents, Jesus carried on a lover's quarrel with some of the traditions of his people. However, he defended but few novel ideas that had not been accepted by at least some of his fellow Jews.

Some of the Israelite prophets inspired Jesus in style and in content. The poetic rhythms by which they conveyed their messages affected his speech. Jesus' focus on love and mercy was no doubt influenced by Hosea's main theme.[115] The "good tidings" lyrics of Isaiah of Babylon had a profound impact on Jesus. He aimed at fulfilling the prophecies of a suffering servant who would become a "light to the nations."[116] The innocent servant would persist in gentle ways to bring justice to the earth.[117]

Jesus attracted "great crowds" in Galilee even though some members of the religious establishment found him subversive. The party of Pharisees (meaning "Separated Ones") thought that devotion to God required aloofness from those who did not have the time or interest to obey the host of details in the Mosaic law. The respectable Pharisees were disgusted that Jesus was kind to those who had been marginalized. In response, he affirmed that his mission in life was to live with the disreputable, extending to them the largest measure of trust possible in order to change their attitudes. He acknowledged that he did not come to work with those who thought they were in excellent spiritual health; rather, he came to associate with the irreligious.[118]

Like John the Baptist before him and Muhammad after him, Jesus proclaimed God's rule and the need for repentance.[119] Repentance involves a radical change in personal values, which results in discarding religious legalism, purifying the inner life, and assisting the needy. In spite of Jesus' unwelcomed message of judgment, he attracted many people because of the therapy (from *therapeuo*, usually poorly translated as "healing") he provided for the sick.[120] In ancient cultures, people commonly believed that disease was caused by demons that invaded their bodies, so Jesus worked to expel them. He tried to make people aware of the psychosomatic causation of some illnesses, and occasionally he informed those who felt healed that their faith was the cause.[121] Jesus recognized his powerlessness to facilitate healing among those who lacked confidence that they could regain health through the help of God.[122]

Consider one type of faith healing: Jesus occasionally encountered individuals who had a skin disease that was psychogenic in nature. It may have been psoriasis or vitiligo, misleadingly called "leprosy."[123] Priests declared those with such dermatological difficulties to be impure and quarantined them.[124] Being socially ostracized until symptoms disappeared was probably more destructive to well-being than the ailments. One so-called "leper" came to Jesus believing that he could be cleansed. Far from shunning him as contaminated and repulsive, Jesus was "moved with compassion" and laid his hand on the man.[125] The therapy in this case appears to have been Jesus assuring him that he was not polluted as defined by Jewish law. A similar disregard for conventional standards is displayed in the story of Simon the leper and Jesus.[126] He identified with that outcast by entering his dwelling and dining with him, an encounter that may have brought healing.

Jesus was not pleased with the fame he was winning by attending to those who were ill, knowing that there is nothing permanent in healing. Since all who regained their health would eventually die, he recognized that transmittable teaching could influence subsequent generations. He left the crowds who wanted to be cured of their ailments, saying: "I must proclaim the good news of the sovereignty of God . . . for I was sent for this purpose."[127] The newly introduced title of "Rabbi" was frequently used in reference to Jesus because he was interested in interpreting scripture and in providing illustrative parables. Synagogue-goers found in his teachings a vitality and boldness that they did not associate with the Jewish scribes.[128]

Bernard Shaw comments on the embarrassment Jesus felt from the popularity he was receiving from his "mighty works":

> When people who were not ill or in trouble came to him and asked him to exercise his powers as a sign of his mission, he was irritated beyond measure, and refused with an indignation which they . . . must have thought very unreasonable. To be called "an evil and adulterous generation" (Matt. 12:39) merely for asking a miracle worker to give an exhibition of his powers, is rather a startling experience. Mahomet, by the way, also lost his temper when people asked him to perform miracles.[129]

Both Muhammad and Jesus had visions of what society should be and an eagerness for change to achieve it. Muhammad's method emphasized restructuring the social structure, replacing tribal bonding with the Muslim community. Jesus' approach focused on individual renewal by selecting a dozen ordinary youths and training them to be carriers of his gospel. Although keenly aware of their deficiencies, his dual perspective enabled him to see the persons they might become.

An example of Jesus' transforming friendship can be found in his relations with a fisherman named Simon, who had an impulsive and vacillating temperament.[130] Jesus saw not only Simon's weaknesses but also his possibilities for becoming a steadfast leader. Thus, Jesus had said to him, in effect: "Your parents named you Simon, but I am nicknaming you *Petros*. You are *Petros* and on this *petros* I will build my church."[131] *Petros*, or Peter, is a Greek word that means rock when translated into English. After long association with the charismatic Jesus, Peter did become rock-like in conviction and did not cave in under the threat of persecution from the Jewish supreme court.[132]

Jesus asked prospective disciples to think carefully before joining his band to ascertain if they had the stamina needed for the arduous days ahead.[133] He said, "He who is near me is near the fire."[134] "Fire" is here a figure for the dangerous testing that the recruits would face. Jesus frankly pointed out that wild animals have more safety and security than he was receiving. That awareness is revealed in this dialogue: "As they travelled along the road, someone said to him, 'I will follow you wherever you go.' Jesus replied: 'Foxes have dens and birds have nests, but the Son of Man has nowhere to lay his head.' "[135] In addition to not having a place to call their own, disciples may find their families to be more threatening than sheltering. Jesus quoted a saying of an earlier prophet: "Your enemies will be members of your own household."[136]

Some of Jesus' opponents accused him of being inspired by the devil, and even members of his own family thought he was out of his right mind. When his mother and his brothers attempted to take him home, Jesus declared that his true family is composed not of his physical kin but of those who do God's will.[137] Jesus' bond with his disciples provided a surrogate family that transcended class, education, ethnic, and gender divisions. Since kinship ties were central in the Semitic culture, the loss of that network was dangerous.

John the Baptist became disenchanted with Jesus because he was expecting his cousin to usher in a sudden divine intervention that would separate out the good "grain" and burn the worthless "chaff."[138] Since Jesus had no interest in being a fierce ruler who would quickly destroy evildoers, John dejectedly asked: "Are you the one who is to come, or shall we wait for another?"[139] Jesus responded by attempting to convince John that he was operating in the gradual way announced by Isaiah, emphasizing God's mercy rather than God's wrath.[140]

Midway through his ministry in Galilee, according to Mark, Jesus visited his hometown. He made Isaiah's manifesto his own in the Nazareth synagogue. Jesus announced his leading motif in this scriptural reading:

> *The Spirit of the Lord is upon me,*
>   *because he has anointed me to bring good news to the destitute.*
> *He has sent me . . . to free the downtrodden,*
>   *and to proclaim the year of the Lord's favor.*[141]

On that occasion, Jesus referred to himself as a prophet and defended his acceptance of gentiles by calling attention to a neglected aspect of the work of two revered prophets who lived nine centuries earlier. Jesus was impressed that both Elijah and Elisha concerned themselves with needy foreigners. During a time of famine, Elijah traveled to the heathen homeland of Jezebel—his greatest enemy—and aided a widow. What made that episode even more significant to Jesus was that no mention is made of his helping people in Israel who were also suffering from severe deprivation.[142] Likewise, Elisha assisted in restoring the health of a Syrian army commander. Then, as in recent decades, citizens of Israel considered Syria to be their main enemy. Again, Jesus noted, the prophet could have expended all his efforts on those of his own culture in similar need. However, scripture does not tell of Elisha providing therapy for any Israelites who had the same dreaded skin disease.[143]

When fellow Nazarenes heard Jesus appeal to historical episodes that they had conveniently overlooked, their earlier admiration ceased.[144] Had he only said that he was at least as interested in non-Nazarenes as in Nazarenes, he would have generated no more than their disgust over his loss of special affection for his native village. But to cite evidence from authoritative sources to prove that the Lord had compassion on Israel's enemies was perceived by those Nazarenes as a threat to their intense regionalism. Uncontrollable rage toward Jesus resulted, and the Nazareth synagogue service concluded with this attempted lynching:

> When they heard this, all in the synagogue were infuriated. They sprang to their feet and put him out of town. They led him to the brow of the hill on which their town was built, intending to throw him off the cliff. But he walked through the mob and went away.[145]

Thus, the religious establishment in Nazareth illustrated what Jesus had said to them: "Truly I tell you, no prophet is acceptable in his own community."[146] Even as Muhammad was considered such a danger to his fellow Meccans that they attempted to kill him, so Jesus was viewed as threatening by those with whom he had lived throughout his life. He left his hometown never to return again.

CHAPTER FOUR

LATER LIFE

The Medinan Statesman

For Muhammad, a decade of increasing humiliation was followed by a decade of increasing success. He arrived in Yathrib with Abu Bakr, his most steadfast comrade, after narrowly escaping assassination. Going to the city called for a ten-day journey north of Mecca, traveling near the main trade route to Syria. The rainfall there permitted orchards of date palms and fields of barley. Yathrib was not as homogeneous as Mecca; the different tribes lived in agricultural settlements with tower fortifications to provide protection when attacked. The city was soon to be renamed *Medinat al-Nabi*, City of the Prophet, and abbreviated as Medina.

The movement of Muslim base operations to Medina is known as the *hijra*. The linguistic meaning of the term is "migration," but "flight" accurately describes the desperate situation. It was as pivotal for Muslim history as the exodus from Egypt was for Israelite history. Muslim calendar-makers subsequently regarded it as parallel in significance to what the coming of Jesus has been in Christianity. The year of the *hijra*, abbreviated "A.H.," has provided for Muslims an option to "A.D." (*anno Domini*, "year of the Lord"), which has been Christians' recognition of Jesus' significance in beginning a new era. The Muslim year, following the lunar cycle, divides the year into months of twenty-nine or thirty days, for a total of 354 days per year.

Muhammad, now fifty-two in 622 A.D. = 1 A.H., headed the emigrants (muhajirun); only after some years did he become the absolute
ruler of Medina. His first decision was to decide where to live without
offending any group. To avoid the appearance of personal favoritism, he
gave free rein to his camel and alighted where it kneeled. An open-air
sanctuary was located on that plot, presumed to be the divine choice. It
was called a mosque (masjid), which in Arabic means a place of worship.
He constructed shelters of unbaked mud-brick around the mosque for
his residence and headquarters.[1]

Originally there appears to have been three prayer times daily: at
dawn, midday, and evening, but soon two more were added.[2] On Friday,
there was a noon service at the mosque.[3] Muhammad promoted congre-
gational prayer by claiming that it was twenty-five times superior to
private prayer.[4]

In the absence of clocks, a reminder of prayer times was needed.
Muhammad considered following the Jewish custom of blowing a ram's
horn or of adopting the Christian custom of ringing a bell.[5] He decided
on instituting a town crier, and many years later the minaret was
constructed as a perch for the one called a muezzin. Bilal, a former
Ethiopian slave who had been ransomed by Abu Bakr, was selected for
the role. That first Black Muslim shouted out with his powerful voice
from a high place.[6]

Muhammad drew up a unilateral proclamation that replaced the
centrality of kinship with the bond of Muslim brotherhood. The emigrants and the Medina Muslims, along with those who would fight
alongside them, formed "one community (umma) to the exclusion of all
other people."[7] Islam, in effect, became a more inclusive tribe. With
Muslim solidarity, the burden of revenge shifted in large part from the
family to the religious fellowship. An offense against any Muslim consti-
tuted a crime against Islam.[8]

All disputes were to be brought to Muhammad for settlement, and
his pronouncements of God's judgment were to be accepted by the
community.[9] A shift in Muhammad's role in Medina is apparent from the
start. The revelation to the prophet at Mecca stated: "You are only a
warner; you have no authority over them."[10] From this point forward,
Muhammad asserts, "Fear God and obey me."[11]

The Jews, who had been prominent in Medina for many generations, had accommodated themselves to pluralism and were well accepted by the polytheistic Arab tribes. Montgomery Watt describes
their importance:

At one time the Jews had had political control of Medina, and the remnant of the previous Arab settlers had become dependent on them. Perhaps it was the Jews who developed agriculture at Medina, as they did in other parts of Arabia.[12]

Dealing with the Jews was a new challenge for Muhammad because in Mecca he confronted only polytheists. He glibly assumed that fellow astute monotheists would join the Muslims, but few did. The Jews quickly discovered that the free practice of their religion was in conflict with accepting Muhammad's role as mediator. They realized that he did not exalt the Torah as the basis of authority and that his knowledge of their traditions was deficient.[13] Muhammad probably envied the Jews because of their prosperity, as well as their claim to superior religious knowledge. He soon realized that he was incapable of assimilating the Jews into the new community. An unending mutual bitterness between the Jews and Muhammad followed. After realizing the Jewish rejection, he reversed the prayer direction for Muslims, so that they turned their backs on Jerusalem and faced Mecca.[14] Also, fasting during the month of Ramadan replaced the Yom Kippur fast that Muhammad had previously sanctioned.[15]

The Muslims in Medina were in desperate need of employment. The jobs in agriculture and trading were already taken by the Medinans. Following a common bedouin means of subsistence, the refugees began preying on caravans. Muhammad's former experience with Meccan caravans gave him an insider's awareness of their routes and vulnerability. The Meccans were targeted because the emigrants had a passionate desire to retaliate for insults and property losses they had suffered in their native city.

After some unsuccessful raids, the Muslims ambushed a small caravan that was traveling without armed escort under the cover of the holy-month amnesty. Of the four Meccans in the caravan, two were captured, one escaped, and one was killed. That murder launched a blood feud that deepened the antagonism of the Quraish toward the Muslims. The hostages were imprisoned until a ransom was paid.

Many Arabs regarded the Muslim attack as scandalous because it violated a widely honored time of peace that made pilgrimages possible. Muhammad received this clarifying revelation: "Fighting during the sacred month is bad in God's sight, but the expulsion of people from worship (at Mecca) by unbelievers is worse."[16] The Muslims were then able to confiscate the raisins, leather, and other merchandise from the caravan with a clear conscience. A revelation from on high settled how spoils should be divided: four-fifths were to be distributed to the ma-rauders; one-fifth was to be given to Muhammad for his family and for his discretionary use with the poor.[17]

Encouraged by the loot that had been taken from the Meccans, Muhammad led an attack at Badr against a large caravan returning from Syria. In this case, the Meccans had sent out troops to protect their caravan and to fight off Muhammad's bandits. Features of that battle are similar to the fight of David and the Israelites against Goliath and the Philistines. It began with combat between representative warriors going forth from the opposing forces and, at the end, the head of the leader of the larger enemy force was removed as a trophy and thrown down before Muhammad.[18]

Before the general slaughter at Badr got underway, Muhammad prayed in this somewhat threatening manner: "O God, if this band perish today You will be worshiped no more."[19] Afterward the Prophet assured his right-hand companion: "Be of good cheer, O Abu Bakr. God's help has come to you. Here is Gabriel holding the rein of a horse and leading it."[20]

Some important Meccans were killed, including commander Abu Jahl. He had bitterly opposed Muhammad from the beginning of his prophetic ministry and had been determined to crush Muhammad. Most of the Meccan prisoners of war were held for ransom since there was no profit in killing them. But Muhammad did execute two captives who had mocked him during his years of preaching in Mecca.[21]

The most celebrated piece of Badr booty was a double-pointed sword that came to be known as Dhu'l Fakar, meaning "vertebrae cleaver." It had hollows on its back edge for penetrating coats of mail. Muhammad wore it at subsequent battles as an encouraging reminder of past enemies' defeat. The sword passed into the possession of subse-quent Muslim leaders.[22]

The Muslims interpreted the triumph at Badr as a providential deliverance. Its effect on the new community was similar to the Is-raelites' claim, as they fled from Egypt, that God had defeated Pharaoh's army. The lengthy account of the Badr battle and the poetic celebration afterward display the intense Muslim interest in taking revenge. Ishaq devotes half of the pages concerning Muhammad's first two years in Medina to this first major victory, during which the number of Meccans slain was several times more than his own losses.

As Muhammad consolidated his power, he began to rid Medina of the three Jewish tribes. He was irritated that no Jews had volunteered to fight the Meccans and that hardly any had accepted him as a gentile successor to Moses. The Quran insultingly compares the Jews holding the Torah to an ass carrying books, oblivious to what they contain.[23]

Muhammad warned the Qainuqa tribe, composed of Jewish merchants: "Beware lest God bring upon you the vengeance that he brought upon Quraish, and become Muslims. You know that I am a prophet who has been sent—you will find that in your scriptures."[24] They replied, "O Muhammad, you seem to think that we are your people. Do not deceive yourself because you encountered a people with no knowledge of war and got the better of them; for by God if we fight you, you will find that we are real men!"[25] After the Jews expressed defiance, Muhammad received this message: "Say to the unbelievers: 'You shall be vanquished and driven into Hell, an awful resting place! You have already had a sign in the two armies which met: one was fighting for God's cause; the other, unbelievers.' "[26]

Biographer Hisham tells of a prank on an Arab woman by some of the Qainuqa. After she refused to uncover her face when seated in the marketplace, a teasing goldsmith fastened her clothes so as to cause an immodest exposure when she stood. The Jewish merchant was killed by a Muslim who, in turn, was killed by some Jews.[27] After this disturbance, Muhammad wanted to punish the whole tribe severely but a Medinan chief interceded on their behalf. The prophet yielded on condition that the Qainuqa leave Mecca within three days without their arms and possessions. The expelled tribe went to Syria, and the Muslims confiscated a large amount of property.[28]

Meccan general Abu Sufyan vowed to have no sex until he retaliated for his defeat at Badr and for a subsequent capture by the Moslems of his caravan, which contained a huge shipment of silver. While near Medina, he was entertained by a leader of the Nadir tribe of Jewish agriculturists who provided some secret information about the Muslims.[29] Believing that the Nadir were plotting to assassinate him, Muhammad had his men besiege their plantations and destroy some of their palm trees. He approved the Jews' request that their lives be spared and that they be allowed to go into exile. They carried as many of their possessions as they could load on camels and appeared to be relieved to leave a city where they were despised by a leader with increasing power. Some went northward to Khaibar, and others went on to Syria. The Muslims divided the remaining Nadir property, which provided houses for the expatriates from Mecca.[30] The Quran tells of the expulsion of those Jews and the hellfire awaiting them because "they resisted God and his Apostle."[31]

Ishaq records an episode that expresses Muhammad's growing hatred of the Jews, the blind obedience he was receiving from his followers, and pagan theological ethics:

> The Apostle said, "Kill any Jew that falls into your power." Thereupon Muhayyisa . . . leapt upon . . . a Jewish merchant with whom they had social and business relations, and killed him. When Muhayyisa killed him, Huwayyisa (his non-Muslim elder brother) began to beat him, saying, "You enemy of God, did you kill him when much of the fat on your belly comes from his wealth?" . . . Muhayyisa answered, "Had the one who ordered me to kill him ordered me to kill you, I would have cut your head off."[32]

At fifty-five, Muhammad suffered a military reversal at Uhud, where the Meccans slayed three times more troops than the overconfident Muslims did. Wearing two coats of mail, Muhammad participated in the battle. He shot his bow until it broke, and he bloodied his sword. In return, Muhammad received superficial head injuries, causing a demoralizing rumor that he had been killed.[33] The crudity of war is displayed in the corpse mutilations after this battle. Meccan women slashed off ears and noses in order to make anklet and necklace trophies. Abu Sufyan's wife cut out and tried to eat the liver of the prophet's uncle, Hamza, who had killed her father.[34]

The Meccan victory was so great that had they taken advantage of the situation, they could have destroyed the Medinan military capability. However, the Meccans withdrew after retaliating, killing a number equal to that of their own forces killed at the previous engagement. Arabs typically fought to get even for some past injustice, not to exterminate their enemy. Abu Sufyan shouted from a mountaintop: "Victory in war goes by turns: today is in exchange for the day of Badr."[35] Muhammad has Umar respond: "We are not equal: our dead are in Paradise; your dead are in Hell."[36]

Since Muhammad had touted that God caused the victory at Badr, some Muslims had come to think they were henceforth invincible. Most Muslims were encouraged that their upstart army was not eliminated by the strongest force the Meccans could muster. Lest it be thought that the defeat at Uhud was due to the weakness of Islam's deity, the Quran provides this theodicy:

> You disobeyed after God had shown you what you crave. Some yearn for the present world; others, the world to come. He allowed you to be driven back in order to test you. . . . Remember how you fled in panic while the Apostle at your rear was calling out to you. Therefore He paid you back with sorrow for every vexation.[37]

Two years after the Uhud battle, the Quraiza Jewish tribe from Medina may have encouraged the Meccans to attack Muhammad again. The Jews allegedly stated that the religion that Muhammad discarded was superior to Islam.[38] Before the invasion, Muhammad constructed a trench across the only approach to Medina that the Meccan cavalry could use. He assisted the diggers, causing sparks to fly as he struck rocks with a pick.[39]

The besieged Medinans encountered hardships after several weeks, causing Muhammad to plan a peaceful way of getting the invaders to withdraw. By bribing some of them with a large payment of dates, he intended to divide the enemies and to persuade some to leave. After the Muslims learned that Muhammad was merely following his own judgment and not divine revelation, they rejected his efforts for negotiating an end to the conflict. They told Muhammed: "After God has honored and guided us to Islam and made us famous by you, are we to give them our property? We certainly will not. We will give them nothing but the sword until God decides between us."[40] After a little bloodshed, the invaders returned to Mecca.

As soon as the "battle of the trench" was over, Muhammad terrorized the Quraiza, the only Jews left in Medina. They denied the accusation that they supported the Meccans from where they lived on the outskirts of the city. In any case, the Jews did not assist the Muslims during the siege of Medina. Ali Dashti comments: "Since their refusal to collaborate with Abu Sofyan (the Meccan commander) had been the main reason for the outcome of the war to the Moslem advantage, they might have been thought to deserve at least the Prophet's lenience."[41]

According to Ishaq, Gabriel appeared to convey God's order that Muhammad fight against the Quraiza. After they surrendered, they were asked to choose between death and accepting Muhammad as God's the prophet whom God forecasted in their Jewish scripture. The Quraiza said, "We will never abandon the laws of the Torah and never change it for another."[42] Ishaq's grisly account of male massacre follows: "The Apostle went out to the market of Medina and dug trenches in it. Then he sent for them and struck off their heads in those trenches as they were brought out to him in batches. . . . There were 600 or 700 in all."[43] Some of the Jewish women and children were sold as slaves to obtain horses and weapons. Muhammad took Rayhana, the wife of one whom he decapitated, for his possession.[44] The Quran gives a theological sanction to these actions: "God brought those scriptural people down from their strongholds and cast panic in them. You (Muslims) put some to the sword and took others captive. He permitted you to inherit their land, their dwellings, and their wealth."[45]

There was no more organized resistance against Muhammad in Medina after the Quraiza were eliminated. Maxime Rodinson comments on the significance of that action:

> From a purely political point of view . . . the massacre was an extremely wise move. The Quraiza were a permanent threat in Medina. To let them go would be to strengthen the hot-bed of anti-Muslim intrigue at Khaibar. Only the dead do not return. Furthermore, the killing would help to frighten and discourage the enemy.[46]

As the undisputed sovereign of Medina, he turned his attention to negotiating peace with his native Quraish tribe. Muslim devotion to the place called by the Quran "the mother of cities"[47] had been deepened by years of praying in the direction of Mecca. The prophet put on pilgrim garb during the traditional truce month and took seventy camels to the city for sacrifice.

On coming within a few miles of the holy city, his party was confronted by Meccans who were determined to block the Muslims from entering. When the envoy attempted intimidation, Abu Bakr responded: "Go suck Al-Lat's tits!"[48] More conciliatory, Muhammad agreed to the Meccan demand that pilgrimage to the Ka'ba be delayed for a year and that Meccans have a decade to decide on becoming Muslims. Deferring to Meccan sensitivities, he did not sign the armistice with his usual title "Apostle of God." This and other concessions were strongly opposed by General Umar, who regarded it humiliating for a superior power to cater to objections of those who were weaker. He said: "Is he (Muhammad) not God's Apostle, and are we not Muslims, and are they not polytheists? . . . Then why should we agree to what is demeaning to our religion?"[49]

That diplomatic compromise over entering Mecca proved to be one of Muhammad's wisest acts. Since the troops accompanying him were comparatively few in number and lightly armed, he avoided a crushing defeat while securing future benefits. To assure peace, the Meccans agreed to withdraw from the city during the next Muslim pilgrimage. "No previous victory in Islam was greater than this," Ishaq writes; "more than double as many entered Islam as ever before."[50]

Overcoming enemies without bloodshed was Muhammad's policy with regard to his home city, but elsewhere he did not grant generous terms in order to avoid war. He displayed no magnanimity in an expedition he led against the Jewish settlement at Khaibar, an oasis far north of Medina where many members of the Nadir tribe lived. Muhammad was aware of the wealth of that community, and he may still have been disgusted over the proud way in which the Nadirs made their forced exit from Medina two years earlier. Ishaq notes that "they went with such pomp and splendor as had never been seen in any tribe" as wives and children sang joyfully while riding on heavily loaded camels.[51] In any case, Muhammad viewed Jewish power anywhere in his region of Arabia as a security threat and was determined to destroy it. His long-range solution to his problem is disclosed in his frank comments to the Jewish community: "If you embrace Islam, you will be safe. You should know that the earth belongs to God and His Apostle, and I want to expel you from this land."[52]

After a devastating attack and victory at Khaibar, the spoils, including wives of slain warriors, were distributed among the victors. Muhammad selected one of the beautiful young widows for himself. Because of their irreplaceable agricultural skills, the conquered people of Khaibar were not exterminated; they persuaded their captors to employ them for half the share of their produce.[53]

Seven years after the *hijra*, the formerly despised Meccan agitator reentered his native city for the first time. In accord with the truce, the Meccans evacuated their city for three days to avoid hostilities with the Muslim pilgrims. Muhammad's uncle al-Abbas, who was head of the Hashimite clan, remained to welcome his nephew. To strengthen clan bonding, Muhammad married Maimuna, the sister of his uncle's wife.[54] Like the ritual he had performed early in life, he circled the sanctuary seven times on his camel and touched the Black Stone.

Muhammad's finest hour may have been when, at the age of sixty, he returned again to Mecca and led thousands of troops triumphantly into Mecca with little killing or looting. Pardon was given to men such as Abdulla who had renounced Islam and returned to Mecca after writing down some of Muhammad's revelations at Medina. Abu Sufyan, formerly the military commander of battles against Muhammad and now his father-in-law, became his loyal supporter for the rest of a long life. Unlocking the Ka'ba, the focal point of ritual prayers, Muhammad had the 360 idols burned or broken. He ordered that only the icon depicting Jesus on his mother's knee be preserved.[55]

From that occasion to the present, the empty Ka'ba at the center of the rededicated Grand Mosque of Mecca has functioned like the Holy of Holies in the temple of ancient Jerusalem. Neither of the small cubical-shaped structures were places for most worshipers to enter. Israelites imagined then and Muslims now conceive of the windowless shrines as housing the earthly invisible presence of the King of Kings, whose rule stretches in all directions. Those sacred buildings were not objects of worship but places to concentrate consciousness on the single God who made their religious history possible.

Why did Muhammad not destroy the Black Stone that he had helped during his pagan years to lodge in the side of the Ka'ba? On his first pilgrimage to the shrine that had been for him the holiest place throughout his life, the Black Stone was "embraced" (*istalama*, the Arabic word here, involves stroking and kissing).[56] His sentimental attachment was so strong that he could not classify it with the other carved and uncarved idols in the Ka'ba. Perhaps he had come to think of the Black Stone not as an object of worship but as a symbol of God's presence. It became for Muhammad's "house of God" (*bait-allah*) what a field stone became for Jacob's "house of God" (*beth-el*).[57] Rock connotes permanence, so it is an occasional metaphor for God in the Hebrew culture. For example, Joshua used a stone as a reminder of covenant renewal with the Lord.[58]

While at the shrine that was as central to Muslims as it had been to Arab pagans, Meccans swore allegiance to the city's new ruler. At that occasion, according to Ishaq:

> The Apostle stood at the door of the Ka'ba and said: "There is
> no God but Allah alone. . . . He has made good His promise
> and helped His servant. . . . O Quraish, God has taken from
> you the haughtiness of paganism and its veneration of ances-

tors. Man springs from Adam and Adam sprang from dust. . . .
Go your way for you are the freed ones."[59]

At this time, a confederacy of twenty thousand Arabs marched
unsuccessfully against Muhammad at Hunain, near Mecca. Their defeat
established him as unquestionably the most powerful leader in Arabia.
The accompanying personal popularity of Muhammad resulted in a
flood of new Muslims, many of whom may have been only nominally
converted. Ishaq associates a Quranic revelation with this situation:
"After God's help and victory came, you see multitudes crowding into
God's religion."[60] Since a one-sentence creed affirming monotheism and
Muhammad's prophetic role was the minimum demanded for joining
Islam, it is understandable that whole towns would suddenly want to be
part of a people who were highly successful politically and economi-
cally. For the first time in history, most of the bedouin tribes of the
Arabian peninsula became united. Muhammad had increased loyalties
from clan or tribe to form a pan-Arabian solidarity, theoretically based
on theocracy. Belligerence was channeled to the cause of protecting the
community of those professing a common religious commitment.

The Quran states that the bedouin were generally not fully converted to Islam.[61] Those who have probed seventh-century Arabian politics have likewise pointed to the gap between outward profession of faith
and inward monotheistic commitment. Iranian scholar Dashti writes:

> Although no reliable statistics of devotees and opportunists
> among the Prophet's followers have yet been compiled, it can
> be inferred that about ninety percent of those who had pro-
> fessed Islam by the time of his death had done so from either
> fear or expediency.[62]

Rodinson has this to say regarding the consolidation of Muslim
power:

> Muhammad was able to bribe influential men with suitable
> presents and, like a true politician, to play on men's ambition,
> greed, vanity, fears and sometimes no doubt (although more
> rarely) on their thirst for idealism and devotion. Some were
> completely converted, others gave their allegiance while re-
> maining pagan at heart. Every tribe bound itself to Medina
> with promises to furnish troops and not to attack the other

tribes which had made alliances with Muhammad. They smashed their idols and undertook to pay either the lawful contribution of the faithful or the tax levied on associates, as the case might be. . . . Every conceivable attitude was there, from firm conviction to downright unbelief. But all these tribes were bound to Muhammad as political entities. That was what mattered.[63]

In less than a decade, Muhammad had risen from a Meccan fugitive to an Arabian potentate. He sent letters to some foreign rulers affirming that he was God's messenger and that any people who accepted Islam would be safe. The letter to Muqauqis, the Coptic King of Ethiopia, was favorably received, and he sent to Muhammad the gift of a concubine, a Christian named Mariya (Mary).[64] She gave birth to a boy, who lived only one year. During that time, Muhammad probably hoped that some day he might be succeeded by this son who was named Ibrahim after the patriarch declared by the Quran to be the paradigm Muslim.

After subduing his fellow Arabians, Muhammad returned to Medina—which remained his political capital—and directed his attention northward beyond Arabia. He wanted to take advantage of the wealth of the Fertile Crescent, which formed an arc around northern Arabia from the Persian Gulf to the Nile Delta. He may have realized that the power vacuum resulting from the weakness of the former mighty empires of that area would make conquest easier.

The campaign that Muhammad led on Tabuk, an outpost of the Byzantine empire south of the Dead Sea, was the beginning of the Muslim wars of international conquest. To penetrate a region ripe for the plucking hundreds of miles north of Medina, he amassed a large army. Getting underway was hampered by the prosperity of the Muslims, which had lowered their motivation to risk death in order to gather more booty. The intense summer conditions en route were almost disastrous. Ishaq states: "When the men had no water they complained to the Apostle, so he prayed, and God sent a cloud, and so much rain fell that they were satisfied."[65]

When the Muslims reached their destination, the Christians in Tabuk and the surrounding region submitted without fighting. Byzantium had so little power left that John, the governor of Aila, took the initiative to make a treaty with Muhammad. The merchants of Aila, now the port city of Aqaba, were guaranteed safety for their ships and caravans in exchange for paying protection money. A precedent was then established for dealing with people with a biblical religion who lived outside of Arabia. While entrusting Muslims with military control by the payment of an annual tax, they could continue to practice their religion.[66]

On returning to Medina, Muhammad treated as apostates those able-bodied men who had not joined him to spread the religious, political, economic, and social system of Islam. He was incensed that some Muslims would rather not go outside their region to conquer. The Quran treats the situation scornfully: "What ailed you when it was said to you, 'March for God's cause,' that you lingered slothfully in the land. . . . If it had been closer by and an easy journey, you would surely have gone."[67]

The Tabuk campaign was the last of the twenty-seven in which Muhammad took part personally; he actually fought in nine battles. There were many other raids carried out by Muhammad's troops.[68] His victories and defeats were rather evenly divided. The prophet's last sermon in Medina was devoted to promoting a military campaign in Syria, which was completed several years later with the capture of Damascus.[69]

At sixty-two, Muhammad made his last trip to his home city. By now, the Quran had added a pilgrimage to Mecca as a basic Muslim obligation: "To make *hajj* to the Ka'ba is a duty to God for believers who have the capacity to make the journey."[70] At Mecca, he ran around the Ka'ba three times and walked around it four times.[71] Then he moved rapidly between Safa and Marwa,[72] hills associated with Hagar's frantic search for water before the Zamzam source was found. On the Arafat plains, a few miles from Mecca, the culminating rituals took place. For hours, the pilgrims stood together in solidarity.[73] Muhammad concluded what would soon be recognized as his farewell discourse with these unifying words: "Know that every Muslim is a brother to every other Muslim and that you are now one brotherhood."[74]

At nearby Mina, the pilgrims threw pebbles at pillars that represented Satan, who tempted Abraham to refuse God's command to sacrifice his son. Then, in recognition that God permitted Abraham to substitute a domestic animal, the pilgrims ritually sacrificed animals and ate the meat or gave it to the needy.[75] After the pilgrims made offerings, they were deconsecrated and could replace their two white seamless loincloths with ordinary clothing. The minimum time for the pilgrimage was two days; afterward they could resume cutting their hair and engaging in marital intercourse.[76]

Shortly after returning to Medina, Muhammad became ill with pneumonia-like symptoms. He confided to friends that God had assured him a place in paradise but had given him the option of going at once or going later, and that he had chosen the former. Aisha, his teenage wife, described his last hours in this way: "His pain overcame him as he was going the round of his wives. . . . The Apostle died in my bosom during my turn."[77]

Muhammad's last words expressed his judgment that Islam alone should survive in his homeland. He allegedly said: "Let not two religions be left in the Arabian peninsula."[78] Aisha reported that "when the last moment of life of God's Apostle came, . . . he said, 'May God curse the Jews and Christians, for they built the places of worship at the graves of their prophets.' "[79] During his illness, Muhammad heard of the adoration of saint statues at an Ethiopian church[80] and he may have been reflecting on the undesirable possibility of Muslims idolizing his relics. The prophet prohibited the use of funeral monuments or inscriptions.[81]

In Muhammad's opinion, he died as an old man. The Apostle had said: "The term of life of my people ranges between sixty and seventy years, and very few live longer."[82] Yet the Muslim community was not prepared for the loss of their leader, and his death came as a profound shock. Immediately after his death, Umar attempted to deny the mortality of his hero by this announcement: "Muhammad is not dead: he has gone to his Lord as Moses did."[83] Umar was not referring to Moses' final disappearance on Mount Nebo, but to his ascent to Mount Sinai before returning a month later. Abu Bakr, Muhammad's closest companion, then spoke to those who had gathered at the Medina mosque. After silencing Umar's frantic proclamation, Abu Bakr put an immediate end to any idolizing impulse. Facing the reality of Muhammad's corpse nearby, Abu Bakr announced: "If anyone worships Muhammad, Muhammad is dead. If anyone worships God, God is alive, immortal."[84] He then recited this Quranic verse: "Muhammad is no more than an apostle, and many apostles have passed away before him."[85] Muhammad was not buried in the Muslim graveyard, but where he died under Aisha's dwelling adjacent to the mosque.[86]

Robert Ellwood offers a fitting tribute to the fulfilled life of this charismatic figure:

> Muhammad died a popular hero among his people, a ruler, a
> successful diplomat, politician, and general. He was a mystic

visionary also, but there was nothing ethereal about him.
Instead he seemed to his people a man larger than life in many
senses: warmhearted, full of cheerful humor, a planner of
stratagems, a marshall who rode into battle with his troops
and held his following together by the force of his personality
when all seemed darkest.[87]

The Peaceful Reformer

After being ousted from Nazareth for his lack of chauvinism, Jesus
made his home in the lakeside town of Capernaum.[88] His friends were
mainly fisherfolk who lived in the area, including Mary of Magdala,
whose town was also on the Galilean lake. Farther along the lake was
Tiberius, which Herod Antipas built as his new capital and named for
the ruling Caesar. Jesus apparently avoided the Galilean cities, Tiberius
and Herod's earlier capital at Sepphoris.

King Herod had provoked anger among many Jews because of his
luxurious lifestyle and adoption of Roman customs. He assumed that
whom he married or divorced was strictly a personal matter that could
be done without consulting even his wife. Before marrying his brother's
wife, Herod decided to divorce the daughter of Arab King Aretas IV.
John the Baptist denounced the marital conduct of his king, which was
incestuous according to Hebrew law.[89] Fearful that John's popularity
with the people in his realm might cause an uprising, Herod had him
imprisoned.[90] Subsequently, with encouragement from his new wife,
the king ordered John's head served on a platter at his birthday party.[91]

Enraged by the desertion, the Arabian princess returned to Petra,
the Nabatean capital. By way of revenge, her father humiliated Herod in
a battle against the Jews. Josephus records a theological interpretation
that was given to Herod's military defeat:

> To some of the Jews the destruction of Herod's army seemed
> to be divine vengeance, and certainly a just vengeance, for his
> treatment of John, surnamed the Baptist. For Herod had put
> him to death, though he was a good man and had exhorted
> the Jews to lead righteous lives.[92]

John's martyrdom had a profound effect on Jesus because he also thought of himself a prophet. This self-understanding corresponded with his public image; some Galileans described Jesus as "a prophet like one of the old prophets"[93] and exclaimed, "A great prophet has arisen among us!"[94] "Prophet," the standard translation of the Hebrew term *nabi* or the Greek term *prophetes*, can be misleading if foretelling the future is presumed to be its primary connotation. Biblical prophets were interpreters of past divine-human covenants and, on the basis of historical patterns, discerners of present and future trends. The prophets who interested Jesus were principally spokespersons for God in their own times. They were mainly not condemners of outsiders but warners to their own people.

Herod thought of Jesus as another troublesome John the Baptist who was critical of the authorities in his realm.[95] Jesus was informed that the king was determined to kill him.[96] To achieve that end, the Herodians had conspired with the Pharisees.[97] Recognizing that his days were numbered, Jesus concentrated on spreading the Gospel rapidly and training twelve disciples to carry on after him. To accomplish both purposes, Jesus sent out pairs of disciples to different places in Galilee on a practice mission. They attempted to give more wholeness to the minds and bodies of those they encountered.[98]

After Jesus' disciples returned, he took them on a retreat into the mountains to the north of Galilee. There he introduced the notion that great suffering, and even death, should be expected for himself and his followers. In spite of the recent ghastly killing of an innocent prophet, the disciples had a mental block against accepting that God would permit good people to face such terrible experiences. Jesus spoke in this frank and paradoxical manner:

> If any want to become my followers, let them deny them
> selves, carry their cross, and follow me. Those who want to
> save their life will lose it, but those who lose their life for me
> and for the gospel will save it. What will they gain by winning
> the whole world at the cost of their life?[99]

In Galilee, there were occasionally scenes of captured terrorists carrying their cross to a place of execution.[100] Jesus introduced the notion of taking up a cross voluntarily, even when it was not inflicted. According to one Gospel, he advocated that the cross be carried "daily,"[101] showing that it symbolized for him not political martyrdom but an ongoing living sacrifice. The cross was a strong image for risking humiliation while advocating Jesus' way. This would involve breaking some of the establishment rules and courageously standing tall without revenge.

Not long after Jesus returned with his disciples from the Lebanese mountains, a slow journey to Jerusalem began. He announced, "It cannot be that a prophet should perish away from Jerusalem."[102] Jesus interacted with the Passover pilgrims who were traveling with him on his last visit to the traditional capital. Those who accompanied him were filled with ebullient nationalism and religious enthusiasm. They sang a psalm that tells of the divine assistance available to Jews as they desperately respond to encompassing enemies. Psalm 118 contains the Hosanna cry, meaning "Rescue now!" The exclamations that follow identify the singers as being in the Jerusalem area:

> O Lord, give us success!
> Blessed be the one who enters in the name of the Lord! . . .
> With branches in hand, move in procession to the Temple altar![103]

A festive crowd carrying leafy boughs accompanied Jesus. They hoped he might be God's agent for driving the Romans out of Palestine. They shouted, "God bless the coming kingdom of our father David! Hosanna in the highest!"[104] During the Passover, the annual celebration of the Israelite defeat of the Egyptians, there was a fervent longing for liberation from contemporary pharaohs. The pilgrims dreamed that the new savior would be like one of God's anointed kings who never lost a battle. David had removed the Philistine threat and had widened the boundaries of the independent Israelite state to the greatest extent ever. Those along the road with Jesus desired a new David who would behave in a similar manner.

After the Roman conquest of Palestine under General Pompey, some Pharisees composed a new psalm to vent contempt for those gentiles. The pilgrims may have sung it also:

> O God, may the son of David reign over your servant Israel.
> Gird him with strength to shatter wicked rulers.
> May he purge Jerusalem from gentiles that trample and destroy it. . . .
> With an iron mace he will crush all their substance.
> He will blot out the lawless gentiles with a word of his mouth.[105]

Some of Jesus' disciples thought that Jesus was going to Jerusalem to expel the Romans and rule from a glorious throne. James and John requested: "Permit us to sit, one at your right hand and one at your left, in your glory."[106] Jesus lamented that they did not discern that his kingdom was associated with suffering and service, not special privilege and secular power. Ironically, James became the first apostle to be martyred, by order of Herod Agrippa.[107]

When addressing his disciples, Jesus contrasted his notion of greatness with the prevailing view:

> You know that the recognized rulers in the world lord it over their subjects, and their great ones are tyrants. It shall not be so with you. Among you, whoever wishes to become great must be your servant, and whoever wishes to be first must be slave of all. For the Son of Man did not come to be served but to serve, and to give his life to free many.[108]

Jesus discerned two irreconcilable hopes imbedded in the scriptures. The popular one was that the Lord's anointed would become king in Jerusalem and "break them (national enemies) with a rod of iron."[109] Jewish warriors would beat "pruning hooks into spears," converting a peaceful economy into a military power, with Jerusalem as the stronghold.[110] The opposite hope was of a "Prince of Peace"[111] who would lead people in beating their "spears into pruning hooks."[112]

In order to signal that his mission was of a peaceful nature, Jesus used a protest strategy that earlier prophets in Jerusalem had employed. They had used crowd-stopping symbolic actions to draw attention to a message that was counter to popular sentiments. Jeremiah once wore an ordinary ox yoke as he walked in the city, explaining to the curious that the freedom-curtailing "yoke" of Babylonian rule should be preferred to the alternative. To picture the alternative of mass destruction by the Babylonian army, he shattered a pottery vase. Jeremiah believed that Jewish nationalists were inviting war, famine, and pestilence because they aimed at political independence regardless of the cost.[113] He was convinced that submission to a foreign pagan army was the Lord's will, even though many thought of him to be a subversive to the Judean religious community.[114]

Jesus wanted the peasants accompanying him and the Jerusalemites to reject the conventional wisdom that patriotism always means belligerence against national foes, presuming that such is God's will. Jesus agreed with Jeremiah, his role model, that there are situations where being conquered by foreign troops is better than being buried by them. At the risk of being called a deserter, Jesus urged: "When you see Jerusalem surrounded by troops, realize that its devastation is near. Then those who are in Judea must run away to the mountains, and those who are inside the city must evacuate."[115]

Jesus also followed Jeremiah in maintaining that the enemies of the Jewish peasantry were, in considerable part, their own rulers. With that elite group in mind, Jesus laments: "O Jerusalem, Jerusalem, city that kills the prophets and stones those who are sent to it!"[116] Both Jeremiah and Jesus declared: "This house shall become a desolation."[117] The ruling "house" in Jerusalem had violently opposed God's messengers.

To counter the zealotry of those approaching Jerusalem with him, Jesus publicly demonstrated for the first time that he was the promised Messiah. To express the qualities of his reign, he dramatized Zechariah's hope by means of a royal entry.[118] Jesus liked the symbols of the prophet's poetry:

> *Shout for joy, people of Jerusalem!*
> *Look, your king is coming!*
> *He is vindicated and victorious,*
> *But humble and riding on a donkey. . . .*
> *He will banish the war horse and the battle bow;*
> *He will make peace among the nations;*
> *His rule will extend from sea to sea.*[119]

Jesus may also have had in mind the concluding words of Zechariah's prophecy: "There shall no longer be traders in the house of the Lord of hosts."[120]

When Jesus obtained a panoramic view of the city from the Mount of Olives, he lamented that his people did not understand or endorse a vision for the future that he shared with some earlier prophets. The Jerusalem dwellers rested their security on two things: the presumed impregnable walls of their mountaintop fortress and the location there of "the House of the Lord," on the verge of completion after decades of reconstruction. Jesus saw parallels between what weeping Jeremiah faced *vis-à-vis* the Babylonian destruction of Jerusalem six centuries earlier and what might be ahead for those who disregarded the lessons of history. Jesus had sad reflections on entering Jerusalem:

When he came into full view of the city, he burst into tears, saying, "If only you knew today the path to peace! But it is hidden from your sight. The time is coming when your ene- mies will build fortifications around you and besiege you. You and the children within your walls will be dashed to the ground. Your enemies will not leave one stone standing upon another because you did not recognize your time of oppor- tunity."[121]

Here, Jesus gives conditional prophecy in the manner of Jeremiah, who believed that forecasted tragedy would not strike *if* sinful people repented. In urging the Jerusalem officials to choose the road of recon- ciliation toward their enemies rather than the road of rebellion, Jer- emiah pleaded: "The Lord sent me to prophesy against this Temple and this city all the things you have heard. If you change your conduct . . . the Lord will revoke the disaster that he has pronounced against you."[122]

By riding into Jerusalem on what was then the common beast of burden rather than on the mount of a military commander, Jesus acted in a highly significant manner. He pointed to a radically new kind of reign: one in which majesty is combined with meekness and peacefulness replaces jingoism. Marcus Borg describes Jesus' procession into the traditional royal capital in this way:

His entry was a planned political demonstration, an appeal to Jerusalem to follow the path of peace, even as it proclaimed that his movement was the peace party in a generation headed for war. It also implied that the alternative of peace was still open.[123]

Prophets Jeremiah and Jesus both attempted to deflate the priests' presumption that the temple was indispensable to God. For the priests, it was unthinkable that God would permit the destruction of his earthly dwelling place, which they were commissioned to manage. They had converted the outer Court of Gentiles from a place of worship to a place of commerce. Jesus was angered over the desecration there by money- changers who issued temple-approved currency in exchange for Roman coins and over vendors who were hawking animals for the sacrificial ritual. Infuriated by the priests who profited from these concession stands, Jesus appropriated Jeremiah's claim that the temple had become a "den of robbers" and that its destruction was justified.[124]

Jesus thought the temple should be cleansed, not *from* the gentiles, but *for* the gentiles. In support of their right to worship at the temple, he cleared out a space for them. He had the audacity to overthrow the booths in the area originally intended for gentile worship. Jesus agreed with the inclusiveness that Isaiah expressed as God's spokesperson:

> As for the foreigners who give me their allegiance, who love and serve me, . . . I will bring them to my sacred hill and make them joyful in my house of prayer. Their sacrifices and offerings will be accepted on my altar, for my temple shall be called a house of prayer for all peoples.[125]

The priests in Jerusalem asked Jesus about his authority to demonstrate at the temple. Perceiving that the question was intended to entrap him, he did not respond. Rather, Jesus infuriated them more by telling a parable that pointed to the historical unfaithfulness of Jewish rulers and their persecution of prophets.[126] The authorities then posed another tricky question: "Is it lawful to pay taxes to Caesar, or not?"[127] Those raising this taxation issue thought Jesus' answer either would alienate him from his peasant supporters or would convince the Romans that he was subverting their rule in Palestine. By way of separating the spheres of government and religion, he responded: "Give Caesar what Caesar is due, and give God what God is due."[128] In a compromising manner, he asserted that civil obedience to a pagan ruler was not always inconsistent with serving God.

On leaving the temple for the last time, Jesus lamented: "Do you see these great buildings? Not one stone will be left here upon another."[129] Howard Kee and Franklin Young provide this interpretation:

> Many of the Jews were seething with a desire to revolt against the Romans, whom they looked upon as hated intruders; yet Jesus continually refused to give in to the popular hopes for revolt and revenge. Not that he was unaware of the oppression of his people. Rather, he seems to have been convinced that armed revolt was not the way out of their difficulties. It would lead only to destruction, motivated as it was by a desire fully as evil as the Romans' desire for power—the desire for revenge.[130]

Priests of the Sadducaic party were comfortable with the status quo and were not in favor of revolt against Rome; they defended the temple huckstering that provided their income. Seeing that Jesus could not be frightened into leaving Jerusalem, they decided to have him killed in a legal manner. Realizing that the crowds were "spellbound by his teaching," the priests bribed one of Jesus' disciples to assist in capturing him under the cover of darkness.[131] John Crossan, a leading current authority on the historical Jesus, finds his "symbolic destruction" of the temple a sufficient action to account for the determined effort to have him executed.[132]

Jesus arranged for a supper with his disciples at Mark's home in Jerusalem. There he set forth the "new covenant" that Jeremiah had announced.[133] Unlike the old Sinai covenant, adherence to internalized principle would take precedence over external law. He broke a loaf of bread and distributed it, saying, "Take, this is my body."[134] While passing around the wine he said: "This is my blood, poured out for many, which ratifies God's covenant."[135] Here, Jesus alludes to the suffering servant of Isaiah who "poured out himself to death, . . . yet bore the sin of many."[136]

After that private farewell meal, Jesus experienced the humiliation of public rejection by the leaders in Jerusalem. In a garden at the city's outskirts, while he was praying to have the fortitude to carry out his mission, Judas led a detachment of temple guards to Jesus and identified him by greeting him with a kiss. The religious authorities had organized an armed posse that night on the presumption that he was another violent revolutionary who would resist arrest. On seeing them, Jesus asked indignantly: "Am I an outlaw that you have come with swords and clubs to capture me?"[137]

The prisoner was then taken in rapid succession before at least two judges at different places in Jerusalem. At dawn, Jesus first appeared before Caiaphas, the high priest. He had assembled the Jewish high court, called the Sanhedrin, at his residence. After conflicting testimony against Jesus was given, Caiaphas asked: "Are you the Messiah, the Son of the Blessed One?"[138] Jesus' affirmative answer was deemed blasphemous, and the enraged Sanhedrin voted for capital punishment. Some opponents spit on him, and the guards beat him.[139] In a similar manner, the Jerusalem elite had responded to Jeremiah by having him beaten and by demanding his death.[140]

Since the Sanhedrin could not carry out death sentences,[141] Jesus was taken before Pilate, the Roman governor. In order to be prepared for a possible insurrection at the Passover feast, the Jewish freedom celebration, Pilate was visiting his military headquarters in Jerusalem. As a civil ruler, he was unconcerned over the blasphemy matter, but Jesus' admission of being the Messiah prompted this question: "Are you the King of the Jews?" "You say so"[142] was Jesus' elusive reply, but Pilate found nothing to indicate that the accused should be punished. The Roman authority tried to resolve the case by offering the release of either Jesus or Barabbas for Passover amnesty. The latter was a convicted terrorist and a murderer, but the lynch mob requested that Barabbas be acquitted. Pilate then made the politically expedient move and permitted the crucifixion of one he knew was innocent of treason.[143] Jesus was put to death by the Romans, but Jewish scholar Claude Montefiore admits that his arrest and "trial" was instigated by the Jerusalem priests.[144] In Raymond Brown's definitive commentary on the narratives pertaining to Jesus' last week in Jerusalem, he shows that a significant factor in Jesus' condemnation was the Sanhedrin's disgust over his anti-temple teachings.[145]

Before giving Jesus a cross beam to carry to the site of execution, Roman soldiers mocked the Jews by showing them their "king." To simulate royal status, they robed Jesus in purple and placed a stiff weed in his hand for a scepter. To parody the laurel wreath worn by the Roman emperor, a crown of thorn branches was pressed down on Jesus' head. The soldiers then alternated between striking him and saluting him in a contemptuous manner. At Golgotha, the cross for Jesus was distinguished from those for two outlaws by the sarcastic inscription over it, "The King of the Jews."[146] The arms of the three condemned men were spread out and nailed to beams, which were then lashed to vertical posts.

To many Jews in Jerusalem, Jesus must have seemed to be more of a traitorous wimp than a triumphant winner. They admired such rebels as Barabbas, but Jesus rejected their violent methods. Before Jesus, no one had been quite so odd as to advocate a loving attitude toward adversaries or to both preach and practice nonviolence toward personal persecutors. Such teachings of Jesus were so distinctive that diverse groups of biblical scholars have ranked them as the Gospel sayings alleged to be by Jesus that are most likely to be authentic.[147] David Flusser, a Jewish authority on Christian origins, finds the "definitive characteristic" of Jesus' ethic distilled in these three words: "Love your enemies."[148]

Jesus advocated that his followers endure persecution while "seeking the divine rule and God's justice."[149] The unpopular Jesus was taunted by those who equated kingship with militant resistance to alien political powers. The Jewish religious leaders inadvertently expressed the truth when they scornfully commented: "He saved others but he cannot save himself."[150] On that crucifixion day, Jesus' frightened male disciples forsook him, but some women stayed with him until his death and assisted with the burial.[151] In accord with the Semitic tradition that would later result in similar treatment for Muhammad, Jesus' body was wrapped in linen cloth and simply buried.[152]

Within a few days of Jesus' death, some of his disciples became convinced that he had appeared to them.[153] Believing that he was now alive and exalted to a position of honor, their despair was changed to joy. They were no longer blinded by their personal ambitions to be part of the power structure of a restored Jewish kingdom. Recalling Jesus' international aim, the apostles gradually radiated out from Jerusalem in pursuit of that goal. Their mission witness extended to the boundaries of the Mediterranean world.

A psalmist composed this cryptic line: "The stone that the builders rejected has become the chief cornerstone."[154] That stone is treated in the New Testament as a metaphor for Jesus, whom the Jerusalem rulers discarded outside the city walls. They perceived that the odd-shaped religion that he embodied could not fit into the scheme they had for constructing Judaism. Ironically, the stone the rulers threw out became the main stone for a new structure, providing the standard for aligning other "living stones" that compose the church.[155]

The Hebrew poet's stone symbol is also apt for describing Muhammad, whom the Meccan shrine builders despised and rejected. Subsequently, the presumed misshapen stone became worth more to Islam than the Black Stone has been to the Ka'ba. Each prophet has experienced an amazing reversal in subsequent history: one who was deemed inferior and destined for the rubbish heap was discovered to be appropriate for setting the lines and carrying the weight for a massive edifice that is still being erected. Members of the separate communities exclaim with the psalmist, who viewed God as the architect for this strange development: "This is the Lord's doing, and a wonderful sight!"[156]

CHAPTER FIVE

SCRIPTURES

The Bible and the Quran are the most widely read and studied books in history. In Islam, the Quran is primary, and Muhammad is a secondary material witness to it; in Christianity, Jesus is primary, and the Bible is a secondary material witness to him. According to the Quran, the Word of God became a book; according to the New Testament, "the Word became flesh and lived among us."[1] Accordingly, Muslims write about "the divinity of the Quran,"[2] and Christians speak of "the divinity of Christ."[3] In discussing the two scriptures, attention will be given to comparing the Quran's treatments of biblical stories with the biblical texts.

The Quran

Affirmed by the Quran is a transcendent source of revelation, called "the mother of the Book."[4] The "glorious Quran, inscribed on an imperishable tablet,"[5] is believed to be a depository of sublime wisdom. "Only the pure can grasp the Lord's revelation."[6] Since it is written in Arabic,[7] early Muslim scribes wrote down a replica of the original text that Muhammad had recited, and all authentic study of it is necessarily in Arabic. By its own declaration, the Quran is flawless,[8] so no human could be its author. It is the continuous monologue of One whose word is absolute truth: "This Quran is not such as could be composed by anyone but God. It verifies and explains the previously revealed Scriptures."[9] The earthly Arabic copy of the heavenly prototype, certified by the seventh-century caliphs, is also presumed to be infallible.

According to the Quran, communication between God and humans is indirect: "It was not given to any mortals to have God speak to them except by revelation, or from behind a veil, or through a messenger who is authorized to make known His will."[10] All that Muhammad recited was allegedly sent down from heaven by the intermediary, archangel Gabriel, who conveyed what was in the original.[11] God is acknowledged as the Quran's creator, but the prophet was indispensable for its manifestation. Regarding that interdependence, Rafiq Zakaria writes: "There could have been no Quran without Muhammad. He is not only its transmitter but also the embodiment of its teachings. . . . There are references in it to his work and mission, his struggles and even his personal affairs."[12] The revelation was sometimes addressed to other Muslim believers or to unbelievers rather than to Muhammad.

From a wife of Muhammad comes a report indicating that both auditory and visionary stimuli were involved in receiving the Quran:

> Aisha asked: "O Apostle of God, how does revelation come to you?" The Apostle of God said: "Sometimes it comes to me like the reverberation of a bell, and that is the hardest on me. . . . Sometimes the angel takes the form of a man for me, and addresses me, and I understand what he says." Aisha continued: "I have actually seen him, at the coming down of the revelation upon him, on an extremely cold day, with his forehead running with perspiration."[13]

Muhammad distinguished between his fallible opinions and the revelation he transmitted. After coming to Medina, he offered some advice on fruit-tree cultivation, a subject he knew little about. His judgment was put into practice, causing the harvest to diminish. The prophet explained: "When I issue any command to you regarding your religion, accept it; but when I issue any command to you based on my own opinion, I am merely a human being."[14]

The Quran recorded by Muslims is composed of revelations that are loosely strung together. Abrupt topic shifts heighten puzzlement over the meaning of particular fragments. For example, chapter (*sura*) twenty-four begins with regulations pertaining to male/female conduct, commenting on slanderous charges against one of Muhammad's wives. Then comes the most sublime paean of praise to God in the Quran, followed by a description of the plight of unbelievers and other topics.

Both hearers and reciters of Quranic verses in Arabic may not understand what is being chanted, but "the sound itself of inimitable sonority and rhythmic power is numinous and sacramental."[15] Like the mantras of the religions of India, the psychic vibrations of God's very words are considered awesome. The Quranic cadences have so much charm that listeners are often indifferent toward analyzing the content.

There is more in the pages of the Book of Books than the prophet received. Muslims believe that the Hebrew Bible and the Gospels are by-products of the quintessential Book and contain partial revelations of God's ideas.[16] Whatever truth there is in scriptures of other religions comes from this archetype, which embodies the totality of the word of God. Jews and Christians are "people of the Book."[17] The relationship between scriptures is declared succinctly in the Quran: "God revealed the Torah and the Gospel earlier to guide humans. Now God has revealed to you (Muhammad) the Book that confirms the truth of what preceded it."[18]

Regarding the integration of Hebraic legends pertaining to Abraham in the early Islamic culture, Reuven Firestone writes:

> Part of the sublimity of the Quran was its success in rendering Biblicist traditions that had found their way into Arabic meaningful to the indigenous non-Biblicist Arab population. . . . Its audience certainly knew many of the Bible-oriented stories and may have enjoyed hearing them told by their Biblicist neighbors, but had not previously considered them relevant to their own history and welfare. Through his recitation of the Quranic revelation, Muhammad taught that the legends were a part of universal history and that they related directly to every individual's personal salvation.[19]

Muhammad had no firsthand knowledge of either the Torah or the Gospels, the parts of the Bible the Quran frequently alludes to. His exposure was by way of oral transmission rather than through study of the written record. Muhammad displays almost no awareness of the many prophets biblical books are named for. All of the Quran's eighteen biblical prophets are males;[20] Lot and Ishmael are included, but not

Miriam or Huldah. In the Bible, the latter two are prophets, but the former two are not. The absence of most of the biblical prophets may be due to the Jews whom Muhammad encountered having little interest in prophets after Moses. Also, the Quran displays no awareness of the apostle Paul, who wrote a large portion of what came to be known as the New Testament. That silence may reflect Arabian or Ethiopian Christians' lack of concern for some biblical writings.

Abraham and Moses are the Torah personalities whom Muhammad found most useful for his situation. He defended himself from his Meccan critics by utilizing the Quranic adaptation of a Jewish midrash about Abraham.[21] According to that story, Abraham emigrated from his hometown after indulging in idol smashing. Young Abraham had denounced those in his community who followed the traditional worship of images, and he had pulverized all except the chief one when they were not looking. When the outraged polytheists confronted him about the vandalism, Abraham confounded them. He claimed that the biggest image broke the smaller ones and that his people should ask them if that was not true. The episode ended with this dramatic exchange:

> They said to Abraham: "You know they cannot speak." He answered: "Would you then worship, instead of God, that which can neither help nor harm you? Shame on you and on your idols! Have you no sense?" They cried: "Burn him. . . ." We (God) rescued him and Lot, and brought them to the land We had blessed for all peoples.[22]

The plural pronouns that are often used to refer to God should not be interpreted as an unwitting relapse into polytheism. The frequent use of "We" and "Us" may be to heighten awareness that God is not human. A similar use of plural pronouns in reference to the single God is found in the Bible.[23]

One biblical story of Abraham and his family in "the promised land" became the basis for considerable Muslim expansion. The patriarch had given Hagar and Ishmael a goatskin of water before they set out for the arid wilderness. When the water was exhausted, Hagar placed her young son under a bush. According to the Genesis legend, she frantically searched for water and wept in despair, whereupon God showed her a well from which she refilled her goatskin.[24]

On returning to Ishmael, according to Muslim lore, Hagar found that God had provided a spring where she had left him.[25] The place is identified with Becca, the early name for Mecca,[26] so Hagar is presumed to have run between hills in that vicinity. Baca, a word meaning "weeping" that is mentioned once in the Bible as the name of a valley, is equated in Muslim tradition with Becca. A psalmist says of some travelers: "As they go through the valley of Baca, they make it a place of springs."[27] Hagar and Ishmael became the first people to settle there.

Muhammad's grandfather found a well within the sacred enclosure of the Ka'ba that he identified with the one that had saved Ishmael's life. It was called Zamzam in imitation of the sound of the water springing forth. After crying out "Allah is great," he cleaned the rubble out of the well.[28] Zamzam has continued to supply worshipers at the Ka'ba to this day.

According to the Quran, Abraham came to Mecca and helped Ishmael build the Ka'ba for worshiping the one true God.[29] Finding Ishmael's family in poverty, Abraham advised his son to divorce his spouse. Ishmael took the advice and after marrying a second wife, he became prosperous.[30] The grand patriarch is given credit for initiating pilgrimages to Mecca, for circumambulating the axial point of world religion, and for instructing sacrificers there to share the meat with the poor.[31] The mark Abraham made in Mecca was indelible for even now pilgrims are shown a stone enshrined in a kiosk near the Ka'ba that allegedly contains his footprint.

The Quran also includes a story about what commitment to the will of the inscrutable God might entail. The characters of the story are aged Abraham and an unnamed son who is to be sacrificed to God as a burnt offering. Muslim tradition is divided over whether Isaac or Ishmael is the sacrificial son.[32] Abraham asked his son to comment on his dream in which the son was being sacrificed by his father. Although the son knows in advance that he will be slaughtered if his father does what they assume God has ordered, he submits in a gentle manner. While Abraham is posed to slit his son's throat, he learns that God was only testing them and that they have proven their devotion.[33]

Regarding the Meccan enhancements to the Abrahamic legend in the Quran, Francis Peters comments:

Muslim and Jew come together in the figure and symbol of Abraham, . . . the father of both Isaac and Ishmael, the former the tribal ancestor of the Sons of Israel, the latter of all the Arabs. This was the biblical genealogy, and it was not disputed by Islam. Where they did disagree was on the fulfillment of the

promise to Abraham, whether it came to term in the Israelites or
the Arabs. There are in fact two Abrahams in the Quran, the
well-known figure from Genesis, embroidered here and there
with what appear to be Jewish legendary *midrash*; and another
Abraham, the product of some other sensibility, who emigrated
to Arabia with his wife Hagar and his son Ishmael to settle in
Mecca, where he built the Ka'ba, the "house of God," and instituted most of the ritual practices of the later Islamic pilgrimage. . . . The historian may note that the Abraham
associated with Mecca appears in the Quran only after Muhammad's first confrontation with the Jews of Medina, and so the
invocation of Abraham may have been a response, a retort to
the Jewish rejection of Muhammad's own prophethood.[34]

Peters's construction seems plausible because it shows Muhammad
reacting in a typically human fashion. He was certainly dismayed over
realizing that few Jews accepted him as the fulfillment of the monotheistic tradition he admired. By way of compensating for this fact, the
Quranic revelations began to relate Abraham to Arabia, and to Mecca
specifically. The Quran treats the authority of the first Semite who lived
in western Asia as superior to that of Moses, the prophet most admired
by his Jewish opponents. The Abrahamic saga is now assigned exclusively to the place where Muslim attention is focused when praying.

Even if not historically accurate, the Arabization of Abraham
served brilliantly to advance Muhammad's diatribes against the Jews.
Since the biblical tradition is silent on whether Abraham and Ishmael
ever went to Mecca to make it the cult center for their unsullied religion,
the rabbis were unable to give historical refutation to the contention of
the Quran. Moreover, it is reasonable to assume that an ancient person
could travel from Palestine to Arabia to live with a son and help him
construct a shrine.

Montgomery Watt provides this perceptive evaluation of the
Quranic treatment of Abraham:

> The conception of Islam as a restoration of the pure religion
> of Abraham offends modern Western standards of historical
> objectivity. Yet from a sociological standpoint it must be
> admitted that it was effective in its original environment. . . .
> Islam belongs in a sense to the Judaeo-Christian tradition, and
> that tradition may be described as the tradition which begins

with Abraham. Islam is thus a form of the religion of Abraham—a form, too, well suited to the outlook of men whose way of life was closer to Abraham than that of the bulk of Jews and Christians.[35]

Joseph is the other Genesis patriarch who is treated extensively in the Quran. Delightful characterizations are given in what it calls "the best of stories."[36] The chapter entitled "Joseph" stands out in the Quran because it deals consistently with only one subject. The sexual aggressiveness of Potiphar's wife and her friends is portrayed more boldly than in the Hebrew account, causing Joseph to request imprisonment to protect his virtue.

Moses, along with other Israelites of his generation, commands more attention in the Quran than all other biblical prophets combined. He is the major figure for more than five hundred verses, or approximately 10 percent of the total text. He is mentioned seven times more often than Jesus. The focus on Moses is no doubt related to the similarity of his personal experiences to those of Muhammad. Both individuals had foster mothers, and both were exiled from the place where they grew up. Both established ways of worshiping God, served as military leaders, and received revelations in the desert that provided regulations for their people. Sociologist Robert Bellah points out how Muhammad had more in common with Moses than with Jesus:

> Muhammad did not begin his preaching in a great and closely organized world empire but rather in a tribal society, which had not yet attained a political structure that could be called a state. He had not so much to work out a relationship to an existing political order as to create a new one.[37]

Exploring specific parallels between Moses and Muhammad is instructive. Each was unexpectedly summoned to pursue difficult tasks that demanded total commitment. The Quran tells of what happened to Moses when he went to light a torch from something on fire: "When he came near, a voice called out to him: 'Moses! I am your Lord. Take off your sandals, for you are in the sacred valley of Tuwa. I have chosen you; listen to what shall be revealed.' "[38] The Muslim custom of barefooted worship originated with the precedent set by Moses at a burning bush.[39] Common ground becomes sanctified when footwear, symbolizing what is handcrafted, is set aside. While secluded in the Sinai desert, Moses also veiled himself after talking with God.[40] Muhammad, on a mountain outside Mecca, wrapped himself in a cloth at the time of his trances.[41]

Muhammad's mode of serving as an intermediary was similar to that of his precursor. The vocation of each prophet involved being a mouthpiece for God against the power structure of his society. The Torah repeatedly tells of Moses receiving instructions like this: "Go to Pharaoh and say, 'Thus says the Lord, "Let my people go." ' "[42] In the Quran the style is frequently similar, as in this example: "Say, 'People, the truth has come to you from the Lord.' "[43] Muhammad could identify with the fact that Moses' teaching was often unfavorably received by the Israelites, as well as by the Egyptian king. The Quran recalls: "Moses said to his people: 'O my people, why do you seek to harm me when you realize that I am God's messenger to you?' "[44]

Catholic theologian Guilio Basetti-Sani observes: "Between Moses and Muhammad profound psychological and spiritual similarities exist. The religious content and the social ethics of the Sinaitic message are similar to those of the message of the Quran."[45] Quranic law contains overtones of the Mosaic code, especially as summarized in the Decalogue. One listing begins and ends with the first and greatest commandment: "Worship no other god beside God."[46] Following this are laws pertaining to kindness to one's parents, giving to the needy, and knowing before acting. Murder, adultery, stealing, and haughtiness must be avoided. Some laws are more specific than the Ten Commandments: murder is related to infanticide, and stealing is related to weight cheating in the marketplace. Also, the younger generation is instructed to return to aging parents the care they once received from them.[47] A comparison with the Ten Commandments shows two main omissions: there is no law pertaining to the irreverent use of the name of God, and there is no sabbath law.

The Quran affirms: "We gave the Book to Moses, a complete code for those who would do good, with guidance in all things."[48] Even so, this explanation is given for some prohibitions in the Torah: "Because of the wrongdoing of the Jews, We forbade them certain wholesome things which were formerly lawful."[49] For example, camel meat was created to be ceremonially clean, although it is a dietary prohibition in the Mosaic code.[50] Also, Abraham did not have to curtail his activities one day each week because he lived before the enactment of laws regulating the Sabbath.[51]

Moses developed military prowess among the ragtag ex-slaves who had fled with him during the exodus from Egypt.[52] Muhammad also molded timid exiles into an attack force for overcoming powerful adversaries. Just as Moses longed to repossess land promised by God to the followers of Abraham, so Muhammad hoped that the Semitic region from Mecca to Palestine would call on the name of the one God. At the time of the deaths of Moses and Muhammad, their armies had invaded land east of the Dead Sea and had ambitions to capture the region where Abraham, Lot, and Isaac had settled. Richard Bell makes this comment about Muhammad:

> The example of Moses had implanted in his mind the idea of a conquering religious people. The *hijra* and the execution of the divine vengeance upon the unbelievers of Mecca had given the immediate occasion for the organization of such a warlike community. The victory of Badr had confirmed it.[53]

Muslim apologists draw upon the precedent of Moses to justify the Quranic statement regarding Muhammad's harsh treatment toward some followers of Moses.[54] As noted earlier, the entire Quraiza clan of Jews in Medina was killed or enslaved, and their property was confiscated. That action continues to be justified by stating that it was merely doing to the Jews what their distant ancestors did to others. Martin Lings comments on the final liquidation of Jewish power in the city named for the prophet by a footnote to his collection of the earliest sources on Muhammad. Lings states that it "coincided exactly with Jewish law as regards the treatment of a besieged city, even if it were innocent of treachery."[55] The Torah passage is then cited:

> When making war against a town, you shall besiege it; and when the Lord your God gives it into your hand, you shall put all its males to the sword. You may, however, take as your booty the women, the children, livestock, and everything else in the town.[56]

Similarly, Cyril Glasse claims that the Quran is in line with the Torah regarding the extermination of the Quraiza. Muhammad, like Moses, was assisting God in giving appropriate punishment: "It is a case of the final judgment overtaking a people while still in this world."[57] Apologists do not explain that the passage in Deuteronomy to which they appeal also states that forced labor rather than slaughter should be the punishment for those who surrender—as the Quraiza did.

David is another prominent figure of the Hebrew Bible who interested Muhammad. He was charmed by the way in which the inexperienced Israelite, with God's wisdom and a weak band of troops, vanquished Goliath and his mighty army.[58] Muhammad saw a parallel between that Israelite battle and his encounter with Meccan forces at Badr. The Quran refers to the latter engagement this way: "The faithful fighters saw with their very eyes that the unbelievers were twice their own number. But God strengthens with His aid whom He will."[59]

The Quran seems to confuse happenings that are chronologically separate in the Bible. The account of King Saul's army confronting the Philistines appears to be combined with the account of Gideon's forces fighting the Midianites. Stories belonging to different eras may be conflated in this passage: "When Saul led his troops, he said: 'God will test you at a river. Whoever drinks its water will not fight by my side, . . . except for him who scoops it up in the hollow of his hand.' "[60] Also, the Quranic Haman is an Egyptian official whom the Pharaoh commands to build a tower of bricks that he can climb to confront the alleged God of Moses. By contrast, the biblical Haman is a Persian official who is separated by geography and many centuries from either Moses or the Tower of Babel.[61]

The Quran occasionally refers to the evangel (*injil*, the Arabicized form of the Greek *euaggelion*), which in English is more commonly called the Gospel. The Quranic gospel refers not to what Jesus said and did according to the four Gospels of the New Testament, but to his words in the Quran. Some of those words are similar to alleged teachings of Jesus as reported by Christian contemporaries of Muhammad.

Only four New Testament figures are recognized by the Quran, and they all appear in nativity stories. Jesus is portrayed mainly as a child who does little to provoke antagonism from opponents. There are about one hundred verses in fifteen chapters about John the Baptist; his father, Zechariah; Jesus; and his mother, Mary. The latter is distinguished in the Quran as being the only woman for whom a chapter is named and the only woman personally named in any chapter. Apart from that "most blessed of women," all the rest are known as the wives of named husbands.

Muhammad's high regard for Mary is displayed in his protecting a Madonna painting at the Ka'ba from destruction.[62] His respect for her is related to a revelation he received: "(Concerning) Mary, the daughter of Amram (*Imran*), who preserved her virginity: We breathed of Our Spirit into her womb. She trusted in her Lord's words to her and His scriptures, and was truly devout."[63] Perplexed as to how she would become pregnant without having intercourse, Mary is told that "God creates what He wills by simply saying 'Be!' and it is."[64] Conception without the semen of a man or the uterus of a woman occurred when God formed a clay figure and blew into it.[65] The way in which Jesus became animated is similar to the way God made Adam, but the presence of a uterus for fertilization simplified the miracle.[66]

Early Muslim interpreters expanded on the Quran's contention that God placed young Mary in the custody of Zechariah the priest.[67] The claim that she conceived as a virgin is made more plausible by isolating Mary from secular men. She was orphaned as a child and was raised until puberty in the temple precincts of Zechariah, her uncle. Lots were cast in the community where the shrine was located to determine who should give Mary financial support, and a carpenter named George was selected. There was a monk in the community named Joseph, but he did not touch her.[68] That legend parallels in some ways what is recorded in the apocryphal *Protevangelium of James*, which was popular in Byzantine Christianity.

According to the Quran, the ministry of precocious Jesus began as soon as he could breathe. Mary was alone in the countryside when her labor pains began. Leaning against a palm tree, she cried out in distress: "Would I had died before now and left without a trace!"[69] She realized that her baby was being born when she heard a voice from below her, saying: "Don't despair, God has provided a stream of water at your feet. Shake the tree trunk, and ripe dates will fall down around you. Eat, drink, and refresh yourself."[70]

When Mary carried her infant to her people, Jesus announced: "I am God's servant. He has given me the Scripture and has appointed me a prophet; His blessing is upon me wherever I am. He has commanded me to be steadfast in prayer, to pay the welfare tax all my life, and to honor my mother."[71] Later, boy Jesus tells of wonders he will perform:

> From clay I will shape for you the form of a bird. It will become a living bird, by God's permission, as I breathe into it. Also by God's permission I will heal the blind and the leper, and raise the dead. I will announce to you what to eat and what to store in your houses.[72]

When the Quranic Jesus became an adult, his disciples wanted him to produce food miraculously. They tested him in this manner: "Can

your Lord send down for us from heaven a tray full of food? . . . We wish
to eat from it so that we may reassure ourselves and know that what you
said to us is true, and that we may be witnesses of it."[73] Jesus responded
with this prayer: "Lord, send down to us food from heaven that it may be
a feast for us and a sign from You for those who will come after us."[74]
God replied by sending provisions and by warning that subsequent
disbelief would result in severe punishment.[75] On the basis of what
surfaces in the Quran, Muslims seemed to regard Jesus principally as a
lifelong magician. Parables were of much interest to several Gospel
writers, but they were apparently unknown to Muhammad. Perhaps the
reason for almost no discussion of Jesus' teaching in the Quran was an
assumption that its content was not different from that of other
prophets, whose teachings are given.

Muhammad apparently presumed that Jews and Christians knew
little of significance about prophets that could supplement what he had
revealed. Thus, the prophet said: "Do not ask the people of the Book
about anything."[76] Curiosity about comparative religion is lacking in
those who presume that they possess the later and purer truth. Apropos
here is John Kelsay's comment on the status of the Quran: "It becomes
more than an Arabic version of the Word of God, equivalent to Torah
and Gospel. The Quran becomes the 'decisive criterion,' by which the
monotheistic communities may resolve their religious disputes."[77]

According to the Quran, Jesus was uniquely "close to God."[78] His
role is revealed in these verses: "Christ Jesus, the son of Mary, was only a
messenger of God, and His Word that He imparted to Mary, and His
Spirit."[79] (Here, Jesus is called *al-masih*, literally "the messiah," but the
Quran shows no understanding of its original meaning as a title of the
anointed ruler promised in Israel. Rather, it connotes what Christ meant
to Christians of Muhammad's day, a proper name of Jesus.) God says of
Jesus, "We confirmed him with the Holy Spirit."[80] God without Word is
expressionless; God without Spirit is lifeless. Thus, if God's Word and
Spirit dwelt in Jesus, then to know Jesus is in some way to be aware of
the living presence of God.

Jesus in the Quran is a harbinger parallel to John the Baptist in the
Gospels. John proclaimed: "The one who is coming after me is greater
than I";[81] "He must increase, but I must decrease."[82] Similarly, the Quran
attributes this prophecy to Jesus: "People of Israel, I am God's messenger
to you, confirming the truth of the Torah and bringing good news of a
messenger who will come after me, whose name is praiseworthy."[83]

Ahmad, the Arabic word for "praiseworthy," contains the same root as the name Muhammad. Thus, Muslims presume that the principal teaching of Jesus' gospel was that Muhammad would be his successor.

Biographer Ishaq attempts to relate to the New Testament Jesus' alleged forecast of Muhammad in the Quran. Recorded in the Gospel of John are these words attributed to Jesus while he was at the Last Supper with his disciples: "It is to your advantage that I am leaving you. Unless I go, the Helper will not come; but if I depart, I will send him to you."[84] The Greek word for helper, *paraklytos*, is also translated in English as comforter, counselor, or advocate. Ishaq alleges that the Greek term does not adequately translate the Aramaic (or Syriac) word that Jesus used: *menahhemana*, meaning "life giver." Thus, when Jesus taught in Aramaic, he allegedly used a word containing some letters of Muhammad's name.[85] Subsequently, the Fourth Gospel writer corrupted Jesus' words when making a Greek translation. European Christians have believed Jesus was promising the Holy Spirit to reinforce his witness, but Muslims have thought he was predicting the coming of Muhammad.

According to Ishaq, a Jewish king named David condemned Jesus to be crucified whereupon Jesus persuaded one of his thirteen disciples to be his stand-in. His name was Sergius—who is not generally known because Christians deny that he existed. Sergius had become Jesus' execution replacement before Judas' betrayal kiss.[86]

Ishaq says of Jesus: "God raised him to Him and garbed him in feathers and dressed him in light and cut off his desire for food and drink, so he flew among the angels, and he was with them around the throne. He was human and angelic, heavenly and earthly."[87] Ishaq thought of Jesus as being taken alive to heaven in the manner of an earlier bird-like ascension: "God wrapped Elijah in feathers and clothed him with fire and removed his need for food and drink, and he flew among the angels, and he was half man, half angel, half earthly, half heavenly."[88]

Just as the Quran views Jesus as a modifier of the earlier revelation, so Muhammad's mission was to announce changes in scriptural revelations and even to alter revelations he had received earlier. The Mosaic dietary law is relaxed, and all foods except pork, carrion, meat offered to idols, and blood are sanctioned.[89] The Quran recognizes the camel as the main animal for religious sacrifices and for providing meat to eat.[90]

The tone of the Quranic revelations delivered in Mecca generally differ from those given in Medina. The earlier ones include advice and

exhortation but not legislation, whereas the later ones contain manda-
tory commandments. Over the decades that Muhammad received divine communiqués, the content occasionally changed. The prophet is
reported to have said: "Some of my traditions abrogate others just as
some parts of the Quran abrogate others."[91] The Quran affirms that
textual revision is the prerogative of the Author: "God abrogates or
confirms whatever He will, for He has with Him the mother of Books."[92]
God takes full responsibility for revisions, acting like a world-class
scholar improving an already excellent manuscript. This doctrine of
abrogation gave some of Muhammad's opponents ground for accusing
him of doctoring the alleged divine revelation to suit his personal needs.
The Quran states: "When We replace one verse for another—and God
knows best what He reveals—they say, 'You have made it up.' "[93]

Interpreters of the Quran would be greatly assisted if there had
been a revelation from on high as to which verses were changed. Most
of the abrogated verses appear to remain in the text as part of God's
word. This is problematic since often there is no divine declaration as to
which text is earlier, and thus temporary, and which is the permanent
injunction. Consequently, there is little consensus among scholars as to
what verses have been modified or discarded. To protect the infallibility
of the Quran, some Muslim scholars claim that what has been super-
ceded is not anything that was revealed to Muhammad, but any biblical
revelation that is inconsistent with the Quran.[94] For example, ancient
Jewish expatriates oriented themselves toward Jerusalem when they
prayed, but Muhammad changed the direction to Mecca.[95] The obvious
discrepancy between the records of two holy books regarding Jesus' final
hours on earth is explained as a falsification by the writers of the New
Testament in order to serve their own interests.

In an effort to absolutize the Quranic revelation, Muslims who
have lived after the time of Muhammad have generally believed that the
Quran called the prophet "illiterate" (ummi).[96] This would stress that he
was a passive transmitter of God's word and exclude the possibility that
his pronouncements came after he studied Jewish and Christian texts.
However, an examination of uses of ummi elsewhere in the Quran shows
that the term specifically means "unscriptured" or "gentile," in contrast to
the "People of the Book."[97] Working as the business manager for his
wife's caravans for a large part of his life, Muhammad most likely shared
at least a basic literacy that was common among traders. Indeed, the
earliest biography of Muhammad occasionally refers to his writing
down something.[98] Apart from the issue of Muhammad's literary abili-

ties, he surely had an active mind. The stories of his early religious retreats show that he had developed extraordinary sensitivity to spiritual impulses.

Awareness of Muhammad's creativity prompted accusations by some adversaries about his source of authority. These are echoed in the Quran: "Those who disbelieve say: 'This is but a forgery which he invented with the help of others.' . . . And they say: 'Stories about ancient people he has written down as they were told him morning and evening.' "[99] Other critics of Muhammad claimed that he got his ideas from a particular human: "They say, 'A mortal taught him' but the man to whom they allude speaks a foreign language, while this is eloquent Arabic speech."[100] The Jews that Muhammad encountered spoke a mixture of Aramaic and Arabic. Since his message was strongly mono-theistic, Maxime Rodinson is probably right in identifying as Jewish the foreign source to which the Quran refers.[101]

A Jewish boyhood companion of Muhammad named Ibn Sayyad might be the person who was thought to have been a source of what Muhammad called God's revelation. According to an early Muslim tradition, Ibn Sayyad also claimed that he was God's messenger and had a throne vision. Muhammad hid behind palm trees in an attempt to hear something that Ibn Sayyad was murmuring when he wrapped himself in a garment to induce a mystical trance.[102]

Muhammad appreciated parts of three religious traditions. From his inherited Arabian religion, he endorsed the sanctity of the Ka'ba and some of the pilgrimage observances. From Judaism, he adapted the sagas of some prophets and approved of their theological ethics. From Chris-tianity, he accepted the prominent roles of Mary and her son. This prompts Khuda Bukhsh to ask:

> What else is Islam but a revised edition of Judaism and Chris-tianity? Muhammed never claimed originality. He insisted . . . that his mission was but to rid Judaism and Christianity of what he regarded as life-destroying accretions—to proclaim their pristine purity—to enthrone in the hearts of men the faith of Abraham, in its undimmed excellence![103]

According to the Quran, Muhammad is "the seal of the prophets."[104] Throughout the centuries, writers have commonly certi-fied their works by impressing their private seals upon them. Al-Bukhari records that Muhammad, to assure recipients of the authenticity of his letters, fashioned a seal in the form of a silver ring on which he engraved, "Muhammad, God's Apostle."[105] As a metaphor, a messenger was called "a seal" if his testimony conveyed the sender's authority. Hence, in John's Gospel, Jesus is referred to as the carrier of God's seal.[106] This means that God attests to the truth of Jesus' teachings, but it does not imply that there would be no subsequent communications. Montgomery Watt suggests that the reference to Muhammad as "the seal of the prophets" meant that he confirmed previous prophets, not that he was the final legitimate one.[107]

Late in life Muhammad may have thought of himself not only as having the divine mark of approval, but also as a bearer of God's final testimony. Another Arab, who claimed prophetic credentials, received a harsh reply from Muhammad after sending him a letter with this salutation: "From Musailima the messenger of God to Muhammad the messenger of God."[108] The response was addressed: "From Muhammad the messenger of God to Musailima the liar."[109] A monotheist and probably a Christian, Musailima was subsequently killed when Muslims led an army against him and his Hanifa tribe.[110]

Muhammad may have been among those Arabs who had been influenced by Mani.[111] Several centuries earlier, he had sought to establish himself in the Middle East as the culmination of a line of divine spokespersons in Asian religions. He claimed that an angel had announced to him that God had chosen him to preach and that he had been made a sealer of a wide range of revealers, including those of the Judeo-Christian culture. According to the founder of the influential Manichean religion:

> Wisdom and deeds have always from time to time been brought to mankind by the messengers of God. So in one age they have been brought by the messenger called Buddha to India, in another by Zaradusht (Zoroaster) to Persia, in another by Jesus to the West. Thereupon this revelation has come down, this prophecy in this last age, through me, Mani, messenger of the God of truth to Babylonia.[112]

The Quranic revelation was initially transmitted from person to person by professional reciters. Muhammad said: "You must keep on reciting the Quran because it escapes from the hearts of men faster than camels do when untied."[113] Memorization was facilitated by the poetic rhythm contained in many of the more than six thousand verses. Some

Muslims must have memorized parts of it during Muhammad's lifetime and recited it in prayers. There was and continues to be the *hafiz*, meaning "keeper," who commits to memory the whole Quran, which is almost as long as the New Testament.

To curb the problem of forgetfulness, fragments of the Quran were recorded on bones, palm leaves, leather, potsherds, and thin white stones.[114] Writing down the oral revelations probably began before Muhammad's death and continued for a generation afterward. Abu Bakr and Umar were concerned over the possible loss or distortion of the revelations that Muhammad received during the last third of his life (610–32 C.E.). Those first caliphs realized that many who knew parts of the Quran by heart were dying; therefore, they arranged for scribes to gather written and oral testimonies so that an official text could be canonized as Islam's ultimate authority.[115] Most Muslims think that the final edition of the Quran was completed during the rule of Caliph Uthman in the mid-seventh century. Oral transmitters were much needed even after the written Quran was completed because the classical Arabic script lacks the vowel signs that are necessary for both reading and understanding.

Some scholars surmise that it was at least the eighth century before the definitive recension was completed.[116] The earlier portions of the written Quran are the short poetic utterances delivered at Mecca, and the last are the prosaic social regulations for the Muslim community at Medina. To understand the Quran in its approximate chronological development, the book should be read from end to beginning. After the Quran's canon was completed, additional records were made of the life and teachings of Muhammad, but these are not considered to be infallible.

Presumably, God has not since added to or erased from Muhammad's recital of the matrix Book. The belief among orthodox Muslims is that the Arabic text of the Quran is literally the word of God. Fresh arguments are occasionally made in support of that dogma. For example, after completing a computer analysis, Naheem Khan concludes that "the Quran could not have been composed by any person except Allah."[117] Included in his purported scientific support for this conclusion is that *irraheem* ("most merciful") is used exactly 114 times, which coincides with the total number of Quranic chapters.[118]

The Bible

The biblical terms for "revelation" (Hebrew, *galah*; Greek, *apokalupsis*), refer to an uncovering by God of what had been hidden. The emphasis in revelation is on divine initiative, but alertness by humans is needed in order to notice the exposure of what previously had been veiled. Most people fail to comprehend spiritual meaning, Jesus observed, because they do not make an adequate effort to find out.[119]

Jesus' parables paradoxically conceal and elucidate, depending on the recipients' capabilities for thoughtful and spiritual reflection. For example, his story of a father with two problem sons does not make explicit the theological message that legalistic obedience to religious regulations can hinder a close relationship with God.[120] Although the story does not mention God, it may subtly reveal more about Jesus' view of God than anything else in the Gospels. For those who have spiritual sensitivity and insight, some characteristics of God are revealed in the parent who is eager to develop mature relationships among alienated family members.

When Jesus quoted from the Torah what he called the first commandment, he added to the Hebrew original. The additional phrase is italicized: "You shall love the Lord your God with all your heart, and with all your soul, *and with all your mind,* and with all your strength."[121] Seemingly, Jesus wished to emphasize that devotees to God should not substitute affectionate gushing or ritualistic frenzy for intellectual discipline. Both devotional and mental persistence are needed for religious discovery. Jesus advised: "Continue to ask and it will be given you; keep seeking and you will find; knock constantly and it will be opened to you."[122]

A dialogue between Jesus and Peter illustrates the close tie between revelation and discovery. After gathering from his disciples a report on how other Galileans regarded him, Jesus asked, "Who do you say that I am?"[123] Peter answered, "God's Messiah."[124] Jesus commented that Peter's affirmation came not so much from human insight but from what God had revealed to him.[125]

In the Semitic culture there was the doctrine that cosmic nature "proclaims God's handiwork."[126] Jesus found that wildflowers and carefree birds disclose some of the glory of God.[127] Muhammad believed that God inspires bees to suck from flowers and produce honey.[128] But nature was not the primary method of God's communication for either prophet, nor did they associate revelation with priestly pronouncements, magical manipulation, or divination declarations.

Jesus found God's purposes usually expressed through events in Israelite history; revelation accompanied the prophetic interpretation of those events. For example, the emancipation of Israelite slaves is interpreted by Moses and Miriam as a mighty act of the God of liberation that should motivate the emancipated to respond by divine worship and by adherence to covenantal law. A Quranic metaphor is apropos here: revelation is a lightning flash at night that illumines everything in the vicinity, assisting in the movement toward the sanctioned destination.[129] The revelation pertaining to the exodus from Egypt enabled discerning Israelites to get a general bearing on the nature of God that made their subsequent activities significant.

The equity theme that was prominent in the struggle of Moses against Pharaoh had an impact on both Jesus and Muhammad. Jesus expressed a Torah teaching when he announced at Nazareth that God had sent him "to free the downtrodden and to proclaim the year of the Lord's favor."[130] Allusion is made here to Moses' designation of a jubilee year when the people of God will "proclaim liberty throughout the land."[131] During that year, a land redistribution would provide a new beginning for those who had become impoverished. Although Jesus did not conceive of his role as an economic redeemer, he warned his disciples against gentile tyrants. He taught them that leaders should administer in the literal sense of ministering to others.[132] The Quran also emphasizes the social-justice message of the Torah in this preface to the story of Moses: "Pharaoh became a tyrant by dividing his people into different castes and impoverishing one tribe. . . . God showed favor to those who were oppressed by providing them leaders . . . and by inflicting on their oppressors what they dreaded."[133]

When arguing with the Sadducees, Jesus appealed to what his scriptures said about God's continuing relationship with Moses' Hebrew ancestors. Jesus presumed that those Jewish leaders could have discovered a clue about life after death from reading carefully a passage from Exodus.[134] To provide authority for his positions when responding to the Pharisees, Jesus cited what David did and what Isaiah said.[135]

According to the Gospels, divine revelation came directly to Jesus as it had to earlier prophets. John the Baptist was regarded by Jesus as the most recent of a long sequence of spokespersons for God. He had great respect for John's supplement to the past divine-human communications that were preserved in Hebrew scriptures.[136] Jesus' direct relationship with God is best revealed in his frequent references to divine fatherhood, a metaphor emphasizing personal closeness rather than oldness or maleness.

Both Jesus and Muhammad belonged to the Semitic tradition in which divine revelation consisted of both vision and audition.[137] Frequently, however, God speaks without appearing.[138] At his baptism, Jesus both saw the "the Spirit's descent like a dove" from an opening in the heavens and heard a heavenly voice.[139] After that special audiovisual experience, subsequent inspiration appears to have had a continual quality. Millar Burrows observes: "Jesus' message seems to be the expression of clear, steady insight rather than the result of separate, particular revelations."[140]

For Jesus, revelation was not primarily associated with mystical dreams or mediating angels. He told his disciples that they were privileged in this respect: "Many prophets and righteous people longed to see what you see, and did not see it, and to hear what you hear, and did not hear it."[141] This shows that Jesus believed that his gospel disclosed more about God's purposes than earlier religious persons had received.

Jesus was convinced that the substance of revelations was in a constant process of revaluation. The theological notions of earlier pivotal biblical personalities might either be rejected or given a fuller significance in light of fresh experience. The presumption is not that God is improving, but that humans are gradually gaining more understanding of God's will. Both the Gospels and the Quran maintain that Jesus confirmed the Torah and developed it further. For example, Jesus expanded the commandment forbidding murder to include the prohibition of hateful attitudes that might result in homicide.[142]

Supplanting rather than supplementing Torah laws is also associated with Jesus' teachings. He distinguished God's intention from human legislation by the way he referred to some laws. Significantly, the Sermon on the Mount does not introduce a quotation from his Bible in this Torah manner: "God said . . . 'An eye for an eye. . . .' "[143] Rather, this and other quotations from the Mosaic law are prefaced by "You have heard that it was said. . . ."[144] Jesus then states a different principle that was, in at least one case, diametrically opposed to a basic Torah law. The way in which Jesus revoked the Mosaic law pertaining to retaliatory justice is discussed later.

As John Meier demonstrates, abrogation is an appropriate way of referring to Jesus' treatment of some verses of the Hebrew Bible.[145] Since the doctrine of verbal inerrancy is not defended in the Bible, no insurmountable problems are posed by biblical figures who champion contradictory principles. For example, Moses, in the name of the Lord, excluded all with mutilated genitals from the Israelite community.[146] Isaiah later replaced that cruel restriction with a merciful judgment. He promises, in the name of the Lord, that eunuchs who cling to the Israelite covenant will have honor more enduring than some who have children.[147] Philip Sigal shows that Jesus was among those ancient rabbis who abrogated specific teachings of the written and oral Torah in pursuit of a fuller understanding of God's will.[148]

Jesus did not strictly adhere to the Mosaic ceremonial law. As the Quran recognizes, he announced that his mission was to confirm what is true in the Torah and "to authorize as lawful some things that had been forbidden."[149] Jesus denounced those who scrupulously observed the Jewish food laws while ignoring personality pollution. Some Pharisees were exceedingly cautious not to contaminate themselves by putting so-called unclean meats in their mouths, but they permitted vile things to flow from their minds and mouths. Jesus asked:

> Do you not perceive that nothing that goes into you from the outside can defile? It enters the stomach, and not the heart, and is excreted. . . . What comes out of you is what defiles. From your heart come evil intentions which lead to sexual immorality, stealing, murder, and adultery. From inside come greed, meanness, deceit, indecency, envy, slander, arrogance, and foolishness.[150]

Mark comments on this teaching: "By saying this, Jesus pronounced all foods clean." Note that the issue of ceremonial purification is unrelated to whether foods are physically dirty or washed.

The basic biographical sources for both Jesus and Muhammad deny that they were omniscient at any stage of life. Jesus warned disciples to be wary of self-appointed prophets who claim to know future scenarios regarding the coming Judgment Day. He commented: "About that day or hour no one knows, neither the angels in heaven, nor the Son, but only the Father."[151] Because eschatological specifics are unpredictable, Jesus recommended continual alertness.[152] A Quranic revelation is virtually the same: "They ask you (Muhammad) about when

the hour of doom will come to pass. Say: 'Knowledge of it is with my
Lord only. He alone will reveal it at its proper time. . . . It comes when
you are unaware.' "[153]

Both Jesus and Muhammad alerted their disciples to the possible
deceitfulness of those claiming to be mouthpieces for God. "Beware of
false prophets," Jesus said, "who come to you in sheep's clothing but
inwardly are ravenous wolves."[154] Muhammad appropriated those same
animal images in his warnings: "In the last times men will come forth
who will fraudulently use religion for worldly ends and wear sheepskins
in public to display meekness. Their tongues will be sweeter than sugar,
but their hearts will be the hearts of wolves."[155]

Early Christian and Muslim spokespersons have interpreted an
announcement about Moses in a parallel manner. He said to the Israelites, "God will raise up for you a prophet like me from among you."[156]
Those who recorded and preserved that saying did not think that Moses
had some particular prophet in mind, but they hoped that a spirit-
inspired person would appear in the future. On separate occasions,
church leaders Peter and Stephen quoted that verse from the Torah
when arguing before Jerusalem authorities that Jesus fulfilled Moses'
longing.[157] Knowing that the Jews continued to look for the prophet
Moses promised, the main biographer of Muhammad helped to legiti-
mize Islam by declaring Muhammad to be the fulfillment of the forecast.[158]

In the New Testament, Jesus is accepted as the decisive prophet,
but revelation did not terminate with his life and death. Since he did not
think of himself as the last prophet, he promised his followers that they
would become divine spokespersons. They should not worry about
testifying before oppressive authorities because, Jesus assured them,
"words will be given you when the time comes; it will not be you
speaking, but the Spirit of your Father speaking through you."[159] Likewise, the Fourth Gospel affirms that Jesus will send the "Spirit of truth"
who will provide fuller theological disclosures.[160] There were female as
well as male prophets who embodied that Spirit.[161] The earliest list of
church offices places the apostles at the beginning, the tongue-speakers
at the end, and the prophets in second rank.[162] The gift of prophecy
continued in the post-apostolic age.[163]

In contrast to Moses and Muhammad, Jesus did not think of himself
as a lawgiver. For example, inheritance laws are set forth by Moses[164]
and by Muhammad,[165] but Jesus stated that his role did not involve
handling legal matters of property division. Rather, he concerned him-

self with moral principles on which family inheritance should be based.[166]

Dealing with social inertia was a problem for both Jesus and Muhammad. Jesus compared the traditionalists' rejection of fresh revelations to wine drinkers: "Nobody who has been drinking old wine desires new wine. 'The old is better,' they say."[167] The Quran likewise describes the Arabs' resistance to change: "When they are bidden to come to the revelation which God has sent down to the messenger, they say: 'We are content with what our forefathers did,' even though their forefathers did not know anything and were not rightly guided."[168]

Jesus thought that biblical interpreters often fail to enlighten. Like blind men who have the audacity to call themselves guides, they cause followers to fall in the ditch.[169] They have not used the key at their disposal for unlocking the treasures of the scrolls and for making scriptural teaching relevant.[170] They honor dead prophets but are unappreciative of live ones.[171] The scribes play trivial pursuits in religion at the expense of justice and love; they burden religious life with regulations but do little to help people bear them.[172]

Occasionally, Jesus differed from his fellow Jews on what was important in biblical revelation. For example, the latter tended to admire military prowess and to dote on David, who defeated many enemies of Israel. They hoped that Jesus might be a latter-day David and vanquish the powerful Romans. But Jesus admired David not so much because he suppressed the Philistines but because he combated legalism. On one occasion, some Pharisees demanded an explanation from Jesus as to why he permitted work on the Sabbath. As his disciples passed through a field, they plucked ripe grain, rubbed it in their hands, blew away the chaff, and then consumed the kernels. They had engaged in a form of reaping, threshing, and winnowing, three of the many types of work prohibited by the prevailing interpretation of the basic commandment pertaining to the holy day of rest.[173]

In response to this criticism, Jesus asked why David's soldiers satisfied their hunger by eating consecrated bread at the Israelite tabernacle.[174] According to the Torah, only priests were permitted to eat holy bread at the shrine.[175] Jesus presented that parallel case pertaining to a revered ancestor in order to goad his fellow Jews into realizing that human need should take priority over sanctified legislation. Jesus concluded: "The sabbath was made to serve humans; they were not made to keep the sabbath."[176] He seems to have viewed David more as a humanitarian than as a warrior with a sling or sword.

Jesus realized early on in his public ministry that his adversaries would soon destroy him, so he trained disciples to transmit his teachings after his death. The Acts, the first book of church history, shows that the leadership was broad-based. Peter, although in a later century recognized as the first pope, was responsible to the whole group of apostles. They sent him to Samaria and demanded that he explain why he went beyond established policy.[177] Like the caliphs during the generation after Muhammad, the apostles of Jesus were considered to be the best spokespersons to spread the public teachings of their religious mentor.

The original gospel took the form of orally communicated teachings of Jesus. Just as the Pentateuch contains the record of Moses' alleged speeches that were long preserved in the Israelite oral tradition before being committed to writing, so the New Testament contains "good news" that eyewitnesses remembered and recorded decades later. The phenomenal memories of preliterate persons is captured by the rabbinical saying, "A good student is like a cistern that does not leak a drop."[178] Even so, pious fabrications were probably used to fill in biographical gaps for Jesus, as well as for Muhammad. Painstaking sifting of biblical material is needed to separate later accretions from what is historically authentic.

Neither Jesus nor Muhammad instructed that his messages be published by other than the usual word-of-mouth method. Emphasis was understandably placed on oral transmission because scrolls or books were not the common mode of circulating ideas in cultures in which only a very small percentage were literate. There is no evidence that Jesus thought his teachings would be recorded and eventually be regarded as holy scripture.

In the Semitic culture, the recording of orally transmitted prophetic proclamations occurred when a severe disruption in the community jeopardized the normal communication. The Hebrew prophets did not write down the "books" that now bear their names. Rather, fragments of their proclamations were gathered by disciples and inscribed on a scroll when ominous times arose. For example, prophet Amos announced the imminent destruction of Israel by the Assyrian army. A generation later, when the invading army did in fact destroy Samaria and the nation surrounding that royal city, survivors who remembered Amos's message jotted down some record of it.

The deaths of both Jesus and Muhammad predate the beginning of writing about those prophets and their revelations by a couple of decades. Literary activity was stimulated by the recognition that followers who had firsthand memories of their leaders' teachings were dying or being killed. Efforts were made to put the Quran into a written form when power rivalry in the Muslim community was resulting in the assassination of caliphs.

The written Gospels began when the oral transmission was threatened by the martyrdom of Jesus' apostles. Even apart from those killings, the natural death of first-generation Christians would result in having to rely exclusively on secondhand reports. The Church became aware that the precious teachings of Jesus lodged in people's minds needed to be preserved in writing. About forty years after Jesus' death, two Gospel writings appeared. One was what came to be known as the Gospel of Mark, which emphasizes the actions of Jesus. The other was a collection of Jesus' teachings, which scholars call "Q" or *Quelle* (meaning "source" in German). The original document is lost, but its existence is hypothesized on the basis of paragraphs that are quoted from "Q" in Gospels written about a decade after Mark, which came to be called the Gospels of Matthew and Luke. Those later Gospels separately incorporated most of what is recorded in Mark, supplemented by more than two hundred verses from "Q." "Synoptic" (meaning "common viewpoint") Gospels is the designation given Mark, Matthew, and Luke because the sequence for Jesus' movements in Mark is generally followed by those in Matthew and Luke. In addition, accounts of what Jesus said and did that are not found in Mark or "Q" are contained in Matthew and Luke. Those stories were apparently gathered from the oral tradition by the editors of Matthew and Luke, who wrote independently of one another.

In addition to the Synoptic Gospels, other Gospels contain some genuine traditions of Jesus' life and teachings. The Fourth Gospel, which has been known as John's Gospel, was written at the end of the first Christian century and is less reliable as a historical source than the earlier canonical Gospels. Discovered in the sands of Egypt this century were a number of documents that may contain traditions as early as those published in the New Testament. The Gospel of Thomas is the most important of these non-canonical writings. It contains many sayings of Jesus that are basically the same as those in the New Testament, as well as others that are not recorded elsewhere but may be authentic. An illustration of the latter is this saying that pertains to revelation: "He who will drink from my mouth will become like me. I myself shall become he, and the things that are hidden will be revealed to him."[179]

Within a decade of Jesus' crucifixion, there arose a need to translate his Gospel from the Aramaic language in which he taught. As church membership spread beyond Palestine and became predominantly non-Jewish, missionaries circulated reports of Jesus' sayings and actions in Greek, the international language of the Mediterranean. They found nothing sanctified or charming about reciting Gospel passages from Jesus' mother tongue or from its first translation into Greek. Unlike Islam, there was no savoring the revelation's sonorous original language. In church history, more attention has been accorded particular vernacular renderings of the Bible, such as the Latin Vulgate, the German translation by Luther, and the King James version. Christians tend to be inspired less by any sublimity of the New Testament's literary style and more by its content as interpreted. Whereas the Quran is presumed to be a verbatim transcript of what God wrote in Arabic on a heavenly tablet, the New Testament contains little of what was regarded as God's direct words.

Beginning in the second century, many Christians have presumed that numerous creations by unknown writers contain historical material about Jesus' life. The Quran echoes some stories about Mary, the mother of Jesus, that are not found in the New Testament. One of these later tales begins with this account of Mary's mother: When she was delivered, she said: "Lord, I have given birth to a daughter and have called her Mary. . . . Protect her and her offspring from Satan."[180] In explaining this verse, Muhammad said: "Except for Mary and her son, no child is born but that Satan touches it when it is born, whereupon it starts crying."[181]

Also, according to the Quran, the angels said: "God has chosen you, Mary. He has made you pure and exalted you above womankind."[182] Edward Gibbon comments on that treatment of Mary's sanctity: "The Latin church has not disdained to borrow from the Koran the immaculate conception of his virgin mother."[183] Although Gibbon errs in suggesting that the Catholic doctrine of the Immaculate Conception is Muslim in origin, he rightly recognizes that it is not a part of early Christianity. It is unlikely that there is any reliable historical data about Mary apart from the New Testament, and even some of its accounts are historically questionable.

Much of Muhammad's knowledge of Jesus and his mother may have come from an encounter with some Christian visitors from Najran, an oasis near Yemen. They came to Medina two years before Muhammad's death in response to a threatening letter from the prophet. He had urged them to convert to Islam or pay the tax he prescribed. He concluded: "If you refuse to pay the tax, then I shall declare war against you."[184] After much consultation, the Bishop of Najran decided to send a delegation to Muhammad to find out if he was a prophet sent by God.[185] Their discussions appear to have been friendly because the Quran claims that, in contrast to the Jews and the idolaters, they appreciated Muhammad: "Among them are priests and monks who are not arrogant. When they listen to the Apostle's revelation, their eyes overflow with tears as they recognize its truth."[186]

The Najran Christians argued for the divinity of Jesus because he had the supernatural ability to speak wisely from his cradle and to create birds that could fly when he was a boy.[187] Those miracle stories originated with an apocryphal Gospel that was composed in the Byzantine region centuries after the canonical Gospels. This note appears at the beginning: "Jesus spoke even when he was in the cradle, and said to his mother, 'Mary, I am Jesus, the Son of God, the Word. . . .' "[188] That non-canonical Gospel also tells of Jesus at the age of seven acting like the Genesis Creator, animating by his command the creatures he had formed from clay.[189] That folktale, like the Quran, seems to regard Jesus' childhood as the most important period of his life. The Quran contains hardly any of Jesus' teachings as an adult. He is usually named in tandem with his mother, conveying the impression that he did not become independent of her. But in the Gospels of the New Testament, the adult Jesus has views that differ sharply from those of his mother.[190]

Both Jesus and Muhammad thought of the messages they conveyed as improvements in some respects over previous disclosures of God. Jesus believed that the Gospel abrogated some of the declarations of the Torah, and Muhammad believed that his proclamations as God's spokesperson abrogated any conflicting statements in the Torah, the Gospels, or his earlier revelations. Many followers of each prophet have maintained that God has not spoken definitively since the time of their respective prophet. It is obvious that interfaith dialogue cannot proceed far until there is adjudication of these conflicting doctrines of revelation.

CHAPTER SIX

PERSONAL
CONDUCT

Prayer and Forgiveness

In most religions, prayer is regarded as a two-way communication, combining listening for divine revelation with making appropriate responses. "To pray" literally means "to plea," so the verb does not adequately express the full interrelationship assumed in Muslim and Christian worship. Both Jesus and Muhammad believed that they could converse directly with God in public and in private, without priestly or angelic intercession.

For Muhammad, every day was hallowed by engaging in frequent communication with God. The Quran indicates that the prophet sometimes spent part or all of a night meditating on God.[1] Although he did not establish a weekly holy day for worship and rest, he advised his followers to interrupt ordinary work one day each week for community worship at noon. The Quran states: "Believers, when you are called to Friday prayers, hasten to remember God and leave your trading."[2] In addition to prescribed prayers independent of mealtimes, there was this Quranic injunction: "Do not eat of that over which God's name has not been pronounced."[3] The importance of prayer to the prophet is illustrated by his response to being told of someone who failed to arise to perform morning prayer. "Satan urinated in his ears" was his comment on the sleeper who was unresponsive when the call to prayer was sounded.[4]

Muhammad and other Muslims engaged in preparatory ceremonial purification. The Quran provides these instructions:

> Believers, when you rise up for prayer, wash your faces and your hands up to the elbows; wipe your heads and wash your feet up to the ankles. If you are sexually polluted, cleanse yourselves. But if you are sick or on a journey, or if you can find no water after you have relieved yourselves or had intercourse with women, take some clean sand and rub your hands and faces with it.[5]

Muslim tradition supplements the Quran in providing details on bodily expressions for prayer. Aisha supplies this information: "When prayer was first laid on the Apostle, it was with two prostrations for every prayer: then God raised it to four prostrations at home, while on a journey the former ordinance of two prostrations held."[6] "Prostration" does not refer to stretching out flat; rather, knees, head, and palms touch the "dust" from which humans are made. Praying begins by exclaiming "God is greater!" (*Allahu akbar*) with hands raised, followed by reciting the opening chapter of the Quran while still in an erect posture. This worship is climaxed by kneeling, lowering the head to the rug or the ground, and saying amen (*amin*). The Quran informs the faithful that a callous on the forehead can result from this habitual homage.[7]

In Jesus' day, Jews were expected to "pray at the dawning of light"[8] and in the evening.[9] Jesus recharged his spiritual batteries by vigils in secluded places: "In the morning, while it was still very dark, he got up and went out to a deserted place, and there he prayed."[10] And, "After saying farewell to them (the crowd and his disciples), he went up on the mountain to pray."[11] His prayer postures included standing, kneeling, and prostration.[12] Following Jewish custom, Jesus said a "blessing" before eating.[13] Although he sometimes prayed with congregations, privacy was often sought for integrating prayer with the ongoing activities at hand. Even though Jesus generally followed the traditional prayer practices of his people, he occasionally displayed independence. He was criticized for not having his followers pray and fast as frequently as pious Jews did.[14]

For Jesus, prayer was a discipline for subordinating human desires to divine wisdom rather than a scheme for getting one's will accomplished. In the garden of Gethsemane on the night before his execution, Jesus requested that he might be relieved, if possible, of the anticipated suffering ahead. Then, with resignation, he concluded, "Yet not my will, but Your will be done."[15] The Quran suggests Muhammad's similar humility when facing the future. Muhammad proclaimed: "Do not say of anything: 'I will do that tomorrow,' without adding, 'If God wills.' "[16]

Jesus recognized that insincerity is a perennial problem in religion. The Sermon on the Mount advises: "Whenever you pray, do not be like the hypocrites; for they love to stand and pray in the synagogues and at the street corners, so that they may be publicly seen."[17] To other Jews, Jesus charged:

> Rightly did Isaiah describe you hypocrites in these words:
> *These people honor me with their lips,*
> *but their hearts are far from me;*
> *Their worship is an empty show.*[18]

The Quran also criticizes ostentation: "Hypocrites seek to outwit God, but God outwits them. When they rise to pray, they perform it unenthusiastically, making a show before the people and are little mindful of God."[19] The Quran also regards the thoughtless ritualizing of words as unacceptable. It advises: "Believers, do not attempt to pray when you are drunk, but wait until you know what you are saying."[20] Muhammad warned against other distractions that could shift the focus of the person praying. He warned that prayers are annulled if a dog, donkey, or a woman pass in front. (Aisha did not appreciate being categorized with animals.)[21] Women who wish to pray at mosques form lines behind the men, which prevents men from observing female posteriors during kneelings.

In the context of encouraging prayer to give inner strength, the Quran compares religion to plant development. The Quran teaches that divine nurture produces firm and mature believers.[22] The Quran develops this organic analogy elsewhere: "Good words are like trees with deep roots and fruitful branches; evil words are like an uprooted tree."[23] This instruction parallels Jesus' comparison of the godly community's gradual growth to seed in fertile and moist soil; its branches become strong enough to support bird nests and eventually to produce abundantly.[24]

The heartbeat of Islam is found on the opening page of the Quran. Called the *fatibah*, the essence of Islamic worship is contained in several sentences:

Praise be to God, Lord of the Universe, the Compassionate, the Merciful, Sovereign of the Day of Judgment. You alone we worship, and You alone we ask for help. Guide us in the straight path, the path of those whom You have favored; not of those who have earned Your anger, nor of those who have gone astray.[25]

Memorized in Arabic by every faithful Muslim, those words are repeated by the devout at each of the five daily times of prayer. This prayer of prayers emphasizes the benevolence of God, even though His wrath is acknowledged. The nature of God is associated with the "path" along which believers walk, showing the relevance of theology to moral conduct.

The corresponding basic prayer for Christians is commonly known as "The Lord's Prayer." While it has been recited over the centuries, some concluding phrases have often expanded its form as recorded in the New Testament. Luke's Gospel explains what prompted that most influential prayer and then gives the original petitions:

After Jesus finished praying in a certain place, one of his disciples said, "Lord, teach us to pray, as John taught his disciples." Jesus replied: "When you pray, say this: Father, may your name be kept holy. Your kingdom come. Give us each day the food we need. And forgive us our sins, as we forgive everyone who has done us wrong. And do not put us to hard testing."[26]

The use of "Father" was not intended to connote gender, but to focus on parents' creative and nurturing powers. Jesus' father image was similar to that of a psalmist who said: "As a father has compassion on his children, so the Lord has compassion on those who revere him."[27] God is separated by holiness but is not removed from earth. Thus, daily bread and other material needs of humans are of God's concern.

The Lord's Prayer and the principal Muslim prayer are considered to be as efficacious when prayer either in private or in a congregation. Both prayers begin with the adoration of God's greatness, and both rise above egocentricity by the use of plural pronouns. The pronouns "we," "us," and "our" significantly display that private concerns are not predominant and that everyone has similar fundamental needs. Neither prayer is comprehensive; both omit thanksgiving, which Muhammad and Jesus considered important.

Jesus' model prayer has been admired in Muslim tradition. Muhammad is represented as praying: "Our Lord God who is in heaven, hallowed be your name; your kingdom is in heaven and on earth; as your mercy is in heaven, so show your mercy on earth; forgive us our debts and our sins."[28] If Jesus prayed what he recommended to his disciples, then he and Muhammad were aware of the need for personal forgiveness.

By means of a weighty conjunction, Jesus coupled acceptance by God with human forgiving-ness: "Forgive . . . *as* we forgive."[29] Pleading for God's mercy while sacrificing an animal is less demanding than working patiently to overcome one's alienation from other humans. Jesus thought it improper to seek divine forgiveness if a similar attitude was lacking in one's own human relationships. He provided this illustration: "If, as you come to worship, you remember a falling out with your neighbor, first go and make peace with him."[30] Jesus' emphasis on reconciliation is conveyed in this exchange: "Peter came and said to him, 'Lord, if another member of the community sins against me, how often should I forgive? As many as seven times?' Jesus said to him, 'Not seven times, but, I tell you, seventy times seven.' "[31] When praying on the cross that his executioners be forgiven, Jesus practiced what he taught.[32]

Vertical and horizonal reconciliation is also connected in the Quran: "Pardon and forgive. Do you not wish God to forgive you?"[33] According to early Muslim tradition, Muhammad advised: "If anyone would like God to save him from the anxieties of the Day of Resurrection, he should grant a respite to one who is in straitened circumstances, or remit his debt."[34] Aisha reported the prophet as saying: "Avert the infliction of prescribed penalties on Muslims as much as you can, and let a man go if there is any way out, for it is better for a leader to make a mistake in forgiving than to make a mistake in punishing."[35]

Muslims also remembered this exchange between Muhammad and one of his followers: " 'How often shall I pardon a servant?' . . . The prophet replied: 'Forgive him seventy times daily.' "[36] "Seventy" was a Semitic way of saying "unlimited." Jesus and Muhammad were using hyperbole, which was prominent in Semitic speech.[37] It is hard to imagine the possibility of more than a small fraction of seventy pardoning interactions with a servant in the course of a day. The seventy sayings attempt to convey that a quantitative limit should not be placed on forgiveness.

Moses, one of Muhammad's mentors, is represented in the Quran as seeking God's forgiveness more often than he does in the Bible. After his impetuous act of killing an Egyptian slavemaster, Moses prays: "Forgive me, Lord, for I have sinned."[38] Again, after the episode of the golden calf and breaking the law tablets, he pleads, "Lord, forgive me, and forgive my brother."[39]

After becoming victorious over an Arabian city, Muhammad received this encouragement: "God may forgive you your past and future sins and perfect His goodness to you."[40] One of the prophet's prayers emphasizes his need for divine forgiveness: "I am Thy servant and hold to Thy covenant and promise as much as I can. I seek refuge in Thee from the evil of what I have done. I acknowledge Thy favor to me, and I acknowledge my sin. Pardon me, for none but Thee pardons sins."[41] Muhammad was instructed to ask his people to pray for more than their own pardon: "Implore God to forgive your sins and to forgive believing men and women."[42] A Quranic prayer suggests the dire consequence that can come from not being forgiven: "Our Lord, we believe: forgive us our sins and guard us from the punishment of Fire."[43]

The Quran sets limits on forgiveness by excluding pagans who are Muslim enemies. Believers should follow the example of Abraham who allegedly said to those who opposed his family in his native town: "We are through with you and all that you worship other than God. We reject you: hostility and hatred have come between us and you forever, unless you believe in God only."[44] However, a nonbelligerent idolater should not be renounced: "God does not forbid you from being kind and dealing equitably towards those who have not made war on your religion nor expelled you from your homes. God loves those who are just."[45]

Muhammad could not tolerate poets who criticized him, and he showed no mercy toward them. At the time, poets had a role similar to television commentators today as molders of public opinion. Muhammad ordered the death of Uqba, who had written verses against him, as soon as he achieved the power to do so with impunity. A bitter response was given to Uqba's plea for mercy: " 'But who will look after my children, O Muhammad?' 'Hell,' he said."[46]

Asma, another poet, composed some lines on the folly of Medinans who "obey a stranger who is none of yours."[47] She asked, "Is there no man of pride who would attack Muhammad by surprise?"[48] Biographer Ishaq writes: "When the Apostle heard what she had said, he said, 'Who will rid me of Marwan's daughter?' "[49] Umair heard him and murdered her that night as she slept with her infant. When told the next morning at the mosque what had happened, Muhammad said to the assassin, "You have helped God and His Apostle."[50] Muhammad responded to Umair's anxiety over retribution from her five sons by assuring him that there was no need to worry.[51]

After describing Muhammad's execution of two Meccan prisoners of war who had composed satires about him, Montgomery Watt comments: "Throughout his career Muhammad was specially sensitive to intellectual or literary attacks of this kind. They were for him an unforgivable sin."[52] Later, after his largely bloodless conquest of Mecca, Muhammad ordered the killing of some women whose songs had provoked him.[53] Exchanging death for insults, Muhammad exceeded the Mosaic equal-retribution limitation. The prophet, who issued a general anmesty toward his former Meccan enemies, appears inconsistent in his treatment of poets who were unsympathetic toward him personally.

Lowliness and Children

Muhammad's lowliness was influenced by revelations that were personally directed to him. The Quran instructed him to describe himself in these ways: "I am only a mortal like yourselves";[54] "I am nothing more than a mortal messenger";[55] and "I am no new thing among messengers, nor do I know what will happen to me or to you; I only follow what is revealed in me."[56] Muhammad best expressed his humility in the body language of prayer. In the movements accompanying that central act of Islam, the cranium—which contains the highest in the human—repeatedly touches the ground.

An ancient sage named Luqman imparted wisdom that Muhammad valued: "Do not treat people with scorn, nor strut about the earth. God does not love the arrogant and the boastful. Behave yourself modestly and lower your voice. The harshest of all sounds is the braying of an ass!"[57] The Quran contains another vivid image for encouraging lowliness: "Do not walk haughtily on the earth. . . . You can never rival the mountains in height!"[58] Internalization of Quranic values is evident in this saying of the prophet: "Do not eulogize me as the Christians eulogize the son of Mary. Just say, 'God's servant and messenger.' "[59]

An episode early in Muhammad's prophetic career taught him not to shun those of low status. While he was trying to persuade a leading Meccan citizen about the truth of Islam, he was annoyed when an earnest blind man requested religious instruction. Afterward, Muhammad received this Quranic admonition: "He frowned and turned away when the blind man approached him. . . . To the one who thought he had no need you were attentive . . . but to him that came to you with godly zeal, you disregarded."[60] Ishaq provides this paraphrase: "I (God) did not specify one person to the exclusion of another, so withhold not the message from him who seeks it, and do not waste time over one who does not want it."[61]

Muhammad was content with the basic necessities of life, even during the last years of his life when his wealth could have provided him an earthly paradise comparable to what some Saudi princes now possess. An early story about Muhammad illustrates his lowliness. An unbeliever whom he invited to dinner "ate with seven stomachs."[62] Muhammad then took the glutton to his guest room to recover. The visitor left the room dirty the next day. On returning to pick up something left behind, he found the prophet cleaning the room himself. Shamed by such humility, the man became a Muslim.[63] There is another story of Muhammad telling his people not to disturb a Muslim who was urinating in the mosque. After the prayer ritual was finished, the prophet simply diluted the spot by pouring a bucket of water on it.[64]

From early Muslim descriptions of Muhammad's austerity,[65] Edward Gibbon culled this description:

> Mahomet despised the pomp of royalty; the apostle of God submitted to the menial offices of the family. . . . The interdiction of wine was confirmed by his example; his hunger was appeased with a sparing allowance of barley-bread. He delighted in the taste of milk and honey, but his ordinary food consisted of dates and water. Perfumes and women were the two sensual enjoyments which his nature required, and his religion did not forbid.[66]

Like Muhammad, Jesus preferred simplicity to luxury. He had little respect for the vast treasures that King Solomon was reputed to have accumulated; wildflowers were more splendidly clothed than the Hebrew Croesus in his dazzling robes. While recognizing that lilies are only temporarily alive, Jesus found in them a more genuine beauty than the permanent gleam of Solomon's gold.[67] In Jesus' leisure time, he

separated from the vulgar human expressions of self-sufficiency in order
to sense the throb of nature. The Nazarene was appreciative of a variety
of commonplace out-of-door experiences: grain being reaped, sheep
wandering from the fold, sparrows in the marketplace, vineyards being
pruned, and a ruddy evening glow filling the sky.

Seeking personal recognition by associating with socially prominent persons did not interest Jesus. He criticized those who sought
respectful greetings in the marketplaces and the best seats at banquets
or in synagogues.[68] Jesus made fun of such self-promoters with this
parable:

> When someone invites you to a wedding feast, do not sit
> down at the place of honor. A more distinguished person than
> you may have been invited, and the host who invited both of
> you may come and say, "Give this person your place." Then, to
> your embarrassment, you would have to go and take the
> lowest seat. Instead, when you are a guest, go and sit in an
> inconspicuous place, so that when your host comes, he may
> say, "Friend, move to a better place." Then all the other guests
> will see the respect in which you are held. For all who pro-
> mote themselves will be humbled, and those who humble
> themselves will be promoted.[69]

When Jesus overheard an argument among his disciples over who
had the most prestige, he responded with a paradoxical statement and a
visual presentation:

> "Whoever wants to be first must be last of all and serve all."
> Then he stood before them a child he had found. Putting his
> arms around the child, he said, "Whoever receives a child like
> this in my name receives me; and whoever receives me, re-
> ceives not only me but also the One who sent me."[70]

Jesus said, "I am among you as one who serves,"[71] and he illustrated
those words in a concrete manner. Having stated that his mission in life
was "not to be waited on but to wait on others,"[72] he dramatized his
humble role by washing his disciples' feet at the Last Supper.[73] The
washing of men's feet is referred to in the Hebrew Bible as a handmaid's
function.[74] The Quran commends Jesus' lowly role: "Christ does not
disdain to be a servant of God."[75]

Lowliness is characteristic not only of Jesus, but of the people who most interested him. The earliest Gospel refers to them individually as fishermen, lepers, women, and blind persons. There are also groups: the hungry, the crowds, the children, the sick, the crippled, and the outcasts. In Matthew's Gospel, Jesus is characterized as one who can assist the "weary and overburdened" because he is "gentle and lowly in heart."[76]

Celsus, a second-century pagan scholar, claimed that Christianity consisted of "only slaves, women, and little children."[77] Although he was expressing contempt by that exaggeration, he pointed to an important characteristic of the new religion. The movement Jesus initiated was directed more toward the lowly than the lofty members of society.

Jesus' teaching on hospitality conveys his identification with street people who are commonly overlooked. He recognized that there is a quid-pro-quo expectation in customary party planning: invited guests are viewed as potential hosts. To encourage hosts to befriend the destitute and the disabled, he advised:

> When you give a luncheon or a dinner, do not invite your friends, or your brothers and other relatives, or rich neighbors; they will invite you back and repay your hospitality. But when you entertain, invite the poor, the crippled, the lame, and the blind. That is the way to happiness, because they have no means to reciprocate. Your repayment will be given when the good people rise from the dead.[78]

Regarding Jesus' radical teachings about the restructuring of society by giving significance to nobodies, Albert Nolan writes:

> The kingdom of God . . . will be a society in which there will be no prestige and no status, no division of people into inferior and superior. Everyone will be loved and respected, not because of his education or wealth or ancestry or authority or rank or virtue or other achievements, but because he like everybody else is a person.[79]

Both Jesus and Muhammad rejected the role of the priesthood, which was presumed to control the channel by which the common person could gain access to God. Bernard Shaw thought that Muslims do a better job than the Anglican Church in avoiding the priesthood. He writes:

> In some ways it is easier to reconcile a Mahometan to Jesus than a British parson, because the idea of a professional priest is unfamiliar and even monstrous to a Mahometan; and Jesus never suggested that his disciples should separate themselves from the laity: he picked them up by the wayside, where any man or woman might follow him. For priests he had not a civil word; and they showed their sense of his hostility by getting him killed as soon as possible. He was, in short, a thorough-going anti-Clerical.[80]

"Son of man," Jesus' favorite self-designation, may have been his modest way of identifying himself with other mortals.[81] Rather than being a title for an eschatological judge, as later interpreted by the early Church, it probably had for him a connotation similar to what it had in a Hebrew poetic couplet. When overwhelmed by the awesomeness of cosmic creation, a psalmist asks God: "What is a mere mortal that You are mindful of him? / A son of man (*ben adam*) that You care for him?"[82] The psalmist is amazed that humans have been made "a little lower than God, crowned with glory and honor."[83] John Meier, after reviewing recent interpretations of the enigmatic "son of man" phrase that frequently appears in the Gospels, concludes that it was Jesus' way of referring to himself "as the lowly yet powerful servant of God's Kingdom."[84] Similarly, John Crossan says regarding "the son of man": "an unchauvinistic English translation would be 'the human one.'"[85] The use of that expression in the Gospels reinforces the idea that Jesus shared a common destiny with the destitute.[86]

The early Church thought of Jesus as sinless,[87] but is there a basis for thinking that he considered himself perfect? He humbly differentiated between himself and superlative goodness, as well as between himself and God, in a reply to someone who addressed him as "Good Teacher." "Why do you call me good?" Jesus asked; "No one is good except God alone."[88] If Jesus believed he had no imperfections, could he have honestly said those words? Jesus' feeling of solidarity with sinners is also evident in his decision to become baptized. John instituted baptism to symbolize the forgiveness of those who were repentant.[89]

Moreover, could Jesus have avoided having a self-righteous

estimation of himself if he were unaware of unrighteous behavior in his life? He treated self-righteousness as a debilitating personality flaw and taught that truly good persons do not contemplate their own goodness.[90] One of Jesus' parables characterizes the righteous as having no self-consciousness of their own virtuous deeds.[91] Both Jesus and Muhammad wanted people to distinguish between the imperfect messenger and the sublime message.

Muhammad frequently displayed a fondness for children. He comforted a boy whose pet nightingale had died. Once he teased his wives by showing them a piece of jewelry he had obtained for the one most dear to him. After arousing hopes and anxieties, he gave it to Umamah, his granddaughter.[92] He allowed her to sit on his shoulder when he was leading in prayer and was not prostrated.[93] When chided for kissing a grandchild, Muhammad countered, "What can I do if God has deprived your hearts of all human feeling? God does not grant his mercy to those who are not merciful."[94]

The fact that Muhammad knew his mother only as a widow and was orphaned helps to explain his special concern for widows and orphans. He went to the home of his cousin Ja'far to inform the children and widow that their father and husband respectively, had been killed. After putting his arms around them and weeping with grief, he arranged for food to be brought to the household.[95] Muhammad once said: "One who looks after and works for a widow and for a poor person is like a warrior fighting for God's cause, or like a person who fasts during the day and prays all the night."[96] The Quran's imperatives include: "Oppress not the orphan, refuse not the beggar; but proclaim the bounty of your Lord."[97] In particular, the Quran stipulates that children are to be nursed by their mothers for up to two years following a divorce, during which time their clothing and maintenance are the responsibility of the biological father.[98]

Jesus' disciples had difficulty understanding their rabbi's affection for children. They attempted to keep children away from him, presuming that he did not want to spend time with those who had so little status in the community. Angered by his disciples' attitude, he told them: "Let the children come to me; do not stop them, for the Kingdom of God belongs to the childlike."[99]

The notion of children being more than breathing pieces of parental property is more properly associated with modern democracy than with the ancient world. Full personhood for children is lacking in the Hebrew Bible. Unlimited retaliation was permitted toward a child who expressed anger toward a parent in word or action.[100] Parents were advised to have "a stubborn and rebellious son" stoned to death.[101]

The harsh treatment that adults often inflicted upon children troubled Jesus. He directed his most outspoken criticism toward verbal or physical child abuse:

> If any of you puts a stumbling block before one of these little ones who has faith in me, it would be better for you to be drowned in the deep sea with a large millstone fastened around your neck. . . . Be careful not to treat with contempt a single one of these little ones.[102]

One of Jesus' many paradoxical teachings states: those who desire a fulfilled life must "become like children."[103] What did he mean when he associated personal development with reviving characteristics of the young? To avoid sentimentality, a distinction between being childish and being child-like is needed. To be childish is to pout, to have temper tantrums, and to be selfishly concerned for one's own pleasure. One of Jesus' parables is about children who sulk, a characteristic he did not admire.[104] It describes children who are determined not to join in a musical game unless they can call the tune. They squabble and end up not playing at all. Jesus probably had observed peevishness at Nazareth among his brothers and sisters.[105] He was talking about something quite different from childishness when he commended childlikeness.

What child-like qualities can be extracted from episodes in the Gospels? Consider first that children tend to express themselves spontaneously. The gospel tells of boisterous children who were shouting praises in the temple. Whereas the religious leaders were indignant over such loud behavior at the most sacred Jewish shrine, Jesus commended their uninhibited enthusiasm.[106]

A second characteristic of the young is that they seek out fresh experiences and are not likely to be fully satisfied with the religious practices of their elders. Many Jewish adults contentedly sang, in effect: Give me that old-time religion; if it was good enough for Moses, it is good enough for me. Jesus compared settled religious routines to old leather; they were inflexible, dry, and faded in vitality. He recognized that if the fermenting "new wine" of his message were poured into old wineskins, an undesirable explosion would occur. "Fresh skins for new wine!" he exclaimed.[107] Jesus proclaimed "good news" for a new day, as Isaiah had at the end of the Babylonian exile.[108]

Most of Jesus' disciples were probably teenagers because he addressed them as "children."[109] Also, it is unlikely that students would have been older than their rabbi, and, according to the Gospel, Jesus was "about thirty years old."[110] He probably selected youth to launch his movement on the presumption that their minds, like new wineskins, would stretch with challenging ideas and experiences.

Simple trustfulness is a primary child-like characteristic. A human infant is the most helpless creature on earth for the longest period of time. Naturally, children ask their parents to satisfy their basic needs. To convey his unsophisticated faith, Jesus unconventionally addressed God as *Abba*,[111] the intimate term for father in Aramaic. That the child in Jesus never died is displayed in his last words: "Abba, into your hands I commit my spirit."[112] That prayer comes from a psalm that was used as a bedtime prayer in Jewish homes.[113] While dying on the cross, Jesus trusted in God's care as he had done nightly over the years, confident that life would be his again when he awakened.

The basic virtues of faith, hope, love, and joy are often better displayed in children than in adults. Perhaps this is what Jesus had in mind in this prayer: "I thank you Father, Lord of heaven and earth, for revealing to little children what you have hidden from the learned and the clever."[114]

Temptation and Self-Discipline

According to the theological ethics of the Quran, humans have the potential for doing either good or evil.[115] Disliking this freedom of choice, the angels protested to God at the time of human creation: "Will You put there one who will do harm and shed blood?"[116] Like Adam, Eve, and Cain, all humans are weak when they rely on their own resources. The Quran does not maintain that humanity is under a curse because of the disobedience of primal humans. They were penalized, but their sin did not cause a congenital moral defect in the human species.

In describing temptation, the Quran personifies the power of evil. Satan, or the Devil (this English transliteration and the Arabic *iblis* are from the Greek term *diabolos*, which is often used in the New Testament), is not a rival deity but a being who works within limits established by

God. After fashioning a clay figure and breathing into it, God commanded Satan to join the angels in bowing respectfully to the human. Satan refused, viewing the human as merely stuff made of dirt. Affronted by Satan's failure to show dignity to humans, God cursed him but allowed him to be a tester of humans.[117] Even those who rely on divine assistance are not immune from temptation. The Quran asks: "Do people imagine that once they say 'We believe,' that then they will be left alone and not tested?"[118]

Muhammad was presumably exposed to more than the usual amount of temptation by Satan and his legions. The Quran asserts: "To every prophet We have assigned opponents—the devils among humans and *jinn*—who inspire in one another attractive talk intended to deceive. Had your Lord willed, they would not have done so."[119] Muhammad endured what other prophets before him had experienced.[120] To defend against difficult moral dilemmas, the Quran advises: "If Satan tempts you, seek refuge in God who hears all and knows all."[121] When Muhammad accused jealous Aisha of being possessed by the Devil, she asked her husband if he had similar struggles. He replied: "Yes, but God has helped me against him so that I may be safe."[122]

The Quran contains a puzzling comment about the Meccans who tempted Muhammad: "They strove hard to beguile you away from Our revelations, hoping to tempt you to invent something against Us. They would then have accepted you as a friend. Had We not strengthened your faith, you might have made some compromise with them."[123] How was Muhammad tempted early in his prophetic career? According to Ishaq's account, as incorporated in some subsequent early biographies of Muhammad,[124] Meccan leaders swayed him to issue a conciliatory oracle about their traditional religion, thereby diminishing their antagonism toward him. He legitimized the adoration of Allat, Aluzza, and Almanat, regarded by the Arabs as "daughters of Allah," and worshiped at three shrines near Mecca. Muhammad allegedly proclaimed that these so-called goddesses are angelic beings who can intercede with God. Muslim persecution then subsided in Mecca, and some exiles returned from Ethiopia.[125] Muhammad soon realized that he had mistaken God's message and substituted another revelation, which superseded the earlier one.[126] The Devil had corrupted the initial revelation, "but God abrogates what Satan interposes."[127]

Jesus' wilderness temptations, which were examined in dealing with his early life, prove that testing of prophets can be intense. In a picturesque manner, Jesus' temptations express Hebrew psychology.

Each person has within, so it was thought, both an evil and a good impulse (*yetzer*), which can be personified, respectively, as a devil and an angel in battle.[128] In the Hebrew Bible, Satan is not presumed to be a rival deity. According to the prologue in Job, Satan makes cynical judgments and initiates ideas on testing those presumed to be faithful to God, but he can do so only with divine permission. The stories of Eve arguing with a serpent, as well as those of Jacob wrestling with an angel, might be interpreted as examples of what Freudian psychology expresses more prosaically and secularly as the ego's confrontation with the id and superego. The horned figure with a forked tail and pitchfork, wearing scarlet leotards and residing in Hell, is not derived from the ancient Judeo-Christian tradition but from later European folklore.[129]

Throughout history, the majority of adults tend toward literalism in interpreting literature, but some serious students grasp a more in-depth meaning. Some Jews did not interpret Satan in a literal manner. One sage, Jesus ben Sirach, made this demythologizing clarification: "When a godless person curses Satan, he really curses himself."[130] Similarly, Jesus ben Joseph affirmed that evil does not come from outside but from within a person.[131] When Peter attempted to dissuade Jesus from risking death by going to Jerusalem, Jesus assumed that his disciple was expressing not his godly impulse, as he had earlier,[132] but his devilish impulse. Jesus said to Peter, "Get behind me, Satan."[133] While Jesus was wrestling in Gethsemane to overcome the internal temptation to avoid drinking the cup of suffering at Jerusalem, he counseled his disciples: "Stay awake and pray that you may be spared the test; the spirit is eager, but human nature is weak."[134]

Self-discipline for both Muhammad and Jesus began with honing receptivity skills. Whereas neither was recorded as urging their disciples to learn to speak persuasively, both men emphasized the need for auditory, visual, and mental openness toward other humans and God. Both would have found this Quranic assessment of the insensitivity of many humans insightful: "They have hearts but do not understand; eyes but do not see; ears but do not hear."[135] In the Semitic as well as some other ancient cultures, the "heart" was considered the seat of the personality, corresponding to "mind" in modern culture.

The Quran stresses the need for mental discipline in these admonitions: "Be not like those who say 'We hear' but do not listen. The worst creatures in God's sight are those whose minds are utterly closed";[136] "Do not pursue things of which you have no knowledge. The hearing, the sight, and the heart—all these will be held responsible";[137] and "Call people unto the path of your Lord with sound reasoning and wise exhortation."[138]

As a boy, Jesus learned from Jewish teachers by combining questioning with listening,[139] and he encouraged curiosity and receptivity among those who observed him as an adult. He told them a parable about different kinds of soils, symbolizing types of human receptivity. The sower's seed, representing sound teaching, was wasted on the hard, the shallow, and the crowded soils; the sower's effort was made worthwhile only by the soft, deep, and clean soil. Jesus interprets his parable in this way: "The seed that fell in good soil stands for those who hear the message and retain it in an honest and generous mind and, with patience, become productive."[140] While telling that story, Jesus urged: "You have ears, so listen! . . . Take care how you hear."[141]

Muhammad advocated physical as well as mental self-discipline. For example, he became increasingly aware of its need in regard to intoxicants. Over the years of Quranic revelation, there was a shift from praise to prohibition of strong drink. The earliest reference comes from Muhammad's Meccan years: "We give you . . . the fruit of the date-palm and the grapevine from which you obtain an intoxicant and good nourishment."[142] After Muhammad moved to Medina, the revelation changed to this: "They inquire from you about intoxicants and gambling. Say: 'In both there is great harm and some benefit, but the harm is greater than the benefit.' "[143] The latest revelation contains still more change: "Intoxicants . . . are an abomination, the handiwork of Satan. Avoid them altogether."[144] Fazlur Rahman, the distinguished Pakistani scholar, comments on this reversal of revelation: "The use of alcohol was apparently unreservedly permitted in the early years. Then offering prayer while under the influence of alcohol was prohibited. . . . Finally, a total ban was proclaimed."[145]

The Quran acknowledges that fasting had long been a religious requirement.[146] In the Jewish tradition, Moses fasted during the weeks he was on Mount Sinai, and fasting was required annually on the Day of Atonement.[147] In the Christian tradition, Jesus fasted for about a month at the beginning of his ministry,[148] and monastic fasts were noted for their rigor. The Quran imposes a fast during the daylight hours of the month of Ramadan; eating, drinking, and marital intercourse are permitted from nightfall to sunrise only. When the lunar calendar causes Ramadan to fall during the summer, abstaining from liquids on long and hot days can be quite an ordeal. The primary purpose of the temporary deprivation is to intensify the faithful's awareness of God's presence.

Meditation on the Quran is emphasized because that revelation originated during Ramadan. The faithful find nights of the fast an especially
appropriate time for slowly reciting long passages of the Quran, thus
fulfilling one of its directives.[149]

Another purpose of fasting is to feel, even if only briefly, the pangs
of those who hunger and thirst, thereby cultivating more sympathy for
the needy. The Quran curtails the severity of fasting by recognizing that
excessive hardships can be counterproductive. Those who are sick or on
a journey are permitted to fast at some other time. An alternative to
fasting is to feed the poor.[150] Many make the fast less stressful by
sleeping more during the day and working more at night. Some Muslims
may consume as much food during Ramadan as during other months
because of nocturnal feasting; a large break-fast dinner in the evening is
combined with a smaller predawn begin-fast. When the sliver of a new
moon signals the end of the sacred month, a sensuous celebration takes
place.

Muhammad was confronted with monastic asceticism, the most
prominent feature of Byzantine Christianity in his day.[151] Basil, the
fourth-century father of Greek monasticism, considered pleasurable
activities to be products of the Devil's workshop, and even claimed that
Jesus never laughed.[152] With regard to celibacy and other renunciations
that were championed in monasticism, the Quran offers the following
revelations: "Those of you who are single shall marry";[153] "Who dared to
forbid you to enjoy good things of God's bounty? . . . My Lord has
forbidden only indecencies";[154] and "As for monasticism, it was invented
by Jesus' followers who sought to please God. We did not ordain it and
they did not observe it rightly. We rewarded only those who were true
believers, but many of them were evil-doers."[155]

The Quran accurately separates Jesus from the monastic movement
that began centuries after his death. He affirmed the goodness of the
world and was neither hedonistic nor ascetic. Jesus advised his disciples:
"Do not worry about your life and what you will eat or drink, or about
your body and what you will wear. Is not life more than food, and the
body more than clothing?"[156] He drank wine but cautioned against
overindulgence. He contrasted his enjoyment of wedding parties with
that of teetotaler John the Baptist.[157] Jesus was criticized for not having
his disciples fast frequently, as some other Jewish groups were doing. He
responded that the religious life should be associated more with feasting
than with fasting.[158] Even so, Jesus thought there was a place for fasting
if the motivation was not to show off. He advised:

When you fast, do not look miserable like the hypocrites, for
they neglect their faces to let everyone know they are fasting.
Believe me, they have received in full their reward. But when
you go without eating, take care of your hair and wash your
face so that no one will know you are fasting except your
Father who sees all that is done in secret.[159]

In sharp opposition to the monks, Muhammad had a positive view
of sexual and other pleasurable passions. He regarded marital sex as a
gift from God for both pleasurable and procreative purposes. The
prophet once encountered a man who told of removing one of his eyes
with an arrow because a temptation to sin came through that eye. That
man was interpreting literally this hyperbole of Jesus: "If your right eye
causes you to sin, tear it out."[160] Muhammad responded: "Our law does
not sanction the plucking out of the eye with which one has looked on a
forbidden thing; rather do we teach that one should ask God for pardon,
and afterwards take care to avoid the sin."[161] As a guard against illicit sex,
Muhammad ruled that "whoever is able to marry, should marry."[162]
Regarding his acceptance of hilarity, Ishaq comments: "He laughed so
that one could see his back teeth."[163] His moderate approach is expressed in this saying: "Is it true . . . that you watch through the night
and fast through the day? . . . Your eye, your guests, and your wife have
claims on you."[164]

Getting and Giving

Among the early revelations in the Quran are those pertaining to
riches. One states: "Woe to those . . . who think that hoarding wealth
will render them immortal."[165] Another one describes Hell as the destiny of those whose preoccupation throughout life is multiplying
wealth.[166] A Quranic verse describes the hoarder on the Day of Resurrection as having a fetter hung on him.[167] Elaborating on this, Muhammad commented: "A poisonous snake will encircle the neck of the
greedy and bite him over his cheeks and say, 'I am your wealth.' "[168]

Muhammad's attack on the misuse of wealth caused more hostility
in Mecca than his denunciation of idols. Montgomery Watt describes
the highest good at that time: "To increase one's wealth and power

became the great aim in life, not only for the few very rich men in Mecca, but also for the great majority of the population who aped them from a distance."[169]

While working with Meccan caravans, Muhammad was a steward, or financial manager. He probably realized that a borrower's fee for the use of private property was essential for that capitalistic enterprise. A Quranic verse commends prosperity, but it also states: "Believers, do not live on usury, doubling your wealth many times over."[170] On his final pilgrimage, Muhammad said: "All usury is abolished, but you have your capital."[171] Some Muslims equate taking any profit on capital with unlawful usury (riba), so there is no consensus on how the Quran should be interpreted on this point. Exorbitant increases on investments have been condemned in Islam, but a modest rate of interest has usually been permitted.[172]

While Muhammad did not presume that being rich was in itself bad, he criticized forgetting the needy and the haughtiness that often accompanies having wealth. He retold the story of a rich man who was properly denounced for stealing a ewe (Bathsheba) belonging to a poor man (Uriah), even though the rich man (King David) had a whole flock (harem) from which to choose for satisfying his needs.[173] One of the earliest revelations Muhammad received affirms that genuine religion is measured by helping the needy in a material way: "Have you thought of those who defy religious duty? It is those who turn away the orphan and have no urge to feed the poor. Woe to those who pray but are heedless in their prayer; who make a show of piety but withhold contributions from the destitute."[174]

Responsible stewardship is an aim of the Quran: "Be neither extravagant nor grudging in spending, but follow a middle path."[175] More specifically: "Give to the near of kin, to the destitute, and to the wayfarers; but do not squander your substance wastefully. . . . If you lack the means to assist them, then at least speak to them kindly."[176] Giving to the needy should be viewed as a dividing of wealth that does not ultimately belong to the human giver. The Quran enjoins: "Spend on others out of that which He has made you trustees."[177] A salutary reminder is given to accomplish this before it is too late. God will not grant a reprieve to those who pray to delay their death until they can share with others the riches they have received.[178]

The giving of alms became recognized as a foundational "pillar" of Islam. One of Muhammad's sayings shows the significance of contributing continually and generously: "Only two men are really to be envied, namely, a man to whom Allah has given Scripture and who sits up at nights with it, and a man to whom Allah has given wealth, which he distributes in charitable alms day and night."[179] Making contributions is obligatory not only because the recipients need help, but also because it improves the character of the giver. This latter quality is displayed in *zakat*, the Arabic word that refers to almsgiving, which means purification.[180]

The Quran recognizes that the motivation for almsgiving varies. Some who contribute to charity are as shallow as soil that is washed off bedrock by a rainstorm, but those who give to the needy out of religious devotion have depth like soil that becomes fruitful after a rainstorm.[181] The spirit in which alms are given is addressed in this revelation: "Believers! Do not nullify your charitable deeds by embarrassing others, as do those who give just to make a public show. . . . It is better to give in hidden ways. God has knowledge of what you do."[182] Another verse in the Quran treats almsgiving as a profitable investment: "Men or women who spend in charity give a loan to God that will double for them, providing a generous repayment."[183]

Giving and receiving should express sincere gratitude to God and kindness toward the recipients. As the Quran explains: "God sends the winds as bearers of good things that you may taste His mercy, sail your ships at His command, seek His favor, and render Him thanks";[184] "Eat only of that which has been consecrated in the name of God";[185] and "A kind word with forgiveness is better than almsgiving followed by insult."[186] Aware of the interrelation between gratitude to God and humans, Muhammad succinctly affirmed: "He who does not thank people does not thank God."[187]

According to the Quran, ingratitude is a common human fault: "God is bountiful toward humans, but most of them show no gratitude."[188] They show little appreciation for God's agricultural benefits:

A sign for them is the dead earth that We revived, from which We brought forth grain for their sustenance. We laid out gardens of date palms and grape vines. We caused springs of water flow to provide fruit for food. Their hands did not make all this, so why do they not give thanks?[189]

Divine assistance can be found at sea as well as on land, yet some who seek God's help when in dangerous waters express no thanksgiving after returning safely to shore.[190] Another Quranic revelation declares:

God brought you forth from your mothers' wombs devoid of all knowledge, and gave you ears, eyes, and hearts, so that you might give Him thanks. . . . They (the Meccans) recognize God's favor and then they deny it. Most of them are ungrateful.[191]

One should derive more joy in life from recognizing God's mercy than from being aware of one's financial holdings.[192]

Thankfulness was also a core value of Jesus. Before having a meal with a crowd or with his disciples, he expressed gratitude to God.[193] After healing ten men of a skin disease, he noticed that only one was thankful. Jesus then announced that only that man had full bodily and spiritual wholeness.[194]

Both Jesus and Muhammad presumed that the quality of a community can be measured by how it treats its most vulnerable, the orphans and widows. In a society in which about one-third of the children died by the age of six, those without parents would have the smallest chance for survival. Jesus once noted that a widow's offering of small coin for religious purposes can be more sacrificial than a large sum of money from a rich person.[195] Jesus' mother may have become widowed during his adult years, so he may have been the breadwinner for a sizable family. For most of his life, Jesus was a laborer who knew what it meant to struggle for a living. "Caring for orphans and widows in their distress" is the main component of the only definition of religion in the New Testament.[196] In one of the earliest accounts of a Sunday gathering for the remembrance of Jesus, Justin Martyr tells of offerings taken for "orphans, widows, those who are in need because of sickness or any other cause, those who are in prison, and strangers who are on a journey."[197] For those Christians, the essence of the Gospel was not professing faith but practicing it in accord with the teachings of Jesus.

Jesus was not opposed to having adequate personal property. He associated with both the well-to-do and the down-and-out, and affluent women who traveled with him helped to supply the disciples' needs.[198] Regarding Joanna, Susanna, and anonymous other women, Ernest Renan notes: "Some were rich, and by their fortune enabled the young prophet to live without following the trade which he had until then practiced."[199] That comment could also apply to Khadija's relation to a later young prophet.

In sequential chapters, Luke tells of the way different rich men interacted with Jesus. He tested a ruler who claimed to have kept God's commandments in order to see if money or God had supreme value in his life. Upon finding the ruler unwilling to sell his property and distribute the proceeds to the poor, Jesus exclaimed: "How hard it is for those who have wealth to enter the kingdom of God!"[200] In a later misinterpretation, some monks cited that episode as giving the basis for making poverty a universal requirement for first-class citizenship in God's kingdom. Luke also tells a similar story about another rich man who was fully accepted even though he did not take a vow of poverty. After wealthy Zacchaeus's values were transformed from swindling to sharing equitably, Jesus said: "Today health has come to you and your family, for you are a true son of Abraham."[201]

Both Jesus and Muhammad admired Abraham, who was recognized in the Bible as "very rich in livestock, silver, and gold."[202] In one of the Gospel parables, Abraham is a prominent person in Paradise.[203] Jesus' comparative values are concisely expressed in this saying: "Happiness lies more in giving than in getting."[204] He regarded wealth as one of the good things for people to receive if they find greater enjoyment in sharing it with those who are less fortunate.

While making benevolence a priority, Jesus occasionally enjoyed receiving gifts. An unidentified woman once came uninvited into a home where he was having dinner and gave him a flask of perfume: "She wet his feet with her tears and wiped them with her hair. She covered his feet with kisses and poured on them the myrrh."[205] Jesus then expressed appreciation for what she had lovingly administered and chided his host for neglecting the customary hospitality toward a guest.[206] Another Gospel tells a similar story of a woman who poured expensive ointment over Jesus' head. Some present reproached her for wasting what could have been sold to benefit some charity. Jesus disapproved of their indignation and remarked: "She has done a beautiful thing for me."[207] Through those examples, Jesus taught his disciples that graciousness and humility are sometimes better expressed by being a recipient of kind gestures; continually doing for others may prevent bonding with those who want to share.

Nearly half of Jesus' parables pertain to the use and abuse of riches. He had more to say about the psychology of wealth than about prayer or faith. Some parables feature stewards who manage the business operations of an estate.[208] While describing one steward who was dishonest, Jesus was still able to commend him for prudential planning.[209] Similarly, Jesus taught that humans were given the liberty to invest their talents and money in accord with divinely established policies.[210] Even though the father in another parable assures a son working on his estate that "all that I have is yours",[211] humans are supposed to recognize and appreciate their privileges. Jesus also taught that his disciples should live by the following voluntary principle: "Having received freely, give freely."[212] Humans are accountable for using what they have been loaned from the Lord's land to benefit all people. Those who are wasteful and dishonest in their stewardship will be held responsible.

Jesus told the parable of the rich fool to illustrate that "an abundance of things does not give a person true life."[213] He surprised his listeners by describing a highly successful farmer and then denouncing him:

> There was a rich man who, having had a bountiful harvest, thought to himself, "What shall I do, for I have nowhere to store my crops? I know what I will do: I will tear down my barns and build bigger ones where I can store my grain and all my other goods. Then I can say to myself, Man, you have great wealth laid up for years to come; relax, eat, drink, and be merry!" But God said to him, "You fool!"[214]

This parable concludes with the observation that those who pile up perishables tend to forget that they will soon die and leave these goods behind. Overtones of this story appear in a Quranic parable about the owner of an abundantly producing vineyard who deceived himself into thinking that his wealth would never cease. Because of his feeling of self-sufficiency and his neglectfulness of the Creator, his vineyard became a wasteland.[215]

Jesus also taught that equating the good life with having more possessions is perilous. Becoming absorbed in one's possessions does not increase one's lifespan and, in fact, may decrease it.[216] In contrast to the squirrel-like rich fool, wise people are like the ravens: "They neither sow nor reap, they have neither storehouse nor barn, and yet God feeds them."[217] Birds are not an example of idleness because few other creatures work harder for the necessities of life. They neither wait in their nests for food to be tossed in, nor do they seem to worry about their supply of food running out.

Estate building is deceptive, Jesus believed, because it tends to increase anxieties rather than security. The cure for being emotionally consumed with personal property is immersing oneself in causes associ-

ated with the rule of God. Psychic wellness can come through sublima-
tion; tensions can be released by participation in more significant en-
deavors.[218]

Recognizing that the hoarding of wealth is unsafe and stressful,
Jesus recommended putting valuables in a highly secure enterprise. This
is his prescription for eliminating worries: "Sell your possessions, and
give to those in need. Provide for yourselves purses that never wear out,
an unfailing treasure in heaven, where no thief steals and no moth
destroys. Your heart is wherever your treasure is."[219] As shown earlier,
the theme of making an everlasting investment in God's causes also
appeared in the teachings of Muhammad. A wry saying of his pertains to
where wealth is stored: "When a man dies the angels ask what he has
sent ahead, but the sons of Adam ask what he has left."[220] Perhaps both
prophets were inspired by this maxim: "Whoever is generous to the poor
lends to the Lord and will be repaid for the kindness done."[221] That
assurance was published in an ancient collection of proverbs gathered
from Arab, Hebrew, and other cultures.

Jesus observed that those who are money grubbers tend to become
possessed by their possessions. He said to those with that obsession:
"No one can belong to two masters; a servant will either despise the one
and love the other. . . . You cannot serve both God and Money (mammon)."[222] Mammon is an Aramaic word for money personified as a deity.
Money-theism—to coin a term—is the idolatry that concerned Jesus.
Like all idols, money is a dumb, lifeless object that its worshipers hope
will save them from the ills of life.

Jesus recognized that some people can be fastidious about religious
rituals and miss the essentials. He described their personalities in this
graphic manner: "You clean the outside . . . but inside you are full of
greed and wickedness."[223] Jesus associated cultic cleanliness with almsgiving rather than with ceremonial washings.[224] But charitable giving
can be tainted by the urge to impress others with one's piety. Jesus
advised: "Whenever you give alms, do not blow your own horn. That is
what religious playactors do in meeting places and on the streets so as to
win applause."[225]

Jesus gave priority to the ethical over the ceremonial,[226] although
he did not object to occasional sanctuary gifts to convey reverence.
Animal sacrifices for cultic purposes became a minor part of the religions
of both Jesus and Muhammad. This Quranic revelation conveys their
outlook: "It is not the sacrificed flesh and blood, but your devotion
which reaches God."[227]

In encouraging an open hand to the needy, Jesus did not advocate coddling those who might be exploiting the people who support them. On the one hand, Jesus taught in the Sermon on the Mount: "Give to anyone who begs and do not turn your back on anyone who wants to borrow."[228] He balanced that hyperbole with the following proverb: "Do not give what is holy to dogs and do not throw pearls to pigs, lest they trample on them and then turn and maul you."[229] In the earliest collection of Christian teachings outside the New Testament, Jesus is represented as advising regarding beggars: "Let your donation sweat in your hands until you know to whom to give it."[230]

For Jesus and Muhammad, personal morality was a by-product of theological conviction. Their prayer habits enabled them to avoid arrogance and have child-like dispositions. These prophets believed that temptations strengthened them to cope with adversity. Muhammad and Jesus were keenly aware that devotion to God is a sham if it does not result in the decent treatment of those who are the most vulnerable members of society. Both prophets believed that sharing one's wealth with the needy is the sine qua non of true religion.

CHAPTER SEVEN

SOCIAL TEACHINGS

Gender Relationships

Elisabeth Fiorenza and some other biblical scholars have plausibly argued that Jesus is responsible for the egalitarianism in early Christianity.[1] He countered a custom that Jews shared with most traditional cultures, namely that a woman's fulfillment is inseparable from her homemaking role. He alarmed his friend Martha by encouraging her sister to learn from a rabbi, properly a male role, rather than serve food.[2] Some female learners were included in his traveling band,[3] and women were later sent out as agents to convey his message.[4] Jesus had high regard for the initiative and wisdom of the Queen of Sheba. He found qualities in this gentile ruler that were lacking in some of his compatriots.[5]

Jesus discarded the widespread double standard of sexual morality. When some Pharisees charged that a woman had been detected in "the very act of adultery,"[6] Jesus was indignant that those men had apprehended only one member of the liaison. The Jewish law they were referring to penalized both parties.[7] It is ludicrous to presume that witnesses saw only one person engaging in sexual intercourse. Obviously, the accusing men had indulgently winked at the male participant. Jesus admonished them: "Let him who is without sin among you be the first to throw a stone at her."[8] He spoke sternly to the self-righteous male accusers but gently to the adulterous woman, although he did not condone her behavior.[9]

Jesus helped women as well as men regain their physical and mental health. To honor one whom he had healed, he called her "a daughter of Abraham."[10] Along with the "sons of Abraham," a designation for men who belonged to the Hebrew covenant, Jesus dignified a hunchbacked woman by including her among God's chosen. Some women who traveled with him felt indebted to him for their restored health.[11]

Toward the end of Jesus' earthly life, he singled out an unnamed woman for exceptional praise. She stands in contrast to his male disciples, who had been uncomprehending when he repeatedly warned them that he would be rejected in Jerusalem and then be killed.[12] When the woman anointed his body with ointment that could be used to prepare corpses for burial, Jesus said: "Wherever the good news is proclaimed in the whole world, what she has done will be told in remembrance of her."[13] John Crossan thinks that she might have been the author of the Gospel now designated as that of "Mark."[14]

The Torah declares a woman to be "impure" during her menstrual period and "whoever touches her shall be unclean until the evening."[15] Moreover, a woman with a discharge beyond her regular period continues to be untouchable indefinitely.[16] Jesus disregarded that purification law of Moses when he accepted a woman with incessant bleeding who touched him. He said to her, "Daughter, your faith has made you well."[17] Jesus did not believe that religious defilement came from physical conditions. Giving personal encouragement to a stigmatized hemorrhaging woman was probably the primary therapy he rendered. By addressing her as "daughter," he included her in his new family that was not based on kinship ties. As Jewish scholar Claude Montefiore notes, "There can be little doubt that in Jesus' attitude toward women we have a highly original and significant feature of his life and teaching."[18]

Empathy with various situations women faced is revealed in a number of Jesus' parables: the ten bridesmaids, the woman working with yeast, and the widow confronting an unjust judge.[19] Jesus attempted to counteract economic discrimination against women; he denounced religious leaders who "devour widows' houses and for the sake of appearance say long prayers."[20] His frequent reference to the plight of widows may have been prompted by his own mother's situation. His father probably died before his public ministry began because Joseph is last mentioned when Jesus was a boy.

Divorce was exclusively a male prerogative in the ancient Jewish culture. According to Mosaic law, a husband could write "a divorce bill" if he found "something obnoxious" about his wife.[21] But a wife could not divorce her husband even if he were cruel, lecherous, or otherwise irresponsible. The Mishnah states that a wife can be "put away with her consent or without it."[22] No hearing was required before a court of justice.

Because of this sexist situation, Jesus was asked, "Is it lawful to divorce one's wife for any cause?"[23] The point of that inquiry is contained in the phrase "for any cause." The Jews disputed not whether divorce per se is right or wrong but what should be legitimate grounds for a husband taking this action. At issue in Jesus' era was what type of conduct made a woman so "obnoxious" that she could be ousted by her husband and separated from her children. Shammai contended that "a husband may not divorce his wife unless he has found unchastity in her."[24] But Hillel affirmed that a husband had the right to divorce his wife for any cause—"even if she spoiled a dish for him."[25] Some other rabbis argued that divorce should be permitted if a wife scolds so loudly inside her house that neighbors hear her voice or if she goes out with her hair unbound.[26]

At a time when the sanctity of marriage was being denigrated by a widespread flippant attitude toward divorce, Jesus declared what he held to be the Creator's reason for making two genders. Focusing on Moses' ordinance was myopic, he reasoned, because the divorce law should be viewed in light of the creation principle. Rather than citing the grounds for divorce championed by Shammai, Hillel, or Moses, Jesus directed his interlocutors to the treatment of the purpose of marriage in a creation story of his culture. Significantly, Jesus considered the last word on marriage to be the first word; he referred to the story of the Garden of Eden that stresses companionship as the reason for marriage.[27] "The two shall become one flesh"[28] is Jesus' quotation from the climax of an episode celebrating monogamous companionship. He extracted from the Eden story the concept that the woman was half of holy matrimony, not that she was the source of sin.

Jesus then stated that the Torah permitted divorce because of "hardheartedness." When such insensitivity persists in one or both spouses, legal controls for divorce are needed. However, Jesus did not find the Mosaic law acceptable. He acknowledged the Roman practice that permitted either spouse to initiate a divorce.[29] Thus, in his discussion of the permanence of marriage, Jesus rose above the legal question to focus on the Eden ideal that had been neglected. While not denying the need for divorces, he was not satisfied with the Mosaic divorce law.

In his view, it provided an easy way for a husband to escape from the difficult task of seeking reconciliation with a wife.

How do Muhammad's views of relationships compare with those of Jesus? He ruled that a guardian of an unmarried woman, whether a virgin or a previously married woman, should not arrange a marriage without obtaining her permission, which was indicated by her saying nothing. This custom is displayed in the patriarchal tradition that influenced both Jesus and Muhammad. When Abraham's servant found Isaac a bride, Rebekah's consent was obtained before she went forth to be the wife of someone she had never met.[30] Mutual parent-daughter acceptance of a groom was required. The prophet said: "If any woman marries without the consent of her guardian, her marriage is void."[31]

According to the Quran, God's purpose in instituting marriage was mutual happiness: "He created partners for you that you might comfort one another, and He ordained between you love and kindness."[32] The Quran may also give a mutual-orgasm directive: "Leave not your wife in suspense."[33] However, the mutuality is lost sight of in another verse: husbands are told that "wives are fields to seed as you please."[34] One Muslim translator uses another horticultural image "Your women are fruits for you; take them and enjoy them whenever you wish."[35] Muhammad explained that this revelation means that a husband may have vaginal intercourse with his wife from in front or behind.[36]

Muslim warriors occasionally took along their wives on an expedition for several purposes: to provide conjugal relief, to cook for them, and to assist those wounded in battle. Some who had no wives with them on an expedition asked Muhammad if they should have themselves castrated. He granted them licence to arrange temporary marriages while away from home if they gave each woman a garment as a dowry.[37]

The Quran permits polygyny if a difficult condition is met and allows men as many slave concubines as they can afford. According to Aisha, her husband established the arrangement of multiple wives and abolished polyandry.[38] The reason, in part, why Muhammad approved of men taking several wives simultaneously was to provide husbands for the many widows after heavy Muslim fatalities at the Uhud battle. The Quran permits limited polygyny as an alternative to monogamy only if each wife is treated equitably: "Marry two, three, or four women who seem good to you; but if you fear you cannot maintain equality with so many, marry only one."[39] The same chapter, however, tells husbands: "You will never be able to treat your wives impartially, no matter how much you try."[40] Another relevant verse elsewhere in the Quran states: "God has not provided two hearts in the body of any man."[41]

A tacit endorsement of monogamy emerges when Quranic verses pertaining to the permissible number of wives are juxtaposed. But in the early centuries of Quranic interpretation, monogamy was not endorsed as the preferred pattern for a just social order. A prohibition of polygamy was found there by Syed Ali, a prominent Muslim modernist, in his 1922 publication.[42] Fazlur Rahman maintains that "monogamy is certainly the ideal form" in the Quran even though polygamy is a permissible accommodation to certain social situations.[43] Ahmed Ali comments that the Quran "virtually restricts the number of wives to one, for treating even two with absolute equality is well-nigh impossible."[44] Karen Armstrong also thinks that the Quranic qualification regarding polygamy "means that no Muslim should really have more than one wife."[45]

The Muslim penalty for illicit sex could be severe. The Quran legislates that a woman convicted of adultery be confined to her house until she dies or "until God decrees some other way for her."[46] In this law nothing is said about the husband who commits adultery. Unless there is confession, adultery cases would be difficult to bring to trial because four male or eight female witnesses to the sex act are required. If public testimony is not available, the male accuser can swear four times that he is telling the truth, and the female accused can counter by swearing denial four times.[47] That Quranic law against the adulteress may conflict with another one, which is usually translated: "The adulterer and the adulteress shall each be given a hundred lashes.[48] The subject of that sentence can also be read, "the fornicator and the fornicatress." In early Muslim tradition, the inconsistency between the two laws was resolved by presuming that the whipping law pertained to illicit sex between the unmarried.[49]

Stoning became a penalty for adultery even though it is not sanctioned by the Quran. Some rabbis tested Muhammad's fidelity to Moses by taking a couple before him who was convicted of adultery. The rabbis realized that Muslim punishment for adultery was more lenient than the one the Torah prescribes. After consulting with the two adulterers, Muhammad had them stoned at the door of his mosque. Ishaq tells of their poignant execution: "When the Jew felt the first stone he crouched over the woman to protect her from the stones until both of them were killed."[50] Muhammad allegedly said: "I am the first to revive the order of God and his Book, and to practice it."[51]

Beating was the common penalty for rebellious wives. Their fear of harsh treatment was intended to encourage mutual reconciliation.[52] The Quran gives theological and economic reasons why husbands can discipline their spouses:

> Men are in charge of women because God has so ordained, and because they spend of their wealth to support women. Good women are obedient, protecting their unseen parts as God has guarded them. As for those whose disobedience you suspect, admonish them and send them to separate beds and beat them. If they cease their insubordination, take no further action against them.[53]

In his farewell speech at Mecca, Muhammad reiterated that husbands have the right to put wives in separate rooms or to beat them without severity if they "defile" the bed or "behave with open unseemliness": "They are prisoners with you (husbands), having no control of their person," Muhammad asserted.[54] If wives are obedient, they have the right to food and clothing. They should be kindly treated as a "trust from God" who has provided them for personal enjoyment.[55] On one occasion, Muhammad said: "None of you should beat his wife as he beats a slave, for you may have intercourse with her before the end of the day."[56]

While the Quran permits divorce, it advises mutual counseling for solving marital disagreements: "If you fear a breach is developing between a husband and his wife, appoint an arbiter from his kin and another from hers. The all-knowing and wise God will bring them together again, if they wish to be reconciled."[57] Husbands are granted unilateral divorce power, which can be used without giving reason or notice. As with the Torah law, no judicial authority is needed for them to repudiate wives. Muslim husbands should divorce pagan wives and take back the dowries given them.[58] Three menstrual periods should pass without cohabitation before a divorce is finalized. If a pregnancy is discovered during those months, then divorce is delayed until maternal delivery.[59] Regarding mutual believers, encouragement is given to renewing the marriage during that time. The repudiated Muslim wife can take with her whatever she possesses. Although a wife has no right to divorce, she might be able to purchase it with inherited wealth.[60] Remarriage is permitted when divorce is completed by the passing of sufficient time to eliminate the possibility of paternity confusion.

In his personal life, Muhammad appears to have lived by the Quran advocacy of forgiveness in family disputes.[61] There is no indication that he divorced or beat any of his wives. Muhammad's personal practice appears to be conveyed in this wry advice: "Treat your women-folk kindly, for woman was created out of a crooked rib; if you try to straighten a rib, you will break it."[62]

Muhammad chose one or more wives to accompany him on military campaigns. On one such trip, Aisha was inadvertently left behind when she was searching for a piece of jewelry. She was accused of scandalous behavior because she accepted a camel ride back to Medina from a helpful soldier.[63] Muhammad cleared Aisha from the charge of adultery once he received a special revelation.[64]

In domestic situations, Muhammad appears to have been remarkably helpful. Aisha provided this information on her husband's lifestyle:

> The Prophet, . . . when he was at home used to be at the service of his household, that is, he used to act as servant to them. He used to delouse his own clothes and patch them, mend his own sandals and serve himself. He used to see to the feeding of his own domestic camel, sweep the house with a broom, hobble the camel, eat with the servant and help her knead her dough, and used to carry his own purchases home from the market.[65]

Of the thirty-seven years that Muhammad was married, he was monogamous for all but the last ten years. After moving to Medina, he acquired about one new wife per year. He did not marry any Medinan women, possibly because they did not accept Islam's condoning of polygyny and its curtailment of their right to inheritance.[66] Muhammad provided ordinary housing for each wife: a hut that contained a single room with a clay floor and a roof thatched with palm branches. Muhammad, like Solomon, did not limit his wives to those who practiced his religion. The Quran states: "You are permitted to marry women who are believers and women who have received the scriptures before you."[67] Muslim men are free to marry Jews and Christians; by contrast, Muslim women can marry only coreligionists.

Muhammad's own marriages illustrate the inability of husbands to give equal consideration to multiple wives. One wife divulged to another wife what Muhammad intended to be kept secret, and the ensuing squabble is echoed in the Quran.[68] He treated Aisha as his "first lady," giving his only virgin bride more personal attention than any other wife.[69] Just to be in her presence inspired him to higher things. Muhammad said: "If the revelation comes to me when I am under the coverlet of a woman, it is only when I am with Aisha."[70] In an excellent biography of Aisha, Nabia Abbott tells of ways in which Muhammad's favoritism contributed to continual jealousies in the harem.[71] Even though Muhammad preferred Aisha over his other living wives during his last decade of life, he irked her by rating Khadija as the best of his wives. Aisha protested: "Why do you have to be always remembering that toothless old Quraishite with her red mouth? Fate made her die and God has replaced her with someone better!"[72]

Muhammad was personally exempted from some general Quranic regulations pertaining to women. He alone was permitted to have unlimited wives as well as concubines.[73] Also, the Quran reveals to Muhammad: "You are free to refrain as you wish from any of your wives . . . and may all be pleased with anything you give them."[74] Taking sexual turns was the customary expectation in multiple-wife marriages, but Muhammad was at liberty to consort with only wives whom he desired.[75]

The Quran requires that women not be forced from their homes during the first year of their widowhood and that provisions for their welfare be supplied.[76] The Quranic expectation of kindness to widows explains some of Muhammad's marriages. His practice of multiple marriages provided a social security for widows. A few months after Khadija died, Muhammad married Sauda, the widow of a Muslim who died in Ethiopia. Probably one reason for marrying Sauda was to have her help in carrying for his young children. Several years later he married Umm-Salama, a war widow; Hafsa, Zainab, and Umm-Habiba were also widows. Umm-Habiba's first husband became a Christian after migrating to Ethiopia and died there.[77]

Another reason for Muhammad's polygyny was to strengthen political alliances. He married Aisha, Abu Bakr's daughter, to show appreciation for his most loyal male follower. Aisha became Muhammad's wife in Mecca when she was seven, but continued to live with her parents there and in Medina. He consummated the marriage when Aisha was just nine; she brought her toys when she came to live with him.[78] Later Muhammad married Hafsa, the daughter of Umar, his top military officer. She was literate and helped to record and collect Quranic verses. The prophet's marriage to Umm-Habiba, the daughter of his archenemy, Abu Sufyan of Mecca, diminished the threat her father posed.

Several of Muhammad's marriages appear to have been principally intended as a further humiliation of vanquished enemies. After the Quraiza massacre, he took Jewess Raihana as a concubine during his fifty-eighth year. That same year he married Juwairiya, the daughter of a tribal chief defeated by a raiding party that Muhammad led. Ishaq reports that her exceptional beauty "captivated every man who saw her."[79] Safiya, the teenaged widow of the vanquished Jewish chief at Khaibar, was subsequently selected as his tenth wife. Muhammad threw his mantle over that spoil of war after discerning that she did not appear to grieve as she was led past the corpses of her husband and father. He rejected the other woman who was brought with Safiya, calling her a she-devil because she shrieked on seeing the sight of her slain spouse.[80]

Muhammad said: "A woman is married for four things: her wealth, her family status, her beauty, and her religion."[81] This saying expresses some of the reasons why the prophet married: he was probably influenced by Khadija's wealth, Umm-Habiba's family status, Safiya's beauty, and Aisha's religion.

Gazing at the prophet's wives was prohibited, and addressing them was permitted only if done through a curtain.[82] Since Muhammad's wives' bedrooms opened onto the mosque courtyard, that regulation helped him to deal with the numerous men who frequently gathered outside. Subsequently, the practice of secluding the prophet's wives was applied widely and became the basis of purdah.

Apart from Muhammad's wives, women were not required to speak to men through a veil. The Quran directs women to lower their gaze and cover their bosoms modestly, displaying their "charms" only to family members and to their eunuch slaves. For protection against public molestation, younger women are instructed to draw their outer garments closely around themselves.[83] Furthermore, they should not stomp their feet so as to call attention to their private parts.[84] Belly dancing, which developed for men's entertainment in Muslim culture, appears to have been a spectacle intended only for a husband to view in his harem.

Sexual desire was a significant ingredient in some of Muhammad's marriages, and his sexual drive remained strong even when he was advanced in years. Abbott's biography of Aisha begins with this sentence: "Muhammad, the prayful and perfumed prophet of Islam, was avowedly a great lover of the ladies."[85] The Muslim tradition maintained that Muhammad was able to have intercourse with all nine wives in one day. In sexual potency, "the Prophet was given the strength of thirty men."[86]

Muhammad appears to have relaxed this Quranic prohibition: "Keep away from menstruating women until they are clean again."[87] On this topic, Al-Bukhari reports:

> God's messenger said: "Do everything except sexual inter-course." . . . Aisha said, "When I was menstruating the Prophet would order me to wrap myself up and would embrace me. . . . She also said, "I would drink when I was menstruating, then hand it to the Prophet, and he would put his mouth where mine had been and drink. . . . The Prophet would recline on my lap when I was menstruating, then recite the Quran.[88]

Fatima Mernissi discusses Muhammad's relations with the wife of a member of his immediate family to illustrate that the physical beauty of women was, in at least one case, the prime factor in marriage.[89] At fifty-six, Muhammad fell in love with a woman named Zainab, whom he had earlier wedded to his adopted son, Zaid. Muhammad found her sexually attractive on seeing her revealingly clad in her home. When Zaid returned, Zainab reported on his father's visit. Zaid, who was obliged to Muhammad for emancipating him from slavery, then divorced Zainab so that Muhammad could marry her.[90]

Divorces violated no mores in pre-Islamic Arabia, but the taking of a son's wife was prohibited.[91] Montgomery Watt comments on the impact of the traditional taboo on the Medinan community: "There is no evidence that the Muslims thought this allegedly sensual and voluptuous behavior inappropriate for a prophet. Frequent divorce, too, was quite normal. What was criticized in this marriage was its incestuous character."[92] The dispute over Muhammad's marriage to Zainab was settled when Muhammad received a special oracle explaining that an adopted son was no longer to be regarded as a biological son.[93]

The Quran gives instructions in manners for Muhammad's parties:

> Do not enter the house of the Prophet unless permission is given. If invited to a meal, do not come before the proper time. Disperse after you have eaten, lingering not to talk. That would annoy the Prophet, but he would be reluctant to ask you to leave.[94]

According to Muslim tradition, this revelation pertains to the wedding feast for Muhammad and Zainab. Eager to lower the curtain and be alone with his gorgeous bride, Muhammad was impatient with several guests who tactlessly delayed their departure too long.[95]

Muhammad's advice to youth gives some insight into his marital outlook:

> Young men who can support a wife should marry, for it keeps you from looking at strange women and preserves you from immorality; but those who cannot should devote themselves to fasting, for it is a means of suppressing sexual desire.[96]

When a man told the prophet that he had married a woman who had previously been married, Muhammad said: "Why did you not marry a virgin with whom you could sport and who could sport with you?"[97] In this regard he also counseled: "Marry virgins, for they have the sweetest mouths, the most prolific wombs, and are most satisfied with little."[98] In addition, Muhammad's collected sayings on marriage state:

> After fear of God a believer gains nothing better for him than a good wife who obeys him: if he gives her a command, pleases him if he looks at her, is true to him if he adjures her to do something, and is sincere toward him regarding her person and his property if he is absent.[99]

Even though most of Muhammad's wives had been married previously, apparently his preference was for fresh brides. He probably realized that older women were less likely to become pregnant. Anxiety over having a son to follow him must have been a concern as Muhammad grew older, especially since the Quran declares that having sons is one proof of God's goodness.[100] Furthermore, many Arabic men died in fighting, so having numerous children was a biological duty.

Muhammad had several exceptional privileges with respect to his wives, and several exceptional restrictions were imposed on them. In addition to those already discussed, the wives who survived his death were not permitted to remarry.[101] Regarding one wife who was widowed at eighteen, Abbott observes: "Aisha, with her zest for a full life . . . was destined to outlive her one aged husband by nearly half a century, to be spent in childless widowhood in a still much-married society."[102]

Scholars have long debated as to whether Muhammad raised the status of women in the Muslim community. On one hand, Edwin Burtt, a non-Muslim without vested interests, asserts that "Muhammad achieved a vast improvement in the accepted rights of women."[103] Karen Armstrong, who also has a Christian background, argues in a recent biography that "the emancipation of women was dear to the Prophet's heart."[104] She describes the pre-Islamic period this way:

> Like slaves, women were treated as an inferior species, who had no legal existence. In such a primitive world, what Muhammad achieved for women was extraordinary. The very idea that a woman could be a witness or could inherit anything at all in her own right was astonishing.[105]

Muhammad received these instructions regarding inheritance:

> As for children, God decrees that a son gets twice as much as a daughter. If there are more than two daughters, they get two-thirds of the inheritance; if there is only one, she shall inherit half. . . . Your wives shall inherit one-fourth of your estate if you die childless; if you leave children, your wives shall inherit one-eighth of your estate after the payment of legacies and debts.[106]

When a wealthy Muslim asked Muhammad if he should leave all his property to charity since his only heir was a daughter, he replied that two-thirds of it should be given to her.[107]

Rahman, along with most other Muslims, finds nothing negative in Muhammad's treatment of women and maintains that "the Quran immensely improved the status of the woman."[108] To support his belief that Muhammad favored sexual equality, Maulana Ali quotes from the Quran. "The Magna Charta of woman's franchise" is Ali's label for a verse that he translates in this way: "Women shall have the same rights over men as men have over them."[109] Ali claims that this revelation came to an Arab people saturated with misogyny. However, a more accurate rendering of that Quranic verse might be: "Women and men have similar rights, although men's rights take precedence."[110]

Compared with the situation of women in pre-Islamic Arabia, discussed in an earlier chapter, evidence suggests that Muhammad improved women's dignity in some ways and lowered it in others. Poor Arabs had considered infanticide to be an acceptable means of population control.[111] Since it was less likely that a male child would be an economic burden on a family, the killing of babies was directed more toward eliminating females. This was the case not only in Arabia but also among the pagans in the ancient Mediterranean culture.[112] For example, a letter written at the time of Jesus by an Egyptian husband to his pregnant wife advises her to discard their baby if it is a girl.[113] The Quran discloses:

> When told of the birth of a daughter, a (pagan) father is angered and he chokes inwardly. Because of the embarrassing news he hides from the sight of people and ponders whether he should keep the girl, in spite of the humiliating disgrace, or bury her in the dust.[114]

However, the Quran also warns that an infant girl who has been buried alive will ask on Judgment Day why she was murdered.[115]

Unwanted females who were not killed in pagan Arabia were frequently sold as sex slaves. Although the Quran approves of concubinage, it requires that a choice be given: "If your slave-girls desire to preserve their chastity, do not force them into prostitution in order to enrich yourself."[116] Muhammad's concern for improving the lot of girls may have been prompted by his own family situation. He had four daughters to whom he was devoted, only one of whom survived her father.

Gender valuation and feminine stereotypes are exposed in some Quran texts that express sarcasm toward idolatry. Meccans who worship three daughters in the pantheon are described in this manner: "They assign daughters to God . . . but they desire them not for themselves"[117] and "They associate with God females who adorn themselves with finery and are tediously argumentative!"[118] Thus, Muslim scripture shows that Arabs who adored female gods were inconsistent by not relating such theology to human relationships.

The Quran lists the following virtues for both women and men: reverence, sincerity, truthfulness, patience, humility, generosity, self-control, and modesty.[119] Women as well as men are included among "believers" who should safeguard each other's dignity. The Muslim slogan, "Believers are a brotherhood," was not intended to connote that Islam is a society in which there is male bonding to the exclusion of women.[120] Women are permitted to participate in the Meccan pilgrimage that aims to promote Muslim solidarity.

Some changes in marital customs by the Quran raised women's status. The levirate was discontinued, so a widow was no longer transferred without her consent to her husband's next of kin.[121] A dowry was no longer given to the guardian to purchase the bride, but was instead given to the woman to protect her should she be divorced or encounter other perils.[122] That dowry could be as little as what a man could quickly earn.[123]

According to the Quran, gender is no barrier to eternal reward: "Righteous believers, whether male or female, shall enter Paradise."[124] Even so, there seems to be an inbalance between the sexes in the two afterworld areas. Muhammad observed: "I looked into Paradise and saw that most of its inhabitants were the poor, and I looked into the Fire and saw that most of its inhabitants were women."[125] The reasons the prophet gave for the preponderance of women in Hell are that they are ungrateful to their husbands, that their menstruation interferes with their religious duties, and that their intelligence is deficient.[126]

The information given in the Quran about Noah's wife and the Queen of Sheba reveals that Muslim scripture has a lower estimate of them than the Hebrew Bible does. The earlier record discloses no misconduct on the part of Noah's wife, but it discusses her husband's bad conduct in the final episode of his life. After getting drunk, he curses an innocent grandson and introduces slavery to his people as the means for punishing him.[127] In contrast, many passages in the Quran, including an entire chapter named "Noah," are devoted to describing Noah's undeviating piety. His wife, however, is portrayed as having no positive qualities and is sent to Hell for betraying her husband.[128]

The Queen of Sheba is represented in the Hebrew Bible as making a dignified state visit to King Solomon. She praises the God of Israel, and the two monarchs exchange gifts.[129] In the Quran, Solomon gives that queen, a sun worshiper who has been seduced by Satan, an ultimatum to surrender to him, and she is humiliated until that is accomplished.[130] When Muhammad was told that the Persians had a queen who was sovereign, he said: "People who make a woman their ruler will never prosper."[131]

Some scholars conclude that the overall impact of the coming of Islam was to increase male superiority. Abbott considers Muhammad a reformer who improved the status of women, but he left "woman forever inferior to man, placing her one step below him."[132] Swedish historian of religion Tor Andrae states in his widely respected book on Muhammad: "The strict patriarchal system and the restriction of woman's freedom of movement which he attempted to enforce would seem to imply a retrogression as compared with the freedom frequently enjoyed by Arabian women."[133] Ilse Lichtenstadter asserts: "In pre-Islamic Arabia, women had played a part in the life of their tribe and had exercised an influence which they lost only later in the development of Islamic society."[134] Through a careful examination of Arabic sources pertaining to gender, Ahmed contrasts women's disempowerment after Muhammad assumed social control with the earlier freedom of Arabian women. She finds evidence of that pre-Islamic autonomy in Khadija's economic independence and employment of Muhammad, in her proposal of marriage to him, and in their subsequent monogamous relationship. With the beginning of the Islamic era after Khadija's death, women's liberty to initiate and terminate marriage was eliminated. Muhammad abolished the polyandry that had been previously permitted.[135] Also, women no longer had the right to serve as priests, prophets, satirical poets, battlefield participants, and shrine keepers.[136] Ahmed concludes that Muhammad intended to transform his society's mores in order to vouchsafe "the absolute empowerment of men in relation to women in all matters relating to sexuality."[137]

Although there is no dispute that Jesus rejected the denigration of women in his culture, the Quran is ambiguous as to whether the genders shared an equal status. Early Muslim tradition generally represents Muhammad as expressing the usual patriarchal sentiments. For example, in one of his sermons, he said: "Women are the snares of the devil. . . . Put women in an inferior position since God has done so."[138]

Outsiders and Violence

Jesus recognized that his religious tradition had long encouraged love toward other Israelites while condoning hatred for foreigners who had been unfriendly to his people.[139] The Torah commands: "You shall not take vengeance or bear a grudge against any of your kinfolks; you shall love your neighbor as yourself."[140] But contempt for some outsiders is also commanded:

> Even to the tenth generation, Ammonites and Moabites (trans-Jordan peoples) shall not be included among the Lord's

people because they did not provide food and water for the
Israelite exodus from Egypt. . . . You shall never promote their
welfare or their prosperity as long as you are a nation.[141]

Gentiles were belittled in the culture in which Jesus was raised.
They could not be excluded entirely from Israelite worship because
King Solomon, in dedicating the first temple, had encouraged foreigners
to come there to pray.[142] A marble tablet recovered from ancient
Jerusalem shows that ethnic segregation at the Herodian temple was
enforced by the threat of capital punishment. The tablet had been on
the wall separating the outer from the inner precincts. Its inscription
reveals intense Jewish animosity: "Let no foreigner enter within the
screen and enclosure surrounding the sanctuary. Whoever is apprehended so doing will be responsible for his own death, which shall take
place immediately."[143]

Norman Perrin points out that most Jews of Jesus' era presumed
gentiles to be "beyond the pale of God's mercy."[144] Even Jews in gentile
employment—tax collectors, for example—were considered to be de-
filing the houses of other Jews when they entered these residences.[145]
Considerable disdain is expressed in this injunction: "An Israelite mid-
wife may not aid a gentile woman in childbirth since she would be
assisting to bring to birth a child for idolatry."[146]

The statement of gentile Luke that Jesus developed socially and in
other ways[147] suggests that he grew beyond his inherited culture. After
struggling with intrinsic ethnocentrism, he transcended it and internalized a prophet's vision for Israel. Isaiah had urged his people to
endure suffering as God's "servant"[148] in order to "establish justice on
earth."[149] As the servant from Nazareth moved beyond a nationalist
mentality, he became "a light to the gentiles."[150]

Mark's Gospel contains a lengthy episode about a psychotic whom
Jesus healed while visiting in a gentile region on the eastern side of the
lake of Galilee.[151] It then tells of a Greek woman living in Phoenicia who
provided a consciousness-raising experience for Jesus.[152] His initial
response to her plea for help for her deranged daughter displayed both
ethnic and gender prejudice. He gave her the silent treatment because
Jewish men shunned talking with women in public.[153] Commenting to
his disciples, "I was sent only to the lost sheep of the house of Israel,"[154]
Jesus insulted the woman by telling her that it would not be proper for
him to throw to gentile "dogs" what belongs to Jewish "children."[155]

When she responded to Jesus' contemptuous remark in a gracious but determined manner, he came to realize her depth of faith. He then provided therapy for the girl, after recognizing that females in a foreign land are as worthy of his concern as males in Israel.

This story about Jesus with the Phoenician woman provides the only record of anyone causing him to change his mind. A broadening of ethnic concern can be detected in the Gospel of Matthew by comparing Jesus' outlook before and after the Phoenician episode. In this Gospel, which is the one most oriented toward the Jews, Jesus charged his apostles to "go nowhere among the gentiles" on an evangelistic mission,[156] but later he commissioned them to "go and make disciples of all peoples (*ethna*)."[157]

Jesus' generous approval of gentiles on many occasions is echoed in Luke's Gospel. Astonished by a Roman centurion's love for Jews and concern for a sick servant, Jesus declared that he had not found such faith among his own people.[158] Non-Jewish Samaritans are heroes in a parable and in an encounter that took place during one of Jesus' journeys.[159] He asserted repeatedly that gentiles are generally more acceptable to God than other Jews because the former, although less aware of the expectations of the one true God, have responded better to their partial knowledge.[160] The purpose of Luke's list of Jesus' ancestors is more theological and anthropological than historical. After the genealogy names many of his Jewish paternal grandfathers, Jesus is declared (unlike the list at the beginning of the Gospel of Matthew) to be a son of Noah and ultimately a "son of Adam, son of God."[161]

Jesus and Muhammad both provided guidance about how to deal with inhospitable outsiders. A Samaritan village once refused to provide accommodations for Jesus' traveling band. Some of his disciples expressed their frustration by asking this question, "Lord, do you want us to bid fire come down from heaven and consume them?"[162] Jesus rebuked his disciples' confrontational impulse and led them to another village. In a comparable situation, this exchange took place between a Muslim and Muhammad:

> "You send us out and we come to people who do not give us hospitality, so what is your opinion?" He replied, "If you come to people who order for you what is fitting for a guest, accept it; but if they do not, take from them what is fitting for them to give to a guest."[163]

Ernest Renan, the famed French interpreter of Jesus in the nine-teenth century, discerned that Jesus' view of outsiders revealed his conception of God as a gentle parent:

> The God of Jesus is not that tyrannical master who kills us, damns us, or saves us, according to his pleasure. . . . The God of Jesus is not the partial despot who has chosen Israel for his people and specially protects them. He is the God of human-ity. Jesus was not a patriot, like the Maccabees. . . . Boldly raising himself above the prejudices of his nation, he estab-lished the universal fatherhood of God.[164]

The Quran also affirms monogenism: "Humans, We have created you from a male and a female, and made you into nations and tribes, so that you might get to know one another."[165] Muhammad Asad com-ments on this verse:

> All belong to one human family, without any inherent superi-ority of one over another. . . . Men's evolution into "nations and tribes" is meant to foster rather than to diminish their mutual desire to understand and appreciate the essential hu-man oneness underlying their outward differentiations; and, correspondingly, all racial, national or tribal prejudice is condemned—implicitly in the Quran, and most explicitly by the Prophet: . . . "Behold, God has removed from you the arrogance of pagan ignorance with its boast of ancestral glo-ries. Man is but a God-conscious believer or an unfortunate sinner. All people are children of Adam, and Adam was cre-ated out of dust."[166]

All humans shared a common religion as well as the same family, according to the Quran. Descendants of idolaters will not be able to plea on Judgment Day that they were following the ways of ancestors who had no opportunity to know the true Lord because children of Adam once acknowledged Him.[167]

During the two decades of Muhammad's prophetic ministry, Mus-lims moved from being scorned as disreputable to shunning those who maintained social relationships with people of other religions. A revela-tion from the Medina period counsels: "Believers, take neither Jews nor Christians for your friends. They are friends of one another and whoever seeks their friendship becomes one of them. God does not guide such wrongdoers."[168]

The Quran assures Muslims that they are superior to all other peoples: "You are the best community that humanity has produced. You command decency, forbid evil, and believe in God. Some of the scriptural people are true believers but most of them are perverse."[169] To enhance the status of the new Muslim religion, a large area around the Ka'ba became forbidden to non-Muslims.[170] Jacques Jomier provides a sketch of a massive inscribed stone that is still used to prohibit non-Muslims from entering the sacred region of Mecca.[171] The restricted precinct extends for a radius of several miles from the Grand Mosque.

Michael Cook points out that the Quran promotes both equality and inequality:

> Human inequality is a common theme in the Koran, both inside and outside the community. Yet if we leave aside the inferior status of women and slaves, the Koran endorses no inequalities among the believers other than those of religious merit. Thus it emphasizes that those who do not participate in holy war cannot be considered the equals of those who do. . . . But there is nothing here to underwrite a privileged position for an aristocracy or priesthood, and the political atmosphere is strikingly lacking in pomp and ceremony.[172]

Throughout most of Arabian history, the institution of slavery has been sanctioned. Most of the slaves have been of African origin, predominantly girls who became concubines. The Quran makes a categorical difference in status between chattel and free people:

> God has favored some more than others. Those who are so favored will not allow their slaves an equal share of what they possess. . . . On the one hand there is the helpless slave, the property of his master. On the other, the man on whom We have bestowed Our bounty, so that he gives of it both in private and in public.[173]

In spite of that divinely approved social and economic distinction, the Quran encourages the emancipation of slaves who have shown potential.[174]

Neither Muhammad nor Jesus was an abolitionist, nor did either man condemn slavery. Muhammad was a slaveholder who was concerned about the treatment of his possessions.[175] After he apprehended the murderers of his slave shepherd, "he cut off their hands and feet and gouged out their eyes."[176] Regarding a slave's rights, Muhammad said: "If anyone beats a servant for an offense he did not commit, or slaps him, the atonement due from him is to set him free."[177] Jesus apparently possessed only his own clothing; however, Jesus praised one slaveholder's attitude and did not suggest that he free slaves he owned.[178] Jesus commended slaves who served their masters diligently.[179] Both Jesus and Muhammad attempted to lessen the inhumaneness of the social institution. Jesus subverted the foundation of slavery by giving high dignity to the servant role.[180]

Jesus not only respected gentiles and slaves, but he was notorious for accepting unrefined Jews who disregarded the "tradition of the elders."[181] Pharisees criticized him for eating with those who neglected the rituals they had prescribed, whom they scornfully called "sinners."[182] Jesus did not accept the Pharisees' view that "the masses, who do not know the law, are accursed."[183] Jacob Neusner, a leading contemporary authority on early Judaism, finds plausible the assertions in the Gospels that the Pharisees stressed eating the right foods with the right people.[184]

Jesus and Muhammad responded in different ways to the outlook on warfare that had long prevailed in the Semitic culture. Moses, who delivered the unconditional command "You shall not kill" in God's name, assumed that some peoples were not included in the prohibition.[185] One such outside group was a shepherd people called Midianites, into whose Arabian territory Moses had led his fellow Israelites after escaping from Egyptian bondage. Believing that the wiles of Midianite women had corrupted Israelite men—perhaps because he had earlier married one— Moses ordered, as the Lord's spokesperson, vengeance against them. According to one legend, twelve thousand warriors attacked the enemy when signaled by a priest's trumpet. Moses was furious after the battle because only the Midianite men had been annihilated. He commanded that all women and children be slain, with this exception: "All the young girls who are virgins, keep alive for yourselves."[186] According to Israelite tradition, Joshua continued Moses' ethnic-cleansing policy when he invaded Canaan. Joshua announced that Jericho was "devoted to the Lord for destruction" and so, with the exception of harlot Rahab's family, all men, women, children, and domestic animals were killed.[187]

Although Jesus' Hebrew name was Joshua, his outlook on violence was completely different from that of this warrior. Jesus condoned neither the plunder nor the piety of holy-war ideology. He also rejected the milder "tooth for a tooth" rule of jurisprudence, which had long been practiced in western Asia. Mesopotamian King Hammurabi had codified the limited-revenge principle in the name of sun-god Shamash, and Moses later reiterated the law in the name of Yahweh for offenses among Israelites.[188] The justice system that Jesus favored was not based on retaliation and did not aim at "getting even." Returning good for evil, a minor theme in the Hebrew Bible, became a major theme in the New Testament.[189]

The founder of Christianity was inspired by an Israelite who declared that God sanctioned neither macroviolence nor microviolence. As Jesus read the scroll of Isaiah, he found there a denunciation of murderous activity within Jerusalem followed by a vision of a world where "nation shall not lift up sword against nation, nor learn war any more."[190] Quietly assuming the irenic messianic role that Isaiah forecast, Jesus proclaimed "a gospel of peace."[191] He aimed at extending reconciliation beyond the bounds of his own Jewish people. Rather than advocating hatred and destruction of so-called enemies, Jesus radically commanded his disciples to love and assist all types of people.

Jesus asserted that God's children should be peacemakers,[192] and he related that principle to a personal situation. After Peter cut off an ear of an officer who had come to arrest his teacher, Jesus commanded: "Put your sword back into its place; for all who take the sword will perish by the sword."[193] The early Christians found a basis for rejecting warfare in these gospel teachings. Tertullian, the first leader of Latin Christianity, asserted that "the Lord unbelted every soldier when he disarmed Peter."[194] While recognizing that Joshua and other Israelites led armies into battle, Tertullian declared military service to be incompatible with Christianity.[195] Church historian Roland Bainton states, "Until the time of Constantine the church was pacifist in this sense: that no Christian writer whose work is extant condoned Christian participation in warfare."[196] The early Christians' attitude toward violence is aptly compared to that of the Quakers in modern times by Arnold Toynbee.[197]

During the fourth century, Constantine became the first Roman emperor to call himself a Christian. He claimed to have been inspired by a vision of Jesus' cross on which a banner was inscribed, "In This Sign Conquer."[198] The emperor then attributed a victory to marching into battle with the cross standard held high.[199] Consequently, the formerly persecuted Christian sect was soon established as the official religion of the Roman empire. Christian rulers from Constantine onward have been as interested in legitimizing war as in making peace. Motivated by pious belligerence, many medieval and modern church members have shifted the direction of the cross. The upright piece that had been stuck in the ground has, in effect, been made into a crude spear for slaughtering. More moderate Christians have followed Augustine's just-war principles and have sanctioned only defensive warfare.[200]

Those who maintain that human sin makes wars inevitable criticize Jesus for advocating a nonviolent ethic that even most Christians have disregarded. Seyyed Nasr, Professor of Islamic Studies at George Washington University and the first Muslim to be included among the prestigious Gifford lecturers in Britain, faults Jesus for his alleged unrealistic assessment of ordinary human nature. He observes:

> Christian ethics is seen by Muslims as being too sublime for ordinary human beings to follow, the injunction to turn the other cheek being meant only for saints. . . . Christian people over the centuries . . . have not shown any more restraint in war than have non-Christians. . . . The ideal preached and the practice followed have often little to do with each other.[201]

The medieval Crusades did almost irreparable harm to the religion of the Prince of Peace. On one occasion, King Richard of England massacred more than two thousand Muslim prisoners of war in Palestine. Bishop Stephen Neill writes of the Crusades: "The halo of martyrdom was set upon death in an ostensibly Christian cause. For those who survived, there was the hope of considerable material rewards."[202] The values of glory, gore, and greed eclipsed the values Jesus championed.

In the Quran, believers are frequently urged to strive (*jihad*) for God's way. Peaceful means are occasionally presumed for the accomplishment of *jihad*. For example, a revelation at Mecca commands: "Worship your Lord and do good, so that you may succeed. *Strive* for God's cause in a manner which is right."[203] Violence is not associated with this injunction delivered in Medina either: "Believers . . . *strive* for God's cause with their wealth and their lives."[204] After a battle, Muhammad is reported to have said: "We have returned from the lesser *jihad* to the greater *jihad*,"[205] meaning that military success is secondary to winning the internal fight. The latter pertains to the struggle to achieve self-control by replacing bad impulses with spiritual attitudes and moral actions.[206] Muhammad also said: "The most excellent *jihad* is when one speaks a true word in the presence of a tyrannical ruler."[206]

When Muhammad began his movement, he advised a nonviolent response to Meccan persecution. Hoodlums sometimes broke up meetings he preached at, and for a period of time the embryonic community was under virtual house arrest in a section of the city. Muhammad's advice to avoid retaliation was pragmatically appropriate because the weak band of Muslims might have been eliminated had they then been militant. The Quran promises Muslims that they will peacefully overcome their adversaries: "Return evil with good, and in so doing your enemy will become a close friend. Patience is needed to attain this."[207]

After a decade, the Muslims discontinued their nonviolent approach because fresh revelations Muhammad received shortly before he went to reside in Medina changed the primary method of *jihad*. As a result, the Quran affirms that "those who avenge themselves when wronged incur no guilt."[208] It is better to endure patiently, but "if you retaliate, do so proportionately to what has been inflicted on you."[209] Muhammad's earliest biographer comments:

> The Apostle had not been given permission to fight or allowed to shed blood before the second Aqaba (at the time of the *hijra*). He had simply been ordered to call men to God and to endure insult and forgive the innocent. The Quraish had persecuted his followers, seducing some from their religion and exiling others from their country. They had to choose whether to give up their religion, be mistreated at home, or to flee the country, some to Ethiopia, others to Medina. When the Quraish became insolent toward God, . . . He gave permission for His Apostle to fight and protect himself against those who wronged them and treated them badly.[210]

Shortly after the *hijra*, Muhammad received a revelation that provides a way of interpreting conflicting messages: "Any verse (*ayah*) We abrogate (*nasakha*) or cast into oblivion, We replace it with a better one or one similar."[211] This chapter also announces that God permits killing those who provoke hostilities: "Fight for God's sake those who fight you, but do not attack them first. God does not like aggressors. Slay them wherever you encounter them and drive them out of the places from which they expelled you. Oppression is worse than killing."[212] The exiled Muslims interpreted this to mean that they were justified in going to war against their pagan persecutors in order to regain the property they had lost in Mecca.

Various punishments for aggressors against Islam are sanctioned in the Quran: "Those that make war against God and His Apostle and persist in their corrupt ways in the land shall be put to the sword, or hanged, or have a hand on one side and a foot on the other side amputated, or be expelled from the country."[213] In addition, sterner punishment is promised in the afterlife.[214]

In a broader context, armed resistance was now permissible for defending the freedom of religion. The just-war concept is explained in this Quranic revelation:

> Some have been driven from their dwellings for no other reason than they affirmed, "Our Lord is God." Had God not defended some people by the might of others, places where God's name is celebrated—monasteries, churches, syna-gogues, and mosques—would have been demolished. God will help those who come to His aid.[215]

Captive soldiers were treated as spoils of war and could be either ransomed or freed.[216] Although the Quran does not address the situa-tion of noncombatants in war, Muhammad followed a just-war principle of prohibiting the killing of captive women, children, and decrepit old men.[217] Those who were granted this immunity could, however, be enslaved.[218]

After the Muslims became established as a power in Medina, another shift in the meaning of *jihad* emerged. At the Badr battle, God allegedly fought against the Meccans: "You (Muslims) did not kill them, but God did; you (Muhammad) did not shoot, but God did."[219] The irenic tolerance of adversaries in earliest Islam, or the subsequent martial endeavor only in defense, is superseded by aggressive holy war. The word from on high now declares: "When you battle unbelievers, strike their necks until you have defeated them. . . . As for those who are slain in pursuit of God's cause, . . . He will admit them to Paradise."[220] The Quran also exhorts: "O Prophet! Stir up the believers to fight. . . . One hundred of you who are steadfast shall rout a thousand unbelievers."[221] One of the latest Quranic revelations contains this statement:

> When the sacred months are passed, take the sword to poly-theists wherever you find them. Capture them, besiege them,

and ambush them wherever you can. But if they convert, perform the prayer ritual, and pay the welfare tax, let them go their way, for God is forgiving and merciful.[222]

Most major interpreters of the Quran agree that verses urging military conquest replaced verses that are irreconcilable with them.[223] The earliest commands were repeatedly to "repel evil with good,"[224] as noted earlier. Faruq Sherif points out that those exhortations were cancelled:

> By far the greatest number of verses held to have been abrogated are those which counsel the Prophet to be patient with the unbelievers and to remember that he is no more than a warner, leaving the punishment of recalcitrants to God. The abrogating verses, on the other hand, are those which command the Prophet and the faithful to fight and kill.[225]

Sherif also shows that the Quran sometimes justifies fighting invaders only, but more often it advocates taking the initiative with the sword. He quotes many Quranic verses in support of this statement, including: "The duty to fight idolaters, unbelievers, and infidels until they surrender to Islam is absolute and not conditional on any act of violence having been committed by the unbelievers."[226]

Contemporary Muslim extremists, who are relatively small in number, have no difficulty finding verses in the Quran that support their acts of mass violence. For example, Sheik Omar Rahman, who was the religious leader of a group convicted of bombing a New York skyscraper, allegedly responded in this way to the charge that he was part of a terrorist group: "We welcome this accusation. And we have to be terrorists'. . . . The Great Allah said, 'Against them make ready your strength to the utmost of your power including steeds of war, to strike terror into the enemies of Allah and your enemies.' "[227]

Moderate modern Muslims consider the following Quranic saying a favorite: "There is no compulsion in religious matters."[228] It is often not explained that some Muslim authorities think that this verse was replaced by a revelation sanctioning the strongest kind of coercion.[229] Also, the saying may have been a comment on human obstancy, that people cannot be compelled to alter their beliefs.[230]

After the Muslim domination in Arabia had been accomplished and Muhammad was at the climax of his career, pagans were not the only ones against whom ruthless action was advocated:

Fight those who have been given the Scripture but do not
believe in God or the Last Day, those who do not forbid what
God and his Apostle have prohibited, those who do not
embrace the true faith. Fight them until they become completely subdued and pay the tax.[231]

Gustave von Grunebaum explains that the replacement of earlier
sympathetic judgments regarding biblical people with this harsh rheto-
ric was psychological preparation for Muhammad's final campaign. To
justify the expedition against Byzantine Christians to the north of
Arabia, negative descriptions of those being invaded helped to prepare
the Muslim troops.[232] The Quranic chapter under consideration assures
that warriors who engage in *jihad* will go directly to Paradise, while their
enemies will be destined for Hell.[233]

Comparing the early history of Christianity and Islam, David
Margoliouth observes: "The Christian martyr is the man who dies
professing his faith, but not resisting; the Moslem martyr is one who dies
for his faith on the battlefield."[234] Muhammad said: "I would love to
fight in God's cause, and then get martyred, and then resurrected, and
then get martyred again."[235] As a tribute to martyrdom, the slain soldier
is buried without the customary corpse-washing and in the same blood-
stained clothing he wore in battle.[236] It is believed that on Judgment
Day, which will follow immediately for martyrs, the clothing can be
exhibited as evidence of heroic merit.

An early Quranic revelation commends some sixth-century people
of Najran in southwestern Arabia who chose Christian nonviolent martyrdom rather than submit to a Yemen tyrant's demand that they re-
nounce their religion. When one Najranite responded affirmatively to
the question, "Are you a Christian?" his right hand was cut off.[237]
Subsequently, the same answer to the same question resulted in a
progressive loss of his other limbs before he died.[238] In addition to
individual butchery, a Najran church was burned with many Christians
inside.[239] That massacre provoked this judgment in the Quran: "Cursed
be the diggers of the trench, who lighted the consuming fire and sat
around it to watch the faithful being tortured . . . only because they
believed in God."[240]

The principal meaning of *jihad* in both the Quran and the *hadith* is
concisely given in a recent Muslim encyclopedia: "A Divine institution
of warfare to extend Islam into non-Islamic territories or to defend Islam
from danger."[241] Every able-bodied man is not only permitted to fight

but is ordered to fight.[242] The Quran castigates those who prefer not to participate in an offensive war against a foreign city. Those who dislike the heat of desert warfare are reminded that they risk facing the more intense heat of Hell.[243]

There are Muslim parallels between the army Alexander the Great led and the Muslim army Muhammad and his successors led. The Quran seems to have adopted the ram's-horn symbol that the Greeks (on their coins) and the Jews had used for that ancient Greek conqueror.[244] "The Two-Horned One" is depicted in this way: "We made him mighty in the land and gave him means to achieve all things. He followed a road until he reached the place of the setting sun. . . . He then followed another road until he reached the place of the rising sun."[245] According to early Muslim tradition, God gave Alexander this assurance: "I will make you able to encompass what I have imposed on you. . . . I will increase your understanding so that nothing will terrify you, and I will spread everything before you so that you can destroy everything."[246] Alexander's army rapidly spread Greek values over much of western Asia and North Africa.

Alexander made no plan for his successor before he died, so his generals took control of his vast conquests. Similarly, Muhammad did not groom anyone to carry on his leadership, so his death precipitated a national crisis. No disciple had been prepared to assume charge of the newly formed Muslim state of Arabia. Regarding the vacuum left by Muhammad's death, Kenneth Cragg writes:

> To the numbed and distraught faithful in Medina and beyond, to the new and sometimes dubious adherents throughout the peninsula, some of whom were ready to withdraw in pagan reassertion, it was as if some giant oak that filled the landscape had been felled, making a great void that left the very scheme of things shorn and unfamiliar.[247]

Even so, to follow Cragg's simile, there was rapid growth of several saplings beneath the great tree, and their limbs were soon to extend over a much wider area than Muhammad had known. Companions who had been with the prophet the longest were presumed to be those who could best administer to the burgeoning Muslim community. According to Muslim doctrine, no one could succeed Muhammad as the divine spokesperson. The office of caliph was instituted to carry out his ruler and warrior roles. Although the term "caliph" means successor, the office paralleled that of Joshua, who carried on only the political and military functions of Moses. The selection of caliph was made from members of Muhammad's extended family. Since none of the prophet's sons survived their father, and since wives and daughters were not considered worthy of having authority over men, Abu Bakr became the first caliph. He was Muhammad's father-in-law, although he was younger than his son!

Abu Bakr died after being caliph for only two years. In rapid succession, two other in-laws of Muhammad served as the second and third caliphs. Umar attempted to fulfill Muhammad's dying request that only Muslims be permitted to live in Arabia. Since there are records of Christians at Najran for centuries after the rise of Islam, he evidently exempted them from expulsion because of Muhammad's treaty with them.[248] Umar strengthened his support by allowing Arab tribal chiefs to distribute the enormous loot that Muslims had seized.[249] Jerusalem submitted to the Muslims during his caliphate, and the Dome of the Rock was constructed there before the seventh century ended. Built on the site of Hebrew temples from Solomon onward, that mosque commemorated the point of departure for Muhammad's alleged nocturnal ride through the heavens when he resided in Mecca.

Ali became the fourth caliph because he was married to Fatima, Muhammad's only surviving offspring. At that time, the partisans (shi'ah) began to separate from the traditionalists (sunnah), who placed their final authority in the first-generation Muslim community. The Shi'ites followed the living prayer-leader (imam), a descendant of Ali and Fatima. Throughout the centuries, the Sunnis have accepted the validity of the first three caliphs, but the Shi'ites have believed that Ali should have been appointed immediately after Muhammad's death. Ali was assassinated, and his son Husain succeeded him for a few years. The greatest martyr for the Shi'ites has been Muhammad's grandson Husain. He was killed when leading his troops against other Muslims at Kerbala, Iraq. Annually, his tomb there is the focus of flagellation and other forms of ascetic piety. Husain's violent death launched a tradition of martyrdom that has profoundly affected the Shi'ites ever since.

The war-weariness of people living in the Fertile Crescent west and north of Arabia made conditions ripe for easy conquest by the caliphs. Persia had taken control away from Byzantium in Palestine, Egypt, and Turkey; Emperor Heraclius then successfully led a holy war and regained lands that had been lost to Persia. Neither kingdom was left with much power, so the Muslims moved with astonishing rapidity and subdued vast territories without major battles. Beginning with Ali, the capital of the mushrooming Dar al-Islam (House of Islam) shifted from Medina to Damascus.

By the end of their first century, the Muslims had brought the Middle East and most of the lands around the Mediterranean under one rule for the first time since the Greco-Roman era. The area was even bigger than that captured by the Romans, who had established the largest of all previous empires. Islam became the Asian response to Alexander's Hellenism, spreading Semitic values over North Africa and southern Europe. The Muslims not only had a political and religious impact, but also brought the teachings of Alexander's tutor, Aristotle, back to Europe.

The Middle East favored the territorial *jihad* that Muhammad launched. Montgomery Watt sums up the historical situation:

> There was the social unrest in Mecca and Medina, the movement towards monotheism, the reaction against Hellenism in Syria and Egypt, the decline of the Persian and Byzantine empires, and a growing realization by the nomadic Arabs of the opportunities for plunder in the settled lands round them.[250]

Those factors in themselves would not have transformed the Muslim community into a world empire and world religion. Watt concludes with this appropriate tribute to Muhammad:

> Circumstances presented him with an opportunity such as few men have had, but the man was fully matched with the hour. Had it not been for his gifts as seer, statesman, and administrator and, behind these, his trust in God and firm belief that God had sent him, a notable chapter in the history of mankind would have remained unwritten.[251]

CHAPTER EIGHT

SANCTIONS

The Nature of God

In Semitic religions, God's omnipresence, omnipotence, and omni-science are the ultimate sanctions for human behavior. Divine omni-presence is expressed succinctly in this Quranic verse: "Wherever you turn, East or West, there is the face of God."[1] Thus, a disoriented person not knowing the direction of Mecca need not be anxious; ritual prayer is efficacious regardless of the direction in which the worshiper is bowing.

The almightiness of the divine is emphatic in the Quran: "God has created seven heavens and like aspects of the earth. His commanding word descends through them, so that you may know that He has power over everything."[2] An oft-quoted Quranic verse affirms God's universal sovereignty: "His throne is as vast as the heavens and the earth, and the preservation of both does not weary Him. He is the Exalted, the Tremendous."[3] God's astral omnipotence is expressed in this way: "Hal-lowed is He who decked the sky with constellations and set among them a beacon and a shining moon."[4] A corollary to this power is the rejection of astrology: "Do not worship the sun and the moon, but worship God who made them."[5]

The Muslim doctrine of omnipotence should be distinguished from the fatalism that was prominent in pre-Islamic religion. According to the Quran, pagans have this melancholy outlook: "We have nothing but this

life; we die and we live, and only fate (*dahr*) destroys us."[6] Here, fate
means, to use Fazlur Rahman's words, "a blind force that 'measured out'
or predetermined matters"[7] but the Quran replaced it with the concept
of "an all-powerful, purposeful, and merciful God."[8] According to the
Quran, a person's death is fixed by God, not by impersonal fate.[9]
Abraham, the Muslim exemplar, gave up the fatalism of Mesopotamia
that was derived from the precise movement of heavenly bodies.[10]

Some verses in the Quran seem to champion a doctrine of God
being the sole agent for everything that happens. Artificial and natural
catastrophes are attributed to God: "Every calamity occurring on earth
or in your own selves is ordained before We cause it to happen."[11] Such
verses appear to endorse extreme predestination, but a preponderance
of texts affirms a moderate predestination that allows for human freedom of choice.[12] The following verse is an example of the latter: "God
does not change a people's situation unless they change themselves."[13]
The Quran claims divine guidance for those who are responsive to the
will of God, but those who do wrong must accept responsibility for their
actions. God is reported to have said: "Whoever goes astray, does so at
his own peril. I am not your guardian."[14]

God's creative power pertains at least as much to ongoing happenings as to cosmic origins. For example, the Quran refers to God's
continual creation of human life in the uterus.[15] God's abiding concern
for the welfare of creation is conveyed in this verse: "It is He who makes
the night a cloak for you and sleep a rest. He makes each day a
resurrection."[16] The divine Sovereign effects His will by decreeing now,
as in the beginning, " 'Be' and it is."[17] Forgetting this, a person may ask:
"When I am dead, how can I be raised to life?" The Quran replies: "Does
he not remember that We have created him once, and that he was
nothing then?"[18]

Providence is a pervading Quranic theme: "God has given you
houses to dwell in, and animal skins for tents. . . . God has given you
shelter from the sun. He has fashioned hills to afford you a refuge,
garments to protect you from heat, and armor to shield you in battle."[19]
While persecuted in Mecca, Muhammad and Abu Bakr hid in a cave.
Muhammad assured his companion: "Do not despair, God is with us."[20]
The account then states that the peace of God descended upon them
and gave them strength.[21] Divine concern is not limited to humans:
"Many animals cannot fend for themselves, but God provides for them
and for you."[22]

Divine omniscience is also related to all of creation: "God knows well the evil-doer. He has the keys of all that is hidden. . . . He knows all that land and sea contain: every leaf that falls is known to Him."[23] Such omniscience provides God with an intimate awareness of ideas presumed to be altogether private: "No three persons confer secretly but He is the fourth among them. . . . Then, on Judgment Day, He will tell them of their doings"[24] "We know persons' innermost thought, for We are closer than the jugular vein."[25]

An extended theological analogy is drawn from the olive-oil lamp on which the people of western Asia depended:

God is the light of the heavens and the earth. His light may be compared to a lamp set in a niche, encased in glass, which shines with star-like brilliance. It is kindled from the blessed olive tree, which is confined neither to the east nor to the west. Its oil almost glows without being touched with fire. Light upon light; God guides to His light whom He will. God speaks in metaphors to humans.[26]

A paradox of the Quran is found in this declaration: "Nothing resembles God; He hears and sees."[27] On one hand, God completely transcends the sphere of earthlings, yet an analogy from animals' ears and eyes is used to describe some functions of God. The Arabic proverb, "Metaphor is the bridge to reality," is amply illustrated in the Quran: human attributes and appearances are occasionally used as a means for understanding God. In this regard, Muhammad said: "When any of you fights he must avoid the face, for God created Adam in His own image.[28]

The anthropomorphisms of the Quran are similar to those of the Hebrew Bible. Physical images are prohibited in Islam as in the Israelite religion, but certain verbal images reoccur. Like a potter, God fashions creatures out of clay with both hands and then breathes into them.[29] He speaks to Moses and writes on tablets for him.[30] Standing watchfully over everyone, God notes the schemes of Muhammad's adversaries and smites them.[31] One of Muhammad's sayings suggests that the divine is also like a parent: "God's pleasure is a father's pleasure and God's displeasure is a father's displeasure."[32]

The biblical leitmotif of God as king is continued in Islam. In both, God has been seated on his throne ever since the six days during which He created the universe.[33] Whereas the Israelite King of Kings is pictured as an elderly, woolly-haired monarch,[34] early Islamic tradition portrays God as youthful. Muhammad described God in this bold way:

"I saw my Lord in a most beautiful form like a youth with exuberant hair, sitting on the throne of grace, surrounded by a golden carpet. He put His hand between my shoulder-blades, and I felt its coolness in my liver."[35]

The God Muhammad worshiped seemed to use both the stick and carrot approaches to enforcing His will. Betty Kelen notes the fluctuations in the prophet's revelations:

> The general tone of the Quran is rather chastising, ranging from mild rebuke through heavy scolding to furious invective—the wrath of God, vibrant and alive. There are also passages of high philosophy and poetry of surpassing loveliness, exhortations to virtue, reminders of God's compassion, and here and there some rather witty comments on the human scene.[36]

Love is an attribute of God as well as of humans. "My Lord is compassionate and loving," the Quran affirms.[37] Almost every chapter begins with acknowledging "compassion" (rahman) as a quality of God. Sometimes "The Compassionate One" (Ar-Rahman) is used as a synonym for God.[38] In a Medina sermon, Muhammad declared: "Love what God loves. Love God with all your hearts, and weary not of the word of God and its mention. Harden not your hearts from it. . . . Carry out loyally towards God what you say with your mouths. Love one another in the spirit of God."[39]

Human obedience is the condition for receiving God's love. The Quran declares: "God loves the righteous;"[40] "God loves those who act equitably;"[41] and "God loves the steadfast"[42] who fight with the Apostle "in the way of God."[43] According to Muslim tradition, Muhammad conveyed this message from God: "My love belongs by right to those who love one another in Me, to those who sit together in Me, to those who visit one another in Me."[44] Unconditional love, however, is not in the Quran because "God does not love the unbelievers."[45] Believers are warned: "If any of you become renegades, God will replace you by others who love Him and are loved by Him."[46]

A century after Muhammad, an Iraqi named Rabia was distressed to realize that many other Muslims acted morally mainly to obtain a satisfactory afterlife for themselves. An intrinsic motivation to express what God valued was lacking in their ethical decision making. Consequently, Rabia went into a street in Basra with a jug of water in one hand

and a flaming torch in the other. When asked what she was doing, she replied: "I am going to quench Hell and set fire to Paradise so that God may be adored and loved for Himself and not for His rewards."[47]

An ethic of response to the goodness of God is occasionally found in the Quran: "Be kind to others as God has been kind to you."[48] In other words, forgive others in imitation of God's mercy,[49] or help the needy in response to God's generosity.[50] The good person is described as "one who does good works for the sake of the Most High only, seeking no thanks from the recipient."[51] Those who love God "give food to the destitute, the orphan, and the captive."[52]

The similarities of the theologies heralded by Muhammad and Jesus are numerous. Neither spokesperson is systematic in his teachings about God; each introduces divine attributes in an occasional manner to fit the consideration at hand. Neither the Quran nor the Gospels contain an attempt to prove the existence of God. Few if any of those to whom Jesus and Muhammad spoke were atheists because they accepted the existence of at least one God. Both prophets believed in a God of history who created the world and governs the course of human events with both power and benevolence. Both men also believed that one's public and private life should be affected by the rule of the divine King.[53] However, Jesus did not think of God's rule as necessarily subversive to pagan Roman rule.

God is known by many names in the Quran,[54] and Muhammad gave ninety-nine of them for Muslims to remember as their passport to Paradise.[55] Most of the personal and impersonal names he lists would also be appropriate for describing the biblical understanding of God. Like the multiple designations for God in the Quran, Jesus refers to Him as "Lord," "Wisdom," and "the Most High."[56] Jesus also alludes to God in an impersonal way through the use of "Power," "Rock," and "Heaven."[57]

Also like Muhammad, Jesus viewed God as ubiquitous. One need not go to the holy mountain in Samaria or to the temple in Jerusalem to worship because "God is spirit" and can be found anywhere.[58] To those eagerly awaiting the future coming of God's reign, Jesus asserted that the King's sovereignty should presently be realized within and among them.[59] God is not aloof but is involved in the lives of mortals and is their bountiful benefactor. "Closer is He than breathing, and nearer than hands and feet," wrote Alfred, Lord Tennyson.[60] That poet's image of divine omnipresence aptly expresses the outlook of both Jesus and Muhammad.

Sovereign-subject relations predominate Quranic theology, but parent-child relations abound in the Gospels. "I thank you, Father," Jesus prayed, "because You have revealed to the childlike what You have hidden from the learned."[61] Although the conception of God as a parent had been occasionally expressed in the Hebrew tradition,[62] it was unusual. Jesus' favorite image for God made plain that unapproachable transcendence should not be viewed as a characteristic of the divine. His designation, "Holy Father",[63] shows that God is separated from human defilement but is not remote.

Theology and ethics were inseparable for Jesus. He expressed this by culling from the 613 Torah laws what he regarded as the two greatest commandments. The first one pertained to loving God with the whole of one's being.[64] The second was "You shall love your neighbor as yourself."[65] Jesus widened the definition of "neighbor" to include not only a person from one's neighborhood but also the scorned tax collector, the immoral adulterer, the shunned leper, and the strange alien. To illustrate that one's neighbor is anyone in need from any nation, Jesus told the parable of the Good Samaritan.[66]

Jesus likened ideal human inclusiveness to the operations of the God of nature. His Sermon on the Mount states: "Love your enemies and pray for your persecutors, so that you may show yourselves true children of your Father in heaven. He makes the sun shine on bad and good people alike, and sends rain on the just and on the unjust."[67] Even as the cosmic sun does not discriminate among what it shines on, so the heavenly Father shows no favoritism among His multi-ethnic children. God loves those who are disobedient to his directives while hating their sins. Humans should also unconditionally love the disreputable as well as the respectable. Jesus concludes this teaching on love's boundlessness with this imperative: "Be all-embracing, as your heavenly Father is all-embracing."[68]

Jesus' God is like a shepherd who knows each member of his flock and is ready to go out into the dark to bring back any who has strayed. No creature is so insignificant as to escape God's agonizing concern. After telling a parable of the shepherd who rejoices over a restored lost sheep, Jesus concludes: "Likewise there will be more joy in Heaven over one sinner who repents than over ninety-nine righteous persons who do not need to repent."[69] Those words were ironically addressed to self-righteous persons because Jesus did not believe that the behavior of any human could not be changed for the better.

In another teaching, Jesus uses an animal comparison to stress the worth of individuals to God: "Are not five sparrows sold for two pennies?

Yet not one of them is overlooked by God. . . . Fear not: you are of more value than many sparrows!"[70] As Jesus watched people purchasing the cheapest meat in the marketplace, he may have reflected on words attributed to God in the Hebrew Bible: "I know every bird in the air, and I care for all life in the fields."[71] The reasoning is this: If God is aware of even each bird, how enormous must be the worth of all humans who are created to reflect the character of God.

According to Jesus, human compassion should be a by-product of theological reflection: "Be merciful, as your Father is merciful."[72] Jesus' story of the father of two sons best conveys his hope that God's disposition will be imitated. The younger son misused his personal freedom by demanding his inheritance while his father was still alive and by living irresponsibly in "a far country."[73] After "he squandered his wealth in dissolute living,"[74] the prodigal became a scavenger among pigs. He then realized that he was destroying himself and contemplated how even his father's servants were better off than he was. The prodigal son then took the initiative to return home and admit that he had done wrong. The father, who had patiently awaited for the alienation of his younger son to cease, "was filled with compassion."[75] The father then ran to meet him, profusely expressed forgiveness, and acted to restore him to the household and celebrate his return.

The righteous elder brother resented his father's acceptance of his younger brother. He thought that each individual should receive exactly what he or she deserved. Fairness demanded that punishment be the compensation for bad conduct and that rewards be reserved for those who had worked hard for the father. The father reminded his older son of the full share he had received and that he should rejoice that the family is reunited.[76] The story illustrates that Jesus thought of God as not being bound by the conventional reward-and-punishment system of justice.

Regarding the nature of God, Jesus' emphasis differs from that of Muhammad. The Quran is similar to the Hebrew Bible in the attention devoted to God's love; the theme can be found in both scriptures after much searching, but God's severity is stressed. When the texts pertaining to Moses, the main revealer of God in the Hebrew Bible, are examined, it is apparent that only a few focus on God's love. Frederick Sontag provides this discerning comparison:

> Muhammad outlines a divinity closer to the God in parts of the Old Testament rather than to the New. . . . A war-like

atmosphere pervades: "Do not falter or sue for peace when
you have gained the upper hand" (Q 47:35). Such statements
make it hard to see the Quran as a purified revelation of
Christianity, when the known words and actions of Jesus have
such a different tone. . . . War is said to be the medium of
eliminating idolatry (Q 8:39), but before we accept this we
must first decide if what is divine uses war and destruction as
an instrument. Certainly not according to Jesus.[77]

Earthly Rewards and Punishments

In Semitic religions, God is sovereign over history and uses the international clashings of His creatures as sanctions to effect His will. The
Quran refers to two armies from outside Arabia that had been defeated
by divine decree. During the year of Muhammad's birth, Ethiopian
Christians attacked Mecca on elephants, hoping to destroy the Ka'ba
with its idols. They retreated after this aerial bombardment: "Did God
not confound them by sending against them flocks of birds that pelted
them with stones, leaving them like withered plants?"[78] The Quran also
announces that the Byzantines would regain control of Palestine from
the Persians and comments on this warring situation: "God is powerful
and gives victory to whomever He wishes.[79]

Theocracy is the theory of government in the Quran; God decides
state as well as interstate matters. Consequently, secular rule has no
legitimacy, and in traditional Islam there is no separation between the
religious community and the political community. In the Quran, "obey
God" is often joined with "and His Apostle." Social control comes from
the top down: "It is not for believers—men or women—to have any
choice in their affairs if God and His Apostle decree otherwise"[80] Also,
Muhammad said, "He who obeys me has obeyed God."[81]

Other humans are occasionally recognized in the Quran as a part
of the governance when obedience is prescribed to "those charged with
authority among you."[82] From that hierarchy come laws that cover all
aspects of corporate life. But the intended result is not a dictatorship
dedicated to giving special privileges to an elite governmental adminis-
tration. Rather, those in the divine-human chain of authority should be
motivated by social justice for all the people. Muhammad warned:

"Anyone who is asked by God to take charge of subjects and does not protect them with good counsel will not smell the fragrance of Paradise."[83]

Islam deviated radically from its traditional Arabic culture by reducing the significance of the extended family. Quranic texts state that what really matters is acting with moral integrity regardless of the customary social sanctions: "Resolutely do justly as witness to God, even though it be against yourselves, your parents, or your kinfolk";[84] and "Be steadfast witnesses for God in equity. Do not let your hatred for any people cause you to pervert justice. Deal justly, for God is aware of what you do."[85] From this political theory came a quick loyalty shift at Medina. John Glubb notes:

> Young Muslims had been remarkably callous where family ties were concerned, and had even urged their fellow-Muslims to kill their own fathers, if they met them in battle. Yet this very callousness had been an extraordinary tribute to the persuasiveness of the Prophet's teaching.[86]

Conflicts in Muhammad's own family resulted from his determination to place God's will over the wishes of his kinfolk. Not only were his Uncle Abu Lahab and wife among his opponents, but also his Uncle Abbas and son-in-law Abu'l-Aasi joined other Meccan idolaters to battle against the Muslims at Badr.[87] These estrangements illustrate well Jesus' forecast that a "sword" will divide the household of those who take God's call seriously.[88]

The Quran refers to only one particular biblical book and quotes from it: "Truly We have written in the Psalms, 'My righteous servants will eventually rule the earth.' "[89] This psalm affirms a common theme of the Hebrew Bible: Those who trust in God will be given vindication, security, prosperity, and abundance in a time of general deprivation. The doctrine is tested in the Book of Job when its hero disputes the conventional wisdom about such sanctions.

Islam endorses the prevailing simple theodicy of ancient Israel, that God grants worldly success to faithful worshipers. Following God is described as a profitable investment in the Quran: "When prayers are ended, go out in quest of God's bounty. Remember God always, that you may prosper";[90] and "Those who recite the Book of God, attend to their prayers, give alms both secretly and openly, may hope for gains that will not fail. He will pay them their rewards and enrich them from His own abundance."[91] Karen Armstrong observes that Christianity's forte is enabling people to cope with adversity, whereas for Muslims worldly success is an outward sign of God's inward grace.[92]

Muhammad believed that too little or too much rain in a region is a consequence of religious disobedience. He proclaimed in God's name: "If My servants obey Me, I shall send down rain by night and cause the sun to shine upon them by day, and I shall not let them hear the sound of thunder."[93] An irrigation dam burst in southern Arabia in the sixth century, causing a productive agricultural area to revert to a wilderness. The Quran interprets the devastation as a result of apostasy: "Sheba turned away, so We sent against them a flood. We replaced their gardens . . . with tamarisk bushes and a scattering of nettle shrubs, punishing them for their unbelief. Do We ever punish any but the unbeliever?"[94]

In contrast to Muhammad and to portions of his Hebrew scriptures, Jesus believed that what individuals regard as destructive or beneficial forces of nature operate independently of just desserts. Not only does needed rain fall on the crops of bad persons, but floods hit the good and bad indiscriminately.[95] Jesus advised his disciples to prepare for the amoral fluctuations of nature, so that they would be able to cope when adverse weather arrives.

According to the Quran, penalties for misconduct, even if severe, can be beneficial; they may cause reformation before a person is confronted with his or her eternal destiny. The Quran states: "We will inflict on them the lesser punishment in this world before the greater punishment in the world to come, so that they may return to the right path."[96] To deter stealing, the Quran asserts: "As for the man or woman who is guilty of theft, cut off their hands."[97] However, following that verse is one that sounds this merciful note: "Whoever repents after doing evil and makes amends shall be pardoned by God."[98] Muhammad decided that an amputation was an appropriate penalty for stealing something worth at least as much as a shield.[99] Exceptions were made for those who take fruit off of a tree, who snatch a cloak, or who plunder while on a war-like expedition.[100] Most who have been convicted of thievery have kept their hands by providing restitution to their victims.

The Quran does not abolish blood revenge, but it provides some alternative penalties. Compensation should be paid for unintentional homicide.[101] For intentional homicide, the next of kin has the right to equal retaliation.[102] Revenge is limited to killing a freeman for a freeman killed, a slave for a slave, and a woman for a woman.[103] In writing to the people of Yemen, Muhammad also permitted that a man be killed in retaliation for murdering a woman.[104] While the Quran acknowledges the Torah law of "an eye for an eye, a tooth for a tooth, and a wound for a wound," it encourages pardoning as an act of charity.[105] Muhammad gave these options: "If a relative of anyone is killed . . . he may retaliate, or forgive, or receive compensation."[106]

One of the most frequent morality teachings in the Quran pertains to God's destruction of Sodom because of male homosexual activity in that biblical city, where Lot, Abraham's nephew, lived.[107] Accordingly, Muhammad taught: "God who is great and glorious will not look at a man who has intercourse with a man or a woman through the anus";[108] and "If you find anyone doing as Lot's people did, kill the one who does it and the one to whom it is done."[109]

In Jesus' era, the "unnatural" conduct of Sodomites was also denounced.[110] But, the Gospels suggest that Jesus viewed homosexual practice as of secondary importance. Although Jesus' extant teachings contain no explicit mention of homosexuality, he did declare that the people of Sodom would fare better on Judgment Day than the Galilean towns that had not responded well when the Gospel was proclaimed.[111]

Jesus thought that revenge—limited or unlimited—was bitter, not sweet. Inspiration for the difficult task of removing vindictiveness should arise, he believed, from reflecting on God's kindness. In one parable, God is pictured as a king who agrees to liquidate an enormous debt owed by a servant. This generosity is displayed with the expectation that the servant will show a similar attitude toward others. However, the pardoned servant treats harshly a fellow servant who had borrowed from him a relatively insignificant sum and who pleas for more time to repay the debt. On learning of this, the royal creditor became angry and cancelled his agreement to be merciful.[112] The parable shows the peril of isolating God's nonretaliation from human relationships.

For Jesus, the reward for acting with integrity and as a peacemaker is not material. Regardless of outward conditions, those with such ethical conduct will enjoy a spiritual vision ("see God") or have the satisfaction of being part of the faithful family of God.[113]

Afterlife Retributions

Semitic religions have been significantly influenced by some views on life after death held by non-Semitic people. Scenes depicted on ancient Egyptian funerary monuments occasionally show a god presiding over a post-mortem court of final judgment. Each individual is judged to determine if there is a balance between his or her records of personal merits and demerits. After reviewing the evidence, the god decides the eternal destiny of the one on trial. A crocodile god awaits to consume the bodies of the wicked. Those who are declared righteous are ushered into a place filled with material delights that the wealthy have been accustomed to. The Egyptians even believed that wives as well as lands would bear abundantly in an afterlife.[114]

When some Jews were in Babylonian captivity, they encountered Zoroasterianism, which contributed profoundly to the mythology they later developed on individual life after death.[115] Prophet Zoroaster had stressed eschatological angels, both good and bad, and had introduced the Persian term "paradise," meaning pleasure park, into religious vocabulary. The sensuousness of that cool, colorful, and fragrant garden, Zoroaster believed, replicates earthly experiences for the righteous. The opposite sensations were experienced by the wicked in an infernal place.

Muhammad was apparently influenced more immediately by the Jewish tradition that conveys the first expression of personal immortality in the Bible. An apocalyptic writer asserts: "Many of those who sleep in the dust of the earth shall awake, some to everlasting life, and some to shame and everlasting disgrace."[116] This verse, one of the latest to be written in the Jewish scriptures, affirms a doctrine of individual afterlife that was to become the norm in Judaism.

According to the Quran, there is an intermediate state of death sleep between death and resurrection for all except *jihad* martyrs. Those warriors go immediately to rejoice over what they have received from their Lord.[117] Other righteous Muslims rest undisturbed for a time in their graves, and the transition period seems brief.[118] In the middle of a night shortly before his death, Muhammad went to the Muslim cemetery in Medina and said, "Peace upon you, O people of the graves! Happy are you that you are so much better off than men here."[119]

In contrast, the unrighteous will not "rest in peace" but will begin to receive their punishment shortly after burial.[120] Two black and blue angels ask the deceased three questions: "Who is your God?", What is your religion?" and; "Who is its prophet?" Those who respond improperly to this interrogation will be given a foretaste of Hell. Infidels will be struck with a sledgehammer, causing them to utter cries that will be heard everywhere. Muslim tradition also tells of Muhammad and the mule on which he was riding hearing the moans of the tortured dead as they pass by a graveyard.[121] The tradition also indicates that punishment in the grave could be for something as small as soiling one's clothes with urine.[122]

After the Badr battle, Muhammad surprised his warriors by addressing dead Meccans whose bodies had been thrown in a common grave: "The Muslims said, 'Are you calling to dead bodies?' He answered: 'You cannot hear what I say better than they, but they cannot answer me.' "[123] Muhammad asked each enemy by name if he now recognized the truth of God's message.[124] The prophet offered another apropos saying: "Ninety-nine dragons will be given power over unbelievers in their graves, biting them until the Day of Resurrection."[125] Those undergoing such agony beg to be sent back to their earthly life for a second chance to perform good deeds, but they learn about an insurmountable barrier (barzakh) that prevents their return.[126]

Since the corpse is believed to be conscious of pain, cremation is no more acceptable in Islam than burning a living person at the stake. Muhammad said: "The breaking of the bones of a corpse is the same as doing it in life. . . . It is not fit for anyone to punish with fire but God."[127] Using white cloth similar to the type pilgrims wear to Mecca, the corpse is shrouded after being washed.[128] After prayers for God's mercy are said over the unembalmed body, it is quickly carried to the graveyard where a few verses from the Quran are recited.[129] Coffins are usually omitted so that the faithful can sit up on Judgment Day when Gabriel blows his horn. Mourners frequently throw earth into the grave and quote what the Quran attributes to Moses: "From the earth We created you and into it We return you; out of it We will bring you forth again."[130] Muhammad prohibited grave markers on the assumption that cemeteries, literally "sleeping places," were not a permanent abode for the bodies of departed Muslims.[131]

At a time that God determines, history will end eventfully. The Quran asserts: "With a blast of the trumpet, the dead will rise up from their graves and hasten to their Lord."[132] While recognizing the prominent roles of Adam, Abraham, Moses, and Jesus on Resurrection Day,

Muhammad asserts that he will be "the first to rattle the knocker of Paradise's (gate) . . . and stand at the right of the throne (of God)."[133]

A sermon of Muhammad provides more graphic description of that final Day: "You will be assembled barefoot, naked, and uncircumcised. . . . Abraham will be the first to be clothed."[134] The Quran declares: "All will be justly weighed on that Day";[135] and "Those whose good deeds weigh heavy in the balance will dwell in bliss, but those whose deeds are light will go to the fiery Abyss."[136] For Muhammad, the most foolish attitude possible is to be unconcerned about Judgment Day. The Quran describes the empty life of those who are flippant about their final outcome: "The life of this world is only a sport and idle talk, a passing show and boasting among you of riches and children. Their growth pleases the cultivator but soon they wither and become stubble."[137]

Jane Smith and Yvonne Haddad, who have made a thorough study of the resurrection views of classical Islam, state that "the vast majority of believers"[138] interpret eschatology literally rather than metaphorically. Muslims have "understood the realities of the Garden and the Fire to be real and specific, anticipating them with terror or with joy."[139] The physical nature of resurrection for Muhammad is revealed in a remark he made about his son Ibrahim, who died in infancy: "He has two foster mothers who will complete his suckling in Paradise."[140] In spite of this comment, Muhammad generally shared Augustine's assumption that the age of the resurrected will be about thirty.[141]

Ancient peoples who believed in physical resurrection had different notions on how it could be achieved. The procedure of Egyptian morticians was to dehydrate the flesh and then make mummies. In contrast, the Jewish rabbis believed that the power of God is sufficient to accomplish a resurrection from unembalmed remains. The former body could be reconstructed even if only a single bone was left.[142] Prophet Ezekiel's dry-bones vision, which originally pertained to his hope for a revived Jewish community,[143] was later used to affirm and describe the resurrection of individuals. After death and burial, bones that had been dismembered would be rejoined in the proper order. A fresco on the wall of a third-century Mesopotamian synagogue depicts a valley where strewn parts of human corpses are being reconnected.[144]

The outlook on the physical resurrection that had developed in Judaism is reflected in these Quranic verses: "We will reassemble bones, even to the fingertips"[145] and "We will raise the bones and cover them with flesh."[146] Endorsing a rabbinical viewpoint, the early Muslims made this claim: "There is nothing of the human body that does not decay except one bone; that is the little bone at the end of the coccyx of which the human body will be recreated on the Day of Resurrection."[147]

When Muhammad proclaimed this resurrection doctrine, he provoked ridicule among the Meccans: "They say: 'If you are telling the truth, bring back our ancestors.'"[148] Ishaq records this exchange between Muhammad and an Arab skeptic:

> Ubayy took to the Apostle an old bone, crumbling to pieces, and said, "Muhammad, do you allege that God can revivify this after it has decayed?" Then he crumbled it in his hand and blew the pieces in the Apostle's face. The Apostle answered: "Yes, I do say that. God will raise it and you, after you have become like this. Then God will send you to Hell."[149]

Regarding eschatology, the pagan Arabs responded to Muhammad and to the Jews in much the same way. A Jew in Arabia at that time spoke about "the resurrection, the reckoning, the scales, Paradise, and Hell."[150] That outlook precipitated this incredulity: "Good gracious, man! Do you think that such things could be that men can be raised from the dead to a place where there is a garden and a fire in which they will be recompensed for their deeds?"[151]

Ascertaining accountability in the Quran is by means of a ledger, which is similar to those used for business in Mecca and in other trading centers. Guardian angels keep a record of the virtues and vices of each person.[152] After the ledger is opened, it is placed in the defendant's right hand if the balance shows a credit, and in the left if there is a debit.[153] On Judgment Day, God announces:

> We have written in this record all you have ever done. Those who believed and did good works, will be admitted into the Lord's mercy. . . . (To the unbelievers it will be said:) "Were not Our revelations proclaimed to you?" . . . The evils they have done will be made apparent to them and what they scoffed at will befall them. We shall say: "This Day We forget you, even as you forgot that you would meet this Day. The Fire will be your home and none will help you."[154]

Some of the Judgment Day imagery in the Quran parallels that of the Bible. Daniel dreamed of God presiding on his throne when "the court sat in judgment, and the books were opened."[155] An early Christian apocalyptic book contains this vision: "I saw the dead, great and small alike, standing before the throne while the books lay open. . . . The dead were judged according to their works, as recorded in the books."[156] Paul tells of the dead being raised in a changed form at the sound of the last trumpet.[157] On that occasion, the New Testament repeatedly states, Jesus will be at God's right hand because he has the highest rank apart from God.[158] In the heavenly court Jesus will acknowledge all Christians and make intercession for them.[159]

According to the Quran, those who appear before God after death are involved in deciding their own guilt or innocence. He will say to every person: "Read your record! You are this Day a sufficient witness against yourself."[160] As Huston Smith explains:

> What death burns away is self-serving defenses, forcing one to see with total objectivity how one has lived one's life. In the uncompromising light of that vision, where no dark and hidden corners are allowed, it is one's own actions that rise up to accuse or confirm.[161]

When the final accounting is made, incriminating evidence is given by one's bodily parts; they expose the persons who are attempting to hide from their record. Consider this example: "Ears, eyes, and skins will testify to their misdeeds. And they will say to their organs, 'Why have you spoken against us?' "[162] Also, the weak will tell about the devious schemes of powerful individuals.[163]

Rahman offers this interpretation:

> (What is) so poignantly portrayed as occurring on the Day of Judgment is what the Quran really desires to take place here in this life; for a man who can x-ray himself effectively and hence diagnose his inner state has nothing to be afraid of if his inner being goes public. . . . The central endeavor of the Quran is for man to develop this keen sight here and now, when there is opportunity for action and progress, for at the Hour of Judgment it will be too late to remedy the state of affairs.[164]

Muhammad is described in the Quran as a proclaimer of the gospel (injil, the Arabicized form of the Greek euaggelios).[165] The good news is that Paradise is ahead for believers. One of its joys is a fuller awareness of God: "On that Day there will be radiant faces, looking toward their Lord."[166] Muhammad claimed that the resurrected will be able to see God as they would the sun at midday in a cloudless sky.[167] The prophet also likened the beatific vision of God to solar light, which, although it cannot be directly seen at night, is gloriously reflected from the full moon.[168] According to Muhammad's gospel, God will announce: "I have prepared for My upright servants what eye has not seen, nor ear heard, nor has entered into the heart of man."[169] That saying is quite similar to these words attributed to Jesus: "I will give you what no eye has seen, no ear has heard, no hand has touched, and what has not arisen in the heart of man."[170]

Another eschatological teaching of Muhammad paraphrases one of Jesus' parables. Muhammad said:

> God will say on the Day of Resurrection: "O son of Adam, I was sick and you did not visit Me." He will reply: "My Lord, how could I visit You, when you are the Lord of the universe?" God will say: "Did you not know that My servant so and so was ill, and yet you did not visit him? Did you not know that if you had visited him, you would have found Me with him?"[171]

This saying, repeated for giving food to the hungry and drink to the thirsty, parallels a parable of Jesus that motivated, among others, monasteries to serve as hospices.[172] The core of that parable pertains to the basis on which eternal life is granted:

> The righteous will answer him, "Lord, when did we see you hungry and feed you, or thirsty and give you drink? And when did we see you a stranger and welcome you, or naked and clothe you? And when did we see you sick or in prison and visit you?" And the king will answer them, "Truly, I tell you, as you did it to one of the least of these who are members of my family, you did it to me."[173]

On Resurrection/Judgment Day, Muslims believe that damnation is imposed for murder, lying, corruption, luxurious living, failure to help the poor, and for disbelief in God's revelations.[174] The hypocrite will have an appropriate retribution. Muhammad said: "He who is two-faced in this world will have two tongues of fire on the Day of Resurrection."[175] The inhabitants of Hell will include all who had been idolatrous, including family members who died before their parents became monotheists. When Khadija inquired about the destiny of her two children who died while she was a pagan, Muhammad informed her that they were in Hell. She then asked: "Messenger of God, what about my son whom I had from you?"[176] Muhammad replied: "Believers and their children are in Paradise and polytheists and their children are in Hell."[177]

The harshest criticism of the Quran is reserved for those who "love wealth with boundless love" and do not care for the orphans or feed the poor. On beholding the punishment before them in Hell, those greedy people will lament on Judgment Day: "Would that we had sent before us some provision for life!"[178] At a barrier separating the saved from the damned, the latter will cry out to those on the other side: "Pour on us some of the water God has provided you. . . . Could we but live our lives again, we would act otherwise."[179] To those who plead for a reincarnation when they would be generous, God says, "No, my revelations came to you but you denied them."[180]

A parable of Jesus contains lines that echo this scenario. A rich man who had little concern for a sick beggar, so the story goes, ends up as a beggar in Hades. He asks Abraham for some cooling water but is refused. The former rich man then requests permission to return to earth to inform his family of the dire consequences of their behaving as he did. Abraham recognizes that the Jewish man had already had plenty of opportunity to respond to social-justice messages. When rejecting the rich man's plea, Abraham asserts: "If they do not listen to Moses and the prophets, neither will they be convinced even if someone rises from the dead."[181] Neither Jesus nor Muhammad thought that supernatural acts were likely to transform the values of people who claimed to see them.

Muslims who qualify for Paradise are taken to a place strikingly different from the Arabian environment. The Quran gives assurance that they will reside "where rivers flow of unpolluted water, unspoiled milk, delicious wine, and clearest honey. They shall eat of every fruit and receive forgiveness from their Lord."[182] Muhammad added: "In Paradise there is a tree so big that in its shade a rider may travel for a century without being able to cross it."[183] Desert people must have been especially dazzled by the promise of perennial water springs and verdant gardens with clusters of fruit ready to gather. With the restoration of the senses in resurrection, the faithful can physically enjoy Paradise, and the faithless can feel the torture of Hell.

Those who feast in Paradise will not suffer any undesirable after-effects. The following exchange took place between Muhammad and a curious individual: " 'The inhabitants of Paradise will eat and drink in it, but they will not spit, or pass water, or void excrement, or suffer from catarrh.' " Asked what would happen to the food, he replied, " 'It will produce belching and sweat like musk.' "[184]

Muhammad promised the faithful that they will enjoy the pleasures of the affluent in the afterlife. He pointed to the advantages of delayed gratifications: "Do not wear silks and satins, and do not drink or eat from gold and silver vessels, for others have them in this world but you will have them in the next."[185] The prophet also said: "He who drinks wine in this world and does not repent of it will be forbidden it in the world to come."[186] While abstinence from intoxicants helps gain admission to Paradise, the Quran guarantees the elect that "they will be served the finest wine" after arriving there.[187]

The Quran promises eternal rewards for both genders:[188] "You and your spouses will enter Paradise and be glad. You will be served with golden plates and goblets. Everything the heart desires and that pleases the eye will be there, where you will abide forever.[189] These immortals will be clothed in silks and fine brocade while they recline under shady trees on green cushions with carpets beneath.

Men will also enjoy virgins with lovely eyes and swelling breasts.[190] Muhammad received these revelations about the beautiful maidens when he was singularly married at Mecca to a woman considerably older than him. Smith and Haddad provide more detail on the girls who are called *hur* in the Quran:

> The man takes his turn with each of his consorts, and none shows any jealousy in waiting for him to return to her. With each he drinks wine but there is no drunkenness. Sleep is unnecessary, the *hur* do not get pregnant (in fact, they never lose their virginal state, despite the clear indication of the physical nature of the union with their husbands), there is no menstruation, the *hur* do not spit or blow their noses, and they are never sick."[191]

Some interpreters presume that family life is not part of the Quranic picture of the afterlife. For example, Ronald Bodley writes:

> Nothing so tedious as marriage is mentioned as a phase of future life. What Mohammed did offer his followers was a

final resting place where they would find all that they had missed on earth: rivers, and lakes and green grass; and fruit trees with fruit always ripe; and wine to drink which exhilarated. . . . Black-eyed girls of resplendent beauty, of virgin purity and exquisite sensibility would be at the disposal of every Moslem believer.[192]

Bodley rightly judges the *hur* to be different from female Muslims, but he wrongly presumes that there are no older females or family bondings in the Quranic Paradise. Puzzlement over elderly Muslim women *vis-à-vis* Paradise is addressed in this teasing story: "The Prophet said to an old woman, 'No old woman will enter Paradise.' . . . She asked him, 'What is wrong with them?' He replied, 'Do you not recite the Quran, 'We have created them and made them virgins?' "[193]

The Quran refers to the presence of believers' wives and children with their husbands and fathers in Paradise.[194] Smith and Haddad tell how Muslim tradition has dealt with earthly wives who are judged worthy of Paradise:

These women, often referred to as the daughters of Eve to distinguish them from the *hur*, are usually said to have one husband each (the men of faith are often portrayed as having all of their earthly wives plus seventy or more of the *hur*). If the woman had more than one husband on earth, the situation is unclear; sometimes it is said that she will get the last one as husband in the Garden, sometimes the best one, and sometimes it is reported that she will have her choice.[195]

Al-Ghazali, the preeminent Muslim theologian, claimed that the promise of sexual pleasures was "a powerful motivation to incite men . . . to adore God so as to reach Heaven."[196] John Glubb comments on the impact of the sensuous Quranic eschatological mythology on Muslim imperialism:

The most powerful factor in promoting Arab conquests, which were soon to follow, was the promise of the immediate admission to Paradise to all Muslims who fell in battle against non-Muslims. Moreover the detailed descriptions of that Paradise with its cool, flowing streams, delicious fruits, and above all its houris, beautiful virgins perpetually young, were

precisely such as to tempt the poor bedouins, whose lives
were an endless struggle against physical hardships.[197]

The Quranic Paradise parallels the fantasizing of Ephraim, the
renowned preacher of the fourth-century Syrian Christians. His paradisaical imagining was especially appealing to other monks because it
pictured a life that compensated for present sensual deprivations.
Ephraim wrote:

> I saw the dwelling places of the just, and they themselves,
> dripping with ointments, giving forth pleasant odors,
> wreathed in flowers and decked with fruits. . . . When they lie
> at the table, the trees offer their shade in the clear air. . . . It is
> a feast without effort, and the hands do not become tired. . . .
> Think, O aged one, of Paradise! When its aroma refreshes you
> and its pleasant odors renew your youth, your blemishes will
> vanish. . . . Whoever has abstained from wine on earth, for
> him do the vines of Paradise yearn. . . . And if a man has lived
> in chastity, the women receive him in a pure bosom, because
> he as a monk did not fall into the bosom and bed of earthly
> love.[198]

Tor Andrae states as "irrefutable fact" that the Quran's paradisaical
description of rejuvenated youth and verdant nature was inspired by
Ephraim's ideas.[199] Muhammad was not an ascetic who dreamed of
being released from self-imposed mortifications, but he may have
longed for a reversal of the privations of his desert environment.

If Paradise is an exquisite oasis, its opposite also shows the influence of the Arabian landscape. Hell resembles the desert at its worst,
scorching winds and no shield from the relentless heat. Some torture is
graphically depicted: the precious metals of hoarders will be heated in
Hell and used to brand their bodies.[200]

The Quran appropriately refers to Muhammad as a "warner" of the
consequences of evil action because Hell is a main theme of his preaching. The threat of Hell is given more attention (367 verses) than the
delights of Paradise (312 verses). Retribution is explained to the infernal
inmates in this way:

> On the day when unbelievers are exposed to the Fire, it will be
> said: "You squandered your good things in your earthly life

and took your fill of pleasure. Now you are rewarded with humiliating punishment because you were disdainful and unjust."[201]

Jahannam, the main Quranic designation for the place for evil people, comes from the Hebrew word *gehinnom*. This term, usually translated into English as "Hell," referred in ancient times to the valley (*ge*) belonging to the Hinnom family. Located on the southern outskirts of Jerusalem, it was considered defiled because children of pre-Israelite Jerusalem residents had been sacrificed there to the god Molech.[202] The ravine became a trash dump where unburied corpses were incinerated.[203] Fire was continuous there, accounting for the rapid decomposition, and worms were ever feasting on the organic wastes.

Recognizing that a fierce fire would soon destroy a physical body, the Quran claims that the damned will be supplied new flesh: "Those who deny Our revelations, We will roast in a fire. As often as their skins are consumed We will give them fresh skins, so that they may taste the torment."[204] The Quran rejects the opinion that wicked individuals will be burned for only a few days[205] and asserts that the doomed will suffer in Hell "as long as heaven and earth endure."[206]

Compared to Muhammad's message, Jesus' teachings have little to do with assurances of a celestial abode for the righteous dead and Hell for the wicked. In the Gospels' only use of "Paradise," the dying Jesus says to the repentant thief on a cross next to him, "I promise you that today you will be with me in Paradise."[207] He may have been speaking about a spiritual condition in which God and humans are one rather than a physical place in the cosmos. Judging from this saying of Jesus, he did not believe in an intermediate state, or purgatory, before the final state.

Jesus' gospel is primarily oriented toward the present world. That note was sounded at the beginning of his ministry: "Jesus came to Galilee, proclaiming the good news of God and saying, 'The time is fulfilled, and the kingdom of God is at hand; repent, and believe in the good news.' "[208] The Gospel of Matthew, which replaced Mark's phrase "kingdom of God" with "Kingdom of Heaven," misleads some modern readers into thinking that Jesus frequently focused on the hereafter. "Heaven" is a circumlocution in a Gospel addressed principally to Jews who might be offended by the uttering of the divine name. Jesus was interested in teaching about God's reign on earth, not about some territory in the sky.

Jesus' outlook on eschatology is rooted in the Hebrew view that eternal life is natural to God alone. In contrast, death is the natural final end for mice and men. According to the story of the Garden of Eden, humans lose spiritual life forever when they separate themselves from God. Because of self-determinism, there is nothing in their future but dusty death.[209] God shares the realm of deathless life with those who desire godly virtues. Thus, each human has the option of "passing on" or passing out of existence. Those who devote themselves to spiritual growth during their physical lives will be given the opportunity for further development after physical death. Life after death is seen as a continuation of the spiritual life that one can begin to enjoy during one's mortal life. For Jesus, as for Muhammad, eternal life depends on just one earthly life; neither suggested the possibility of reincarnation cycles.

Jesus did not adopt the Greek view that the soul (psyche) is inherently immortal. He believed that the ultimate result of rejecting the divine gift of eternal life is the destruction of the self's immortable potentiality, which concludes at death.[210] Jesus used several images to picture the extinction option for the ungodly.[211]

Jesus continually taught his disciples that God should be thought of as a caring parent, so any notion of his dispensing cruel and vindictive punishments must be rejected. Jesus presented this lesser-to-greater logic:

> Is there anyone among you who, if your child asks for bread, will give a stone? Or if the child asks for a fish, will give a snake? If you then, bad as you are, know enough to give your children what is good for them, how much more will your heavenly Father give good things to those who ask him.[212]

Like Muhammad, Jesus occasionally used a Hebrew term when referring to an eschatological place of punishment. Gehinnom becomes geenna in the Greek Synoptic Gospels. The Jews drew a metaphor for the final liquidation of the unrighteous from the geographical gehinnom. In the Mishnah, for example, murderers and deceitful persons "inherit gehinnom and go down to the pit of destruction" whereas the righteous "inherit the Garden of Eden and the world to come."[213] The Jews did not presume that an everlasting Paradise for the good must be balanced by an everlasting torment for the bad. Jesus used gehinnom as a figure for disgraceful annihilation, and once he explicitly associated it with the complete destruction of all that makes one a human being.[214] It is unlikely that Jesus intended to describe a literal spot on earth, beneath the earth, or separate from the earth, where the damned are perpetually burned. Paul's letters, in which he never mentions *gehinnom*, assists in explaining Jesus' ideas on divine retribution. For the apostle, Hell was not the payoff for living an evil life. He states: "The wages of sin is death, but the gift of God is eternal life."[215]

In *Jesus Before Christianity*, Albert Nolan writes perceptively:

> The imagery of fire and worms is derived from the rubbish dump of Gehenna. It should be noted that according to this imagery it is the worms that never die and the fire that is perpetual or eternal. Everything and everybody else in Gehenna dies, decomposes and is destroyed. Gehenna is the image of complete destruction, the extreme opposite of life.[216]

Jesus' most insightful teaching on life after death was given in response to a *reductio ad absurdum* question pertaining to Torah interpretation. Included in the record of Jesus' last week in Jerusalem is this episode:

> Some Sadducees—who deny that there is a resurrection— came to him and inquired: "Teacher, Moses prescribed for us that if there are brothers, and one dies leaving a wife but no child, the next must take the widow to have children for his brother's sake. Now there were seven brothers; the first took a wife and died childless. The second took the widow, and he too died childless; it was the same for all seven. Finally the woman died. At the resurrection, when the dead rise to life, whose wife will she be?"[217]

The priestly party of Sadducees raised this question because they were enraged by Jesus' denunciation of temple commercialization, which was their source of wealth. Rather than seeking information, they wanted to trap him into advocating publicly an absurd idea. To ridicule the notion that corpses revive and carry on what formerly had been their customary life, the Sadducees modified an old Jewish tale of a woman with sequential husbands.[218]

The Sadducees recognized that Moses had sanctioned polygyny but not polyandry. A husband could have multiple spouses concurrently, and the remarriage of a childless widow to her deceased husband's brother was required.[219] Being strict constructionists with respect to the Torah, the Sadducees found in it no basis for an afterlife doctrine. According to Josephus, they believed that "the soul perishes with the body and they disregarded the observation of anything except what the Law enjoins."[220]

Jesus' interlocutors presumed that anyone accepting a resurrection doctrine must think in a literalistic way. The term that is translated "resurrection" in this passage, as well as elsewhere in the New Testament, is a compound Greek word meaning "up" (*ana*) plus "stand" (*stasis*). Thus, "resurrection of the dead" literally means the standing up of corpses that had been recumbent. Belief in a reanimation of relics on the day of God's final judgment was popular in apocalyptic Judaism.[221]

Jesus' view of the afterlife differed from the prevailing views of his time. He believed in a life-after-death doctrine that could be supported by the nature of God as revealed in the Torah. To the Sadducees, Jesus charged: "You know neither the scriptures nor the power of God."[222] He twitted them by asking if they had read the "passage about the bush"[223] from a scroll they accepted as the word of God. Jesus then quoted from the burning-bush story about God's call to shepherd Moses: "I am . . . the God of Abraham, the God of Isaac, and the God of Jacob."[224]

Regarding that verse, Jesus commented: "God is not God of the dead but of the living; you are quite wrong."[225] Jesus claimed that God, being faithful and powerful, does not permit the covenant He has established to be severed by the physical death of "those who are judged worthy."[226] Hence the present tense—"I *am*"—is used to prove that the Hebrew patriarchs, who had physically died centuries before the time of Moses, continue to have a personal relationship with God. To be dead to humans does not necessarily mean to be dead to God, and to be alive to humans does not necessarily mean to be alive to God. By stressing the undying presence of God, Jesus followed the verbal emphasis of an Exodus writer. After inquiring about God's name, Moses received this disclosure: "Say to the Israelites, 'I AM has sent me . . . the God of Abraham. . . .' "[227] Jesus chided the priestly party for lacking a contextual understanding of their scriptures. The Sadducees did not comprehend the way in which the character of the eternal God they professed implied a doctrine of human-life continuance.

Contrary to the outlook of some Jews who had been influenced by Egyptian and Zoroastrian notions of resurrection, Jesus believed that the postmortem existence is not a revival and extension of physical life.

Jesus affirmed: "Those who are judged worthy of a place in the other realm and in the resurrection from the dead take neither husband or wife."[228] One purpose of marriage is removed because "they can no longer die."[229] Reproduction is needed only in a mortal society that must replace the perpetually dying in order to avert biological extinction.

Of course, partners enjoy sharing in one another's company quite apart from procreation. Jesus suggested that personal interaction in the afterlife would have a quality similar to that of divine messengers.[230] Angels communicate as spirits in ways that mortals find difficult to imagine. The intense communion now widely experienced in marriage could be a distant simulation of the relationships in the transformed heavenly community.

Jesus envisaged an ultimate family in which biological and marital ties are transcended. Although "loved ones" are often defined as spouse, children, parents, siblings, and other kin, Jesus did not think of eternal-life companions here or hereafter as primarily one's relatives.[231] He valued those who serve God faithfully more than those bonded by marital covenant or by blood relationship.[232]

Temporal as well as spatial considerations are irrelevant in the eternal community. Even as the Hebrew patriarchs are alive to God while long dead to earthlings, so Abraham and his children are in living fellowship with other mortals who lived in a different age. To convey this idea, Jesus told a parable that pictured a recently deceased beggar leaning on the "bosom" of Abraham. In this fictitious story, intended to express nonliteral truth, Jesus also showed that class differences do not ultimately matter because poor Lazarus and wealthy Abraham share the same status.[233] Elsewhere, Jesus taught that at the end of time "many will come from east and west and feast with Abraham, Isaac, and Jacob."[234] Individuals who once were spread across centuries, continents, and classes are together in a timeless, egalitarian community. Fidelity to the will of the divine Host is the glue binding them together.

CHAPTER NINE

ENLARGEMENTS

Of Muhammad

During the last years of his life, Muhammad was treated in an awesome manner that distinguished him from others in his community. The Quran establishes this protocol:

> Believers, do not raise your voices above that of the Prophet, nor speak loudly to him as you would to one another, lest all your works miscarry without your perceiving it. Those who speak softly in the presence of God's Apostle are those whose hearts have passed God's test for reverence. Forgiveness and an immense reward await them.[1]

Several Quranic verses commanded Muhammad to say to his people: "If you love God, follow me; then God will love you and forgive your sins";[2] "He that obeys the Apostle obeys God";[3] and "In the Apostle of God you have a noble pattern of conduct."[4] By equating devotion to God with allegiance to Muhammad, he became the ultimate human authority before his death.

Since Muhammad had been exalted far above his companions even during his lifetime, it is understandable that the reverential trend would continue afterward. Popular Muslim tradition transformed Muhammad into the prototype of all human perfection. Josef van Ess describes the eclipsing of the historical Muhammad "That the Prophet had been a mere human being was not, in the end, enough. That he had been a pagan himself for forty years was completely hushed up; that he was capable of sinning was no longer believed."[5]

Muhammad was presumed to be the exemplar par excellence of how one ought to live. He transposed abstract principle into concrete personality. Accordingly, devout Muslims began to revere anything that had come into contact with him. When Muhammad returned to Mecca as a hero, companions treated him in this way: "Whenever he performed his ablutions they ran to get the water he had used; if he spat they ran to it; if a hair of his head fell they ran to pick it up."[6] Annemarie Schimmel has researched the role of Muhammad in the lives of devoted Muslims. She notes:

> Veneration of the Prophet and the interest in even the smallest details of his behavior and his personal life grew in the same measure as the Muslims were distanced from him in time. They wanted to know ever more about his personality, his looks, and his words in order to be sure that they were following him correctly. The popular preachers enjoyed depicting the figure of the Prophet in wonderful colors, adding even the most insignificant details.[7]

Maxime Rodinson provides the following information on Muhammad, the saint:

> A multitude of relics of him are preserved everywhere: hairs, teeth, sandals, his cloak, his prayer rug, a sword hilt, an arrow used by him. Constantinople, when it had become the capital of the Muslim world, boasted of the number of these relics to be found there. Two hairs from his beard were kept there in forty bags sewn one inside the other, and were solemnly shown to worshipers once a year.[8]

Al-Ghazali, the most outstanding theologian in the history of Islam, not only championed Muhammad's religious principles but also imitated meticulously even his grooming habits. Al-Ghazali wrote in the eleventh century:

He (God) said: "What the Apostle has brought you, receive;
and what he has forbidden you, refrain from" (Q59:7). So you
must sit while putting on trousers and stand while putting on a
turban. . . . When cutting your nails . . . you must begin with
the little toe of the right foot and finish with the little toe of
the left.[9]

Veneration for Muhammad in popular Islam is difficult to separate
from worship. The widely translated poem by Al-Busiri, a thirteenth-
century Berber, suggests that Muhammad is more worthy of adoration
than Jesus:

Muhammad, Lord of the two worlds . . . surpassed the (other) prophets in
  physical and moral qualities,
Nor did they approach him in either knowledge or magnanimity. . . .
In him the essence of goodness is undivided.
Leave aside what the Christians claim for their prophet.[10]

In the twentieth century, there has been no diminishing of adoration of Muhammad. His name continues to be the most common male
name in Muslim culture. This tribute by Kamal al-Din is often reprinted:

History fails to point out any personality other than him
where we find the assemblage of all the virtues that consti-
tuted an evolved humanity. His simplicity, his humanity, his
generosity, his frugality, his broadmindedness, his forbearance, his earnestness of purpose, his steadfastness, his firmness
in adversity, his meekness in power, his humility in greatness,
his anxious care for animals, his passionate love for children,
his bravery and courage, his magnanimity, his unbending
sense of justice. Volumes are needed to do justice to this
Superman.[11]

Commenting on contemporary conduct, Karen Armstrong writes:
"Just as Christians have developed the practice of the imitation of
Christ, Muslims seek to imitate Muhammad in their daily lives in order
to approximate as closely as possible to this perfection and so to come as
close as they can to God Himself."[12] Armstrong notes that this results in
Muslims throughout the world sharing a particular lifestyle: "The way

they pray or wash, their table manners or personal hygiene follow a common, distinctive pattern."[13]

Some also see Muhammad as the precursor of modern discoveries about nature. Qassim Jairazbhoy argues that all science originated in Muhammad's teachings.[14] Robert Gulick claims that Muhammad's knowledge was so advanced that "it took scientists a thousand years to learn the truth of that which the Prophet had revealed."[15] In his translation of the Quran, Ahmed Ali attempts to show that Muhammad revealed what is now recognized as a sophisticated understanding of genetics and geophysics.[16]

Growing up as an African during the past generation, Lamin Sanneh testifies that he offered intercessory prayer to Muhammad, frequently addressing him as "the Lord of Mankind."[17] Sanneh adds: "Everywhere in the Muslim world the name of God and that of the Prophet stand at the pinnacle of devotion and obligation. . . . Early Muslims were first identified as the *ummatu Muhammadiyah*, "the Muhammadan community."[18] When Hamilton Gibb, the widely respected Islamic scholar, entitled a text *Mohammedanism*,[19] he was following a development that is rooted in Muslim tradition.

Rafiq Zakaria, a prominent Muslim living in Bombay, discusses the anger in Islamic nations over Salman Rushdie's disrespectful characterizations of Muhammad in *The Satanic Verses*. Observing that some of his fellow religionists hold Muhammad "dearer than God,"[20] Zakaria agrees with this assessment of Wilfred Smith: "Muslims will allow attacks on Allah; there are atheists and atheistic publications, and rationalist societies; but to disparage Muhammad will provoke . . . a fanaticism of blazing vehemence."[21]

Ninian Smart, an outstanding comparative religions scholar, observes: "Although Islam regards attempts to deify the deadliest sin, in practice he (Muhammad) is the supreme ethical idea and more closely followed than Christ, partly because of the accumulation of biographical stories about him."[22] By 1981, some 2,713 biographies of Muhammad existed.[23] Many of the alleged life stories are not based on the earliest records. As Rodinson observes: "Over the centuries, thousands of ideas have been consecrated by being attributed to the Prophet: although actually inspired by the spirit of the times and by the widest cultural influences, they have nevertheless been blanketed with his authority."[24]

Rodinson describes the way in which honor was given to the house where Muhammad was allegedly born:

His birthplace in Mecca was turned into a mosque and was especially honored. In 1184 the Spanish pilgrim Ibn Jubayr came to marvel at the green marble slab ringed with silver, which marked the exact spot. "We rubbed our cheeks," he wrote, "on that holy place where the most illustrious of new-born babies dropped to the ground and which was touched by the purest and noblest of all infants."[25]

The scene showing pilgrims at Muhammad's birthplace was proba-bly influenced by what is enshrined in Bethlehem's Basilica of the Nativity. A silver star on a marble slab of that fourth-century church allegedly designates where Mary gave birth to Jesus. Even as the cele-bration of Christmas began several centuries after the birth of Jesus,[26] so the annual commemoration of Muhammad's birthday was initiated in the tenth century.[27] A library now stands at the birthplace site in Mecca.

In many Muslim nations, a public holiday and a street celebration has become customary for *Mawlid an-Nabi* (the Birthday of the Prophet). Al-Busiri's laudatory poem (quoted above) is frequently recited at that time.[28] Rodinson provides these details:

> It was fixed arbitrarily for a Monday, the twelfth of the month of Rabi I. . . . The festival differs in detail from one place to another, but in most places there are torchlight processions, free meals for the poor; sweets are distributed to all. . . . Children are dressed up in new clothes and people exchange visits, let off fireworks, drench themselves in scent and show themselves off on richly caparisoned horses. . . . Speakers demonstrate how the world was plunged in darkness and ignorance before the coming of Muhammad, and how he brought the light of truth to shine in the hearts of men.[29]

Muhammad would have been embarrassed by the claims of some followers that he possessed supernatural powers. He distanced himself from the miracle workers of the past, even though the Quran relates— and expands on—the marvelous deeds of some biblical figures from Abraham to Jesus. For example, Moses engaged in magic to impress the Egyptians and as proof of his office. And like the Bible, the Quran states that Moses' staff became a snake when he threw it down.[30] Although according to the Bible Solomon did not perform any miracles, the Quranic Solomon had a *jinn* army to instantaneously convey the Queen of Sheba's throne to Jerusalem. When a pool of water was transformed into an area of grass, she was converted to Solomon's religion.[31]

In spite of the historical Muhammad's candid acknowledgment that he was no wizard, his own community soon attributed supernatural marvels to him. Pious Muslims were not content with a wholly human prophet, and within a century after Muhammad's death, fantastic stories were accepted as part of the orthodox doctrine. Ali Dashti, who studied to be a Muslim leader in Iran, explains what many Muslims have done to Muhammad: "They have continually striven to turn this man into an imaginary superhuman being, a sort of God in human clothes. . . . As the years advanced, myth-making and miracle-mongering became more and more widespread and extravagant."[32]

The following statement from the Quran inspired one supernatural tale: "The hour of doom is near, for the moon is split. Yet, when unbelievers see a portent they turn away, calling it sorcery."[33] Some have imagined that when Muhammad made that pronouncement at Mecca, the moon circled about the Ka'ba in two parts.[34] In another version of this story, one part of the moon remained over the top of a mountain while the other part went beyond the mountain.[35]

Ishaq's biography describes a tree that responded to Muhammad's command to come to him and then return to where it had been planted.[36] According to Tabari's biography, Muhammad proved his prophethood by summoning to himself a cluster of dates from its hanging place. With just a magical snap of his fingers, the cluster came to him and reattached itself to the tree at his command.[37] When Muhammad's camel wandered off, its return resulted from his clairvoyance: "God has shown me. It is in such-and-such a glen caught by its rope to a tree."[38] And when diggers on a battleground were having difficulty removing a large rock, Muhammad spit on it to cause it to pulverize. He provided an abundant lunch for his troops by taking a few dates in his hand, which then multiplied.[39] One legend is reminiscent of stories about Moses who produced water in the desert by striking rocks with his rod.[40] During Muhammad's last campaign, he rubbed a rock and prayed, after which water burst forth for his famished troops.[41] Al-Bukhari tells of Muhammad praying for rain during a drought. Suddenly it rained for a week, causing houses to collapse. The prophet then pleaded: "O God! Round about us and not on us."[42] So the sky became clear at Medina but there was rain beyond his city.[43]

Ironically, a miracle challenge that Muhammad rejected may have been the origin of the most fascinating of all stories in the Muslim tradition. At Mecca he told the Hebrew story of Jacob who dreamed of a ladder reaching to heaven on which angels were descending and ascending.[44] Some Meccans then wanted Muhammad to produce what Jacob had envisioned.[45] One challenger asserted: "I will never believe in you until you get a ladder to the sky and . . . four angels shall come with you, testifying that you are speaking the truth."[46] Ishaq writes: "The Apostle went to his family, sad and grieving . . . because of their estrangement from him."[47]

That disappointing experience may have triggered in Muhammad a dream of heavenly vistas and of persons who gave him encouragement. Ishaq records that Muhammad, while asleep near the Ka'ba, had "a true vision from God" in which his spirit soared while "his body remained where it was."[48] To transport him on a night flight, Gabriel brought a winged steed named Buraq, who was between a horse and donkey in size. Abraham, Moses, Jesus, and other prophets assembled in Jerusalem where Muhammad alighted, and he led them in prayer.[49] Starting at the rock at the summit of Mount Moriah, where Solomon built the temple, Gabriel took Muhammad up a grand ladder to multiple levels of outer space. The vision follows the ancient cosmology of seven spheres through which the soul ascends toward God.[50]

In the lowest sphere, Muhammad joined Adam to view the horrors of Hell. He beheld various tortures:

> I saw men with lips like camels; in their hands were pieces of fire, like stones which they used to thrust into their mouths. . . . I was told that these were those who sinfully devoured the wealth of orphans. . . . Then I saw women hanging by their breasts. These were those who had fathered bastards on their husbands.[51]

Muhammad also saw people who had scorned Muslims being forced to eat the flesh of the damned. Wantons who tempted strangers by exposing their hair are hanging by it. Women who were not docile toward their husbands are being bitten by snakes. Poison is being poured into the mouths of former winebibbers. Misers who failed to pay their religious tithes have millstones hanging on their necks.

In Muhammad's space odyssey, highlights of other heavens included encountering Jesus and his cousin John in the second; Joseph, Enoch, Aaron, Moses, and Abraham were, in sequence, in the third, fourth, fifth, sixth, and seventh heavens. When Muhammad reached the ultimate heaven, Paradise, Gabriel showed the prophet "a river whiter than milk and sweeter than honey, with pearly domes on either side of it."[52] Abraham offered Muhammad either milk or wine and praised him for being on the right path when he chose the nonalcoholic drink.[53] The patriarch then escorted the Meccan to a damsel with dark-red lips who belonged to his son Zaid. Details of a vision of God's throne are not given.

On returning home at the end of the night, Muhammad reported: "I have never seen a man more like myself than Abraham. Moses was a ruddy-faced man, tall, thinly fleshed, curly haired with a hooked nose. . . . Jesus, son of Mary, was a reddish man of medium height with lank hair with many freckles on his face."[54]

Muhammad's out-of-body mystical experience has been associated with the Quranic revelations about God, "who brought His servant by night from the holy mosque to the distant mosque,"[55] and about seven heavenly spheres surmounted by God's great throne.[56] Muslim orthodoxy has generally transposed the prophet's flight of the imagination into a physical journey, and details of his alleged experiences have developed.

Sixty-one exquisite pictures of Muhammad's overnight ride were produced in fifteenth-century Persia.[57] Buraq has the body of a mule, the face of a woman, and the hooves and tail of a camel. In the third heaven he meets David and Solomon; in the fifth heaven, he finds Ishmael and Isaac in a golden chamber; and in the sixth heaven, he sees Moses, who is weeping because there are more Muslims than Jews in heaven.

As in Judeo-Christian apocalyptic literature, the number seven symbolizes the ultimate level. In the seventh heaven, Muhammad sees beautiful girls in flowering gardens. That sight is soon eclipsed by the glory of God's throne, which is too brilliant for morals to behold. After Muhammad came close to the throne and prostrated himself, God placed his hand upon the prophet's shoulder and said:

> I take you as a friend. . . . I am appointing the earth for you. . . . I am giving your community the right to booty which I have given as provision to no previous community. I shall aid you with such terrors as will make your enemies flee before you while you are still a month's journey away. . . . I shall exalt your name for you, even to the extent of conjoining it with My name, so that none of the regulations of My religion will ever be mentioned without you being mentioned along with Me.[58]

The materialization of Muhammad's internal conceptualizing in Muslim tradition parallels what has happened to an experience Jesus' disciples had on a mountain in Lebanon. The Gospels tell of Jesus and his disciples separating from the crowds at the Galilean lakeside and heading for the hills of northern Palestine to relax. While there it seems that one of his disciples, when "heavy with sleep,"[59] had a dream about Moses and Elijah talking with a transformed Jesus. Although Jesus called this a "vision",[60] Christian tradition has generally assumed that Moses and Elijah came in a supernatural way from where they were residing in Paradise and were literally present to confer with Jesus at a summit conference.[61]

Some of Muhammad's alleged miracles were probably generated to combat criticism from Christians. Thomas Aquinas, for example, discredits Muhammad because the Quran admits that he could not perform miracles. According to Aquinas, a premier Christian theologian: "Muhammad did not bring forth any signs produced in a supernatural way, which alone fittingly gives witness to divine inspiration."[62] In order to compete in an era when supernaturalism was rampant, Muslims fabricated miracles. Mohamed al-Nowaihi, a Muslim professor from Cairo, discusses this development in an address he gave at Harvard on an occasion of *Mawlid an-Nabi*. He regards the attempts to associate miracles with Muhammad's birth as denigrating to one who rejected such. He likens them to weeds that have overgrown a valuable original planting. Credulous Muslims love fantastic tales, some of which emulate those of Christians. Among them, Al-Nowaihi notes, are stories of Muhammad being created before any other human and of stars coming near to earth at his birth. "They distract . . . from the true character and merit of Muhammad," Al-Nowaihi concludes.[63]

A story of Muhammad's mother is also similar to a birth story of Jesus. Amina finds Abdullah, her husband, repulsive because he is dirty from working with mud. When he returns after bathing to have sex, another wife of Abdullah notices a white blaze between his eyes. This brightness is transferred to what Amina conceives, resulting in this comment: "As she was pregnant with him, she saw a light come forth from her by which she could see the castles of Busra in Syria."[64] The light image is given more ultimacy in Muslim mysticism because God creates Muhammad from a handful of light before the creation of the world.[65] The motif of Muhammad's birth story is somewhat parallel to Luke's nativity narrative. Gabriel informs Mary that the child she has conceived will be exceptionally holy.[66] The story concludes with a

devout man recognizing in baby Jesus the fulfillment of Isaiah's prophecy, when a glorious "light to the nations" would come.[67] The creche,
depicting mother and son surrounded with a radiating halo, has been
featured in Christmas traditions to express this holiness.

The source of one miracle story is this Quranic imagery regarding
Muhammad: "Did We not cause your breast to open and relieve you of
the burden that weighted you down."[68] From that verse, the following
tale is spun about angels performing open-heart surgery. Boy Muhammad tells a companion:

> Two men in white raiment came to me with a gold basin full of
> snow. They seized me and opened up my belly, extracted my
> heart and split it; then they extracted a black drop from it and
> threw it away; then they washed my heart and my belly with
> that snow until they had thoroughly cleaned them.[69]

That operation was presumed to have made this testimony possible:

> He grew up to be the finest of his people in manliness, the best
> in character, most noble in lineage, the best neighbor, the
> most kind, truthful, reliable, the furthest removed from filthi-
> ness and corrupt morals, through loftiness and nobility, so
> that he was known among his people as "the trustworthy"
> because of the good qualities which God had implanted in
> him.[70]

The favorite lore from Muhammad's childhood tells of a holy man
from outside Arabia who was aware of the boy's future eminence. Bahira,
a Christian monk, invited Meccan caravanners to a meal while they were
in Syria. Muhammad was left to care for the camels, but the monk
insisted that the camel driver be brought in for examination. Bahira had
received a sign pertaining to a coming great prophet, and he found on
Muhammad's back, between his shoulders, a confirming supernatural
mark.[71]

Islamic tradition has often attempted to hide Muhammad's feet of
clay. Even though the Quran treats him as no more divine than Moses,
devout Muslims often preferred to think of him as unfettered by human
limitations. When those miraculous trappings are discarded, the true
personality of Muhammad is seen more clearly.

Of Jesus

In the teachings of the Galilean apostles, Jesus was primarily presented in the manner in which he understood himself: as God's suffering servant.[72] Questioning the popular view that the Messiah was David's descendant, Jesus suggested that he was not the heir of that prominent king.[73] Regarding Jesus' self-understanding, Thomas Sheehan expresses the consensus of contemporary Catholic and Protestant scholarship: "As far as can be discerned from the available historical data, Jesus of Nazareth did not think he was divine."[74]

Within several decades of Jesus' death, Christians made efforts to raise the Galilean peasant to a higher status. This attempt at elevation can be detected in the Gospels, in which Jesus' nativity legends display a desire to identify him with Jewish royalty. Luke declared that Mary's son "will reign over the house of Jacob forever."[75] In Matthew's lore, foreign astrologers (*magi*) come to Judea, asking "Where is the child who has been born king of the Jews?"[76] It is unlikely that Jesus shared the birthplace of Israel's greatest king, even though two Gospels claim that he was born in Bethlehem, the town of David's origin.[77]

Both the earliest Gospel, Mark, and the latest Gospel, John, assume that Nazareth was the place of Jesus' origin. Both refer to it as Jesus' native place or fatherland (*patris*).[78] That small town had no importance; it is not even mentioned in the Hebrew Bible. Josephus does not refer to Nazareth even though his historical writings tell of numerous Galilean towns in Jesus' day. John suggests that Jesus originated as a Galilean rather than as a Judean; Nathanael asks, "Can anything good come out of Nazareth?"[79] Responding to that question, Philip does not reply that Jesus was from a famed town in Judea. Also, some critics asked the following about Jesus: "Surely the Messiah does not come from Galilee, does he? Has not the scripture said that the Messiah is descended from David and comes from Bethlehem, the village where David lived?"[80] No attempt is made to inform the questioners that Jesus indeed was born in Bethlehem, probably because that was not John's understanding.

Bethlehem was a more prestigious place to be born: not only was it associated with the most noted of the earlier anointed rulers and with his ancestress Ruth, but Micah had prophesied that a future Messiah will originate in the birthplace of David.[81] For political and theological reasons, Luke wished to contrast the reigning Caesar, known as lord and savior to his subjects, with Jesus, the true lord and savior.[82] In his gospel, Luke refers to a regional census, ordered by Augustus and administered by Roman Governor Quirinus, which has been dated about 6 C.E. The custom was to register people where they lived, not in their ancestoral homes; the purpose of the enrollment was not to satisfy genealogical curiosity but to form a tax roll.

The earliest Christian writings contain no happenings that can only be explained by divine causation interrupting the regular operation of nature, whether physical or psychical. The letters of the apostle Paul, which were written about a decade before the earliest Gospel, do not suggest that God interferes with the natural order. In his letters, Paul disappointedly writes that "Jews demand signs";[83] that is, they crave supernatural happenings. Fascinated by the legends of magical acts by Moses, Elijah, and Elisha, they hoped that a new prophet would perform likewise.[84] The Jewish authorities of Jesus' day associated religious proof with the occurrence of something known to be impossible, such as a man escaping from crucifixion by tearing out the binding nails and subduing the armed executioners surrounding him.[85] For Paul, however, the wonder-working of God is not displayed in erratic marvels but in Jesus' suffering humanity.[86]

Soon after the beginning of Christianity, embellishments of the biography of Jesus the adult grew rapidly. By Jewish reckoning, Elisha performed sixteen miracles, including curing a leper, opening blind eyes, restoring the dead to life, and multiplying a small amount of food to feed a multitude. Accordingly, as portrayed by Mark, Jesus also performs sixteen miracles, some of which are quite similar. When Matthew expanded on Mark's earlier Gospel, he heightened the supernaturalism in some episodes.[87] In Mark, for example, Jairus tells Jesus that his daughter is dying and requests that she be healed. But in Matthew, Jairus states that she has died and requests that she be resurrected.[88] Again, Elijah is alleged to have miraculously supplied food for a woman and revived her dead son. Luke's Jesus, as a greater Elijah, produces a meal for thousands from five loaves and two fish, and raises two youth from the dead, one of whom was a widow's son.[89]

Such enhancements of Jesus' powers in the New Testament Gospels are mild in comparison to the fantastic stories from the second and later centuries that are found in the New Testament Apocrypha. In contrast to the Gospel account of Jesus' boyhood, which contains nothing supernatural, the Apocrypha includes fabrications that completely misrepresent both Jesus' outlook and actions. For example, when irritated by a boy who brushed against him, a revengeful Jesus said words that caused the boy to drop dead. In another instance, Jesus assisted in Joseph's carpentry shop by creating out of nothing additional length for boards that were too short.[90]

In medieval folklore, Jesus had powers now associated with Superman. Even as a child, he assisted his family in their journey across the Sinai desert. While they traveled, Joseph said to him, "Lord, we are being roasted by this heat." . . . Jesus replied, "Fear not, Joseph, I will shorten your journey, so that what you were going to traverse in the space of thirty days, you will finish in one day."[91] While this was being said, behold, they began to see the mountains and cities of Egypt.[92]

Milo Connick's observation about ancient cultures applies to both Jesus and Muhammad: "Miracle stories clustered like grapes about the stem of historical personages. Their aim was to inflate the personal status of the hero. It was even considered legitimate to manufacture miraculous tales for this purpose."[93] In prescientific cultures, people have generally believed that the more contrary an event is to the perceived natural pattern, the more it indicates the presence of divine power.

Even before the New Testament era ended, a tendency arose in gentile Christianity to minimize the human nature of Jesus. Some thought that he only appeared to have the qualities of full humanity. Thus, rather than developing through a human childhood, Jesus was presumed to be omniscient from infancy onward. He must have only pretended to suffer because a divine being must be above such passion. Basilides, a Gnostic teacher who lived in Alexandria during the second century, was convinced that Jesus did not get involved in the material realm. Since matter is evil, the good Jesus could not have had a real physical body. Basilides changed Jesus' last earthly narrative in this way: "Simon of Cyrene was constrained to bear Jesus' cross for him. It was Simon who was crucified. . . . People thought he was Jesus, while Jesus took on the appearance of Simon and stood by and mocked them."[94] Only the first sentence of this quotation conforms to the Gospel record.[95]

Basilides was judged to be a heretic of the docetic variety. "Docetic," from the Greek verb *dokein* "to seem," means that Basilides thought of Jesus as seeming to be human while in reality he was purely divine. The majority position crystallizing in the Church maintained that a fully human Jesus confronted temptations and "suffered under Pontius Pilate."[96] Even so, docetism was more easily condemned by the orthodox than eliminated. The mainstream of Christian tradition has been frequently sidetracked by doceticism from Basilides's time onward. In the third century, Mani endorsed the docetic heresy that Jesus had a phantom body that could not be crucified.[97]

Many in the Eastern Church did not accept the Christological definition of the fifth-century Council of Chalcedon that Jesus was paradoxically both fully human and fully divine. They were called monophysites because of their contention that Jesus had only one nature, which was entirely divine. Believing that his body was made of a substance different than that of other human bodies, the monophysites continued the heterodoxy of the docetics. The monophysites disregarded the Gospels' accounts of Jesus experiencing hunger, thirst, weariness, and weeping. In the century before the rise of Islam, the monophysites had considerable influence from Ethiopia to Syria.[98] The sixth-century bishops of Arabia were monophysites.[99] Thus, Jesus' human personality was belittled by most of the Christians to whom Muhammad was exposed.

The Quran, in spite of its determination to deny that Jesus was a deity, accepts some of the tales that were invented to prove the opposite. The stories of baby Jesus performing miracles, as well as the denial of Jesus' crucifixion, were perverse ideas transmitted by Christians with a docetic orientation. Their view is apparent in this Quranic statement about Jesus: "They (the Jews) did not kill him or crucify him, but it appeared so to them."[100]

A deputation of monophysite Christians came to Medina from Najran in southern Arabia to discuss the status of Jesus with Muhammad Biographer Ishaq writes:

> They argued that he is God because he used to raise the dead, and heal the sick, and declare the unseen; and make clay birds and then breathe into them so that they flew away. . . . They argued that he is the Son of God in that they say he had no known father; and he spoke in the cradle.[101]

Muhammad had no difficulty accepting the amazing miracles that the Najran Christians believed Jesus performed. This conformed to the revelation Muhammad received regarding Jesus. God had declared: "He shall be a sign to humanity and a token of Our mercy."[102] Muhammad also accepted that Moses performed miracles, but agreed with Jews and

Christians that Moses was not God. Muhammad disagreed with the Najran Christians about their "Jesus is God" conclusion.

What happened in the course of early Christianity that caused the shift from the assumption that Jesus is subservient to God to equating Jesus with God? A full answer to this question requires an extensive examination of the development of Christian doctrine during several centuries. In the earliest Gospel, Jesus affirms the Shema, which was and continues to be the basic creed of the synagogue.[103] The Shema expresses devotion to a single deity, "the Lord," even more strongly than the Ten Commandments do. The First Commandment, "You shall have no other gods before me,"[104] is actually a statement of henotheism, the worship of one god without denying the existence of other gods. During the early history of Christianity, the simple monotheism of Jesus acquired much complexity, and multiple gods emerged in some heretical developments.[105]

The ambiguity of the word "lord" in ancient languages (*adon* in Hebrew, *Kurios* in Greek), which continues in modern languages, has caused problems in understanding the role of Jesus. The term has both a secular and a religious significance. *Kurios* could designate the owner of a vineyard[106] or of a house[107], as in the English expression "landlord." *Kurios* was also a term of polite address, as when a son responds to his father, "I go, *sir*."[108] *Adon* also had the same commonplace meanings in the Hebrew culture.[109] Complications began when that term was substituted for *yhwh* in the reading of the Hebrew scriptures. As a protection against violating the Mosaic commandment that prohibits the use of Yahweh in an irreverent manner, Jewish scribes before the time of Jesus hallowed that covenantal name by reading *Adonai* ("my Lord") wherever Yahweh occurred.

Jesus is represented in the Gospels as discussing the meanings of "lord" in interpreting a line from the Psalms, then commonly assumed to have been written by David.[110] Consider the puzzling verse: "The Lord (God) said to my lord, 'Sit at my right hand.' "[111] Who is "my lord," who functions as God's right-hand man? The early Christians identified the "lord" with Jesus and considered him to be the primary human agent through whom the will of God is accomplished on earth. Presumably, Jesus expressed that meaning of "lord" when he asked his disciples to borrow a donkey so the *kurios* could demonstrate the nonviolent nature of his kingdom.[112] When the earliest Christians confessed "Jesus is Lord," they meant that he, not some other ruler, was the one who had control over their lives.

The non-physical nature of God was assumed in both the Hebrew Bible and the New Testament. A Hebrew prophet succinctly separates God from humans in this oracle: "I am God and no mortal."[113] Consequently, the theological use of "Son" or "Father" was metaphorical. An Israelite scribe represented God as declaring with regard to a Jewish king: "I will be a father to him, and he shall be a son to me. When he commits iniquity, I will punish him."[114] A psalmist, praising the messianic covenant, has God say to a Jewish king: "You are my son; today I have fathered you."[115] Another psalmist has a king exclaim: "You are my Father, my God, and the Rock of my salvation!"[116] Although God is literally neither a father or a rock, deity has benevolence like a caring parent, and permanence like a hard rock.

Regarding the messianic hope in Judaism at the time of Jesus, Hans Kung comments:

> A successor of David was expected, who as "Son" of God would ascend the ancestral throne and establish the Davidic rule over Israel forever. This title is now applied to Jesus. . . . Originally therefore the title of "Son of God" had *nothing to do with Jesus' origin but with his legal and authoritative status.* It is a question of function, not of nature. Originally the title did not mean a corporeal sonship. . . . "Son of God" therefore did not designate Jesus any more than the king of Israel as a superhuman, divine being, but as the appointed ruler.[117]

Jesus' self-designations included "son of man"[118] and "servant",[119] but probably not "Son of God." At his trial in Jerusalem, he was asked if he was the "Son of God," but the Gospels are unclear as to whether he accepted that designation.[120] In any case, "Son of God" is symbolic language similar to "sons of light," an expression Jesus used in his teaching.[121]

Orthodox Christians do not think of themselves as idolaters when they speak of Jesus as God's Son, even though outsiders may view this as polytheism. It is a means of expressing that one human has become uniquely close to God and that all have the potentiality of becoming adopted children of God.[122] Similarly, Islam does not intend to be idolatrous when it exalts the Quran as infallible, even though it may appear as bibliolatry to outsiders.

The commonplace, traditional understanding of "Trinity" may have obscured rather than clarified the relation of Jesus to God. The term "Trinity" wrongly suggests that Christians are tritheists. To avert the erroneous idea of triple gods, a "u" should be placed in the midst of "Trinity." "Tri-unity" (from the Latin *tria*, threefold, plus *unus*, one) more accurately preserves the oneness notion the fourth-century ecumenical councils intended than "Trinity" does. The official formulation of Christian doctrine rejects tritheism, like the Quran does.

Muslims have often presumed that Christians worship separate gods. One African Muslim whom I encountered jovially commented that the main difference between his religion and mine was that he had several wives and one God, but I had one wife and several gods! Although that Muslim held Jesus in high regard, he was scornful of Christianity because he believed it espoused polytheism. His outlook is similar to that of Muhammad, who thought that Christians believe in three different deities, one being the goddess Mary who was impregnated by intercourse with the father God.[123] Muhammad may have inferred this notion from observing the piety of some Christians. He did not realize that monotheism is affirmed in the Nicene Creed, the Christian core doctrine. Its beginning, "We believe in one God,"[124] parallels the first article of the Muslim creed, "There is no god but God,"[125] and the Jewish Shema, "The Lord is our God, the Lord alone."[126]

Misrepresentations of the Christian doctrine of God by outsiders may have arisen from the confusion of beliefs of many early Church members, as well as from the consequent efforts of Christians to resolve puzzling questions arising from their oral and written traditions. Was the God of the Old Testament a different God from the God of the New Testament? Did One have no beginning and the other have His nativity in Palestine? Was the God of law separate from the God of grace? Were divine beings sent from heaven to earth like relay runners, one carrying on after another one finished? Also, if Jesus is God and if God is nonphysical Spirit, does that mean that Christ never *really* was flesh and blood? There is no full discussion of these questions in the Bible, the acknowledged source of Christian doctrine. Consequently, conflicting answers were given to these theological questions, and Christians themselves were in a dilemma as to what to believe.

Beginning with Sabellius's effort in the third century, attempts have been made to provide simple, natural analogies to assist in comprehending the Christian doctrine of God. Sabellius, a Greek Christian leader, illustrates his theology via the sun and its rays:

> The Father, Son, and Holy Spirit are one and the same being, in the sense that three names are attached to one substance. A close analogy may be found in . . . the sun: it is one substance, but it has three manifestations, light, heat, and the orb itself.[127]

Thus, there is the transcendent God who, like the solar disk, is too brilliant to be gazed at directly; there is Jesus who is "the Light of the World;"[128] and there is the warmth of the Holy Spirit within believers.

Comparing God to the material sun is deficient, however, because an impersonal analogy is inadequate for pointing to a personal God. More helpful is an analogy drawn from classical drama, in which one actor often wore masks to play several roles. Those masks were called *per-sonas*, literally, "through which the sound comes." Sabellius also conceived of a succession of divine impersonations sent forth from heaven to earth during three acts of the cosmic theater. During the Israelite act there was God the Creator; then during the Gospel act there was Emmanuel, "God with us"; and after both the Holy Spirit came on stage.

Constantine, the first Christian emperor, decided that the problems over the relationship between the Creator and Jesus must be resolved. Constantine had converted to Christianity hoping that the religion would help to unite his Roman government, which was disintegrating from civil wars. However, he found that Christians themselves were much divided over questions of doctrine. In an effort to settle this matter, he called together leaders from the entire Church. In the year 325, he gathered hundreds of bishops at a central city named Nicea to debate theology and agree on a creed. It is called the First Ecumenical Council because representatives from churches in Asia, Africa, and Europe were there.

Two months of discussion centered on the difference made by one iota, that is, the Greek letter "i." One group maintained that the Son and the Father were of the "same" (*homo*) substance, and another group argued that they were of a "similar" (*homoi*) substance. At last, the bishops at Nicea voted on the relationship, and the majority approved of the former position. A second Ecumenical Council then met in Constantinople to deal with the relationship of the Holy Spirit to the Father and the Son. What all orthodox Christians call the Nicene Creed contains an additional paragraph about the Holy Spirit that was added in 381.[129]

In contrast to Sabellius, the Nicene council ruled that the three expressions of the divine substance are simultaneous, not sequential.

Consider several roles that a woman can play on the stage of life. To her parents, she is a daughter; to her employers, she is a worker; and to her spouse, she is a partner. Daughter, worker, and partner are quite distinct roles, but all three can be simultaneous expressions of her true self.

To provide a rational explanation of the settled Christian doctrine of God, Augustine, the preeminent fifth-century bishop, uses a botanical analogy:

> The root is wood, the trunk is wood, and the branches are wood, while nevertheless it is not three woods that are thus spoken of, but only one. . . . (Thus) no one should think it absurd that we should call the Father God, the Son God, the Holy Spirit God, and that these are not three gods in the Trinity, but one God and one substance.[130]

A medieval diagram often found in cathedral windows expresses the gist of the Nicene formulation. A central ring is featured within an equilateral triangle. The ring affirms the single essence of God, and the points of the triangle show the equality of three simultaneous expressions of the divine substance.

There is a profound complexity in the orthodox Christian doctrine of God, but it is not incomprehensible. Although humans do not have a full understanding of God—or of anything else that is profound—a reasonable basis for belief in the triune God exists. Since this doctrine has been repeatedly thought through over the centuries to express genuine monotheism, it is hoped that it will not continue to impose a bewildering barrier to ecumenical understanding. Indeed, Christians share with Judaism, Islam, and some other world religions more that theologically unites them than separates them.

For Christians who have misunderstood their own monotheistic doctrine, the Quran's criticism of some Christological developments is helpful. Orthodox Christians would agree completely with this salutary corrective: Unbelievers say, "God is the third of three." There is but one God. . . . God said: Jesus, son of Mary, did you say to the people, "Worship me and my mother as gods apart from God?" He (Jesus) said: "It is not for me to say what is not true."[131] Jesus is then quoted in the next verse as saying: "Worship God, my Lord and your Lord."[132] To say that "Jesus is God" is to affirm a creed that goes beyond the New Testament, as well as to impose a barrier to understanding the historical Jesus.

The Quran is somewhat like the New Testament in that it does not analyze the relationship between Jesus and God. In the Quran Jesus is the only one who is closely associated with "the Holy Spirit." Also, Jesus is referred to as the Messiah eleven times. But the meanings of those terms are not explained in the Quran. Discussing Jesus' "divinity," a term from pagan Greco-Roman theology, is not helpful for comprehending either the New Testament or the Quran.

Muhammad's affirmation of Jesus' roles may have been closer to the New Testament than some doctrines that were championed in churches of his day. The italicized part of a saying of Muhammad illustrates this point:

> If anyone testifies that there is no god but God alone, that Muhammad is His servant and messenger, that *Jesus is God's servant and messenger, the son of His handmaid, His word which He cast into Mary and a spirit from Him*, and that Paradise and Hell are real, God will cause him to enter Paradise no matter what he has done.[133]

There is a parallel between the function of cardinal names for deity in Muslim and Christian theology. The Quran states: "Call on God (*Al-Lah*) or call on the Compassionate One (*Ar-Rahman*). To whomever you pray, it is the same; His names are the most beautiful."[134] Those names do not refer to two different gods but to different attributes of divine oneness. Similarly, in Christianity, the Tri-unity is not a triple-headed monstrosity with three centers of divine consciousness, but a recognition of different aspects of godness.

After the bishops at Nicea had agreed upon a formulation pertaining to the nature of Jesus *vis-à-vis* God, another theological problem demanded attention. The Greek title *Theotokos*, meaning "God-bearer" or "Mother of God," was becoming a popular designation for Mary of Nazareth. This elevation came as Asian shrines of the earlier widely adored mother goddesses of paganism were being closed. In the wake of that development, Mary was worshiped by some women who were known as Collyridians. The name of the sect came from offering cakes (*killyrida*) to Mary, probably in imitation of a ritual for Demeter, the grain goddess. Epiphanius, a fourth-century patriarch of Constantinople, wrote a letter to refute those who "wished to exalt the Ever-Blessed Virgin and put her in the place of God."[135] Epiphanus, a Byzantine bishop who came from Palestine, states that the Collyridians spread into

Arabia. Some Arab Mariolatrists took over a shrine formerly used to worship Ashtaroth, the female consort of Baal.[136]

Nestorius, a fifth-century patriarch of Constantinople, attempted to curb the excessive veneration of Mary by replacing *Theotokos* with *Christotokos* ("mother of Christ").[137] He wished to avoid making her appear to be a goddess, or Jesus appear to be an incomplete human. However, Nestorius was unable to stem the tide of Marian devotion, and the Ephesus Council made *Theotokos* part of church dogma in the year 431. After Nestorius was deposed, he returned to his home region of Syria, where he continued to emphasize Jesus' humanity. The Nestorian Church remains in the Middle East to this day. Ironically, "heretic" Nestorius may have been closer to original Christianity about the role of Mary than the ecumenical council that opposed him.

Significantly, that ecumenical council met in Ephesus where the worship of virgin goddess Artemis or Diana had been centered. After vanquishing the "Queen of Heaven" cult, the most developed in the Mediterranean culture, this affection was transferred to Mary, who was also called the Queen of Heaven. Reviewing the history of devotion to one who still carries the "God-bearer" title, the Vatican II Council observed: "After the Council of Ephesus the cult of the People of God toward Mary wonderfully increased in veneration and love."[138] Kung points out that theologians have distinguished the "hyper-veneration" proper for Mary from the worship due God, "but in practice Mary's createdness and humanity often played a very slight role."[139]

In Ethiopia, there was an "unbounded cult of the Virgin Mary" that reflected the worship of an ancient goddess. Many centuries earlier, Jeremiah had censured the worship of the "Queen of Heaven," an astral deity who was given cakes by devoted women.[140] The pagan Arabs called her Al-Lat.[141] Thus, Mary arose like a phoenix from the ashes of banished goddesses. Some of the earliest Muslims became aware of that form of Christianity when they spent some time in Ethiopian exile before returning to Mecca.

Muhammad came from a background of paganism, and he was probably a polytheist himself for half of his life. Myths about copulating divine couples and the godlings they sired were common in ancient Asia. Muhammad was told to taunt the Meccans in this way: "It is a lie to claim that God has fathered children. Would He prefer daughters to sons? What ails you that you should judge so badly?"[142] That pronouncement was prompted by those who spoke of their idols as "God's daughters."[143] The Quran frequently denounces polytheists who ascribe

partners to God, including those who engage in Jesusolatry and Mar-
iolatry.

Understandably, Muhammad interpreted biblical and church doctrine according to the pagan Arabian pattern of thought. Unschooled in
trinitarian scholarship, he presumed that "persons" of God were individual personalities within a celestial pantheon. From the prominent adoration given to Mary in Ethiopia, the nearest Christian nation to Mecca,
he concluded that she was a member of the divine family that Christians
worshiped. Khuda Bukhsh relates this to the Quran: "As for Jesus, He is
always mentioned in connexion with Mary—in fact, there is a tendency
to exalt Mary as the chief character. Nor is this altogether surprising, for
in Arabia the Collyridians invested her with the name and honors of a
goddess."[144] Even though the Quran describes Mary in a sublime way,
the thought of God originating in her body would have been blasphemous to Muhammad after he became a monotheist.

Christian theology, as Muhammad received it, must have seemed
to parallel the mythology of Egyptian husband Osiris and wife Isis
producing Horus as their divine offspring. He may have talked with
Christians like one a Muslim encountered in Jerusalem later during the
medieval era. Usamah tells of a Christian showing a picture of Mary
with the infant Jesus and provides this explanation: "This is God as a
child."[145]

The Greeks had no difficulty picturing father Zeus physically
siring offspring, but Muhammad thought that it was proper only for
humans to procreate sexually. The Quran occasionally speaks of humans
conceiving by means of the implantation of physical semen in a woman's
body. For example: "The sperm drop is placed in a womb and created
into tissue. This is fashioned into bone, then clothed with flesh, thus
bringing forth a creature."[146] The notion of God developing from a baby
or performing sexually like a human father was unacceptable to Muhammad.

The Quran treats "Son of God" in a literal manner; therefore,
Christians who use that title for Jesus are sometimes presumed to be
guilty of *shirk*.[147] *Shirk* is frequently denounced in the Quran as the
supreme and unforgivable sin.[148] A murderer would have more chance
of avoiding eternal punishment than a *shirk*-er. The sin consists of
ascribing divine qualities to anyone or anything beside God. *Shirk* has
been committed even if a human is regarded as an associate rather than
as a co-equal of God.

Misunderstandings are conveyed in this Quranic curse:

The Jews say, "Ezra is the Son of God," while the Christians say, "Christ is the Son of God." In such assertions they follow previous unbelievers. God damn them! How perverse they are! They make lords besides God of their rabbis, monks, and Christ, Mary's son, though they were commanded to worship only one God.[149]

Given this literary heritage, it is difficult for Muslims to think of "son" in a symbolic manner. Muhammad possibly heard some Jews call Ezra "God's son," but the idiom surely did not mean that they treated the respected priest as divine. Rather it meant that Ezra, along with other worthies of the Hebrew tradition, was close to God because he was a pious human.[150] To assume that Jews or Christians believed that any of their holy men were physically procreated by God would be to grossly misunderstand biblical literature. Just as "son of a gun" or "son of a bitch" in the modern vernacular have a completely nonliteral meaning when applied to humans, so "son of God" in Hebrew psalms or Christian prayers simply means one who is in unity with the purposes of God.

In the Fourth Gospel, Jesus prayed to his "Father" the night before his execution that his disciples "may be one, as we are one."[151] This comparison illuminates what Jesus meant by theological oneness. The bond he hoped for among his disciples was not metaphysical. Much as Jesus thought of marriage as two becoming one,[152] so he longed for close working relationships among his companions after his physical departure. While recognizing that their separate personalities would not be obliterated, Jesus prayed that they would unite by sharing the love and joy of God.

In light of the perennial tendency to misrepresent admired leaders by glorifying them, those interested in historical biography must imitate art restorers who carefully flake away paints and varnishes added to great paintings during subsequent centuries. For example, well-meaning but uninspired painters have attempted to brighten and preserve "The Last Supper," Leonardo da Vinci's masterpiece on a dining room wall in Milan. In recent years, layers of glossy overlays have been carefully removed, and some splendid soft pastels of the original fresco have been exposed. Likewise, when the pious but abusive enlargements of Muhammad and Jesus are eliminated, one can better glimpse the genuine portraits of their earliest biographers. The intrinsic glory of those humans can best be seen without the supernatural glow and unauthentic halos.

In at least one way, Jesus' image has suffered more than that of Muhammad. Since both prophets came from the same global region, it is likely that they resembled one another in general physiognomy. In accord with biological evolution of *Homo sapiens*, their skin pigmentation would have been lighter than that of people of central Africa but darker than that of people originating in northern Europe. The men's hair type and eye color would probably have been like those of Jordanians today. According to early Muslim tradition, Muhammad was of medium height, his skin was neither light nor dark, his eyes were large and black, and his hair had little curl.[153] When European artists wanted to paint Jesus, they lacked both historical descriptions of his appearance and knowledge of the typical features of a Palestinian. Consequently, Jesus has often been represented as a blond, blue-eyed, white-skinned person from their culture, and God has been similarly portrayed. Thanks to Islam's prohibition of human depictions of the prophets and God, Negroid and Mongoloid Muslims can contemplate God without such anthropomorphic limitations.

Any hero naturally attracts accretions from followers that often are a disservice to the humanity of the adored person. For example, there is the familiar lore about young George Washington, who chopped down a cherry tree and then confessed, "Father, I cannot tell a lie." The inventor of that story was attempting to separate the savior of the American Republic from the very human tendency to be deceptive. Likewise, the boyhood and adulthood legends of Jesus and Muhammad display the deifying fiction of hagiographers.

Neither Christianity nor Islam has originated most of the supernaturalism with which they have been associated over the centuries. The adoration of divine men who claimed to perform wonders that were contrary to the natural order was commonplace in ancient Mediterranean cults.[154] Astrology began in the Middle East many centuries before Moses by people who were fascinated with alleged astral deities who could determine destiny.[155] The Torah rejects the consulting of diviners who predict events by gazing at the positions of planets on auspicious occasions.[156] Both Christianity and Islam inherited that Hebrew legacy.

Much of what is called New Age spirituality, with its attention to self-deification, horoscopes, crystal gazing, seances, and other irrational magic, is just a current phase of Old Age superstition that is global in scope. Many people, longing for simple ways of guaranteeing happy outcomes, find reality too complex, too demanding, and too tragic. The continual human dilemma has not been primarily about choosing to be religious or non-religious. Rather, it has been about choosing the religion that focuses on learning to live within the Creator's order and to assist the vulnerable, or choosing the religion that presumes that individual agendas can be accomplished by manipulating rituals. Muhammad and Jesus opted for the former, but many of their followers have preferred the latter.

CHAPTER TEN

CONCLUSION

Theological Differences

Significant differences as well as similarities between Muhammad and Jesus in the area of social teachings and practices have been discussed. In addition, there are two major theological differences. The first one, which also involves a historical judgment, is starkly expressed by Seyyed Nasr an acclaimed contemporary Islamic scholar:

> The Quran . . . does not accept that he (Jesus) was crucified, but states that he was taken directly to heaven. (4:157–58) This is the one irreducible "fact" separating Christianity and Islam, a fact which is in reality placed there providentially to prevent a mingling of the two religions.[1]

If the Apostles' Creed had been revised on the basis of Quranic revelation, then "Born of the Virgin Mary" would be followed by "He ascended into heaven." The in-between affirmations would be considered false: "He suffered under Pontius Pilate, was crucified, died, and was buried. He descended to the dead. On the third day he rose again."[2] In addition, "He will come again to judge the living and the dead" conforms to Quranic revelation.[3] Muhammad is reported to have taught the following: "The son of Mary will descend as a just judge, and will break crosses. . . . Spite, mutual hatred and jealousy will certainly depart, and when he summons people to accept wealth not one will do so."[4] Another saying attributed to Muhammad provides these personal details: "Jesus, son of Mary, will marry, have children, and remain forty-five years, after which he will die and be buried along with me in my grave."[5]

Maulvie Ali, following the doctrine of the Ahmadiya sect of Islam, has modified the early Muslim understanding of the end of Jesus' life. At the Jerusalem execution site, Ali claims, Jesus "was likened to one dead and thus escaped with his life, afterwards dying a natural death."[6] Originating in India in the nineteenth century, the Ahmadiyas believe that Jesus recovered from his crucifixion wounds and migrated to Kashmir. After teaching there successfully for several generations, he died at the age of 120 and was buried at Srinagar. Ghulam Ahmad, the sect's founder, claimed that he found Jesus' tomb there and that he was a reincarnation of Jesus.

The Quran presupposes that God, being omnipotent, will not usually allow true prophets to be destroyed by their foes. Exceptions are admitted because some prophets have unjustly been killed by the ungodly.[7] A Muslim remembered Muhammad telling about an unidentified prophet who was treated much like the way found in the New Testament records of Jesus' last hours.[8] He recalled: "I can see myself looking at God's messenger when he was telling of a prophet who, when his people beat him and covered him with blood, was wiping the blood from his face and saying, 'O God, forgive my people, for they do not know.' "[9]

Jesus should have had a triumphant entry into Jerusalem like the one Muhammad had in Mecca, with the streets lined with kowtowing former enemies, intimidated by his overwhelming power. If Jesus was trapped by the opposition, a *deus ex machina*, like that in classical Greek drama should have intervened. The thought of the humiliation and torture of Jesus through naked exposure on a cross in a prominent public place is completely unacceptable in Islam. The Quran alleges that at the last moment, God swept Jesus away up to the sky to confound those who plotted evil.

The Quran's treatment of Jesus' last earthly day is consistent with what it tells about other biblical prophets. From Noah onward, the theme is that God rescues the innocent.[10] Regarding Abraham and Moses, the Quran states: "We gave them help so that they became victorious."[11] In spite of much initial tribulation, the two prophets eventually succeeded in their mission before they died. Of John the Baptist, the Quran affirms: "Blessed was he on the day of his birth and on the day of his death."[12] In the several Quranic references to that prophet, no mention is made of how he died even though the Grand Mosque in Damascus claims to possess his head, which King Herod removed. As Muhammad reflected on his own career, as well as that of God's earlier spokespeople, he had difficulty accepting that earthly defeat should be the destiny of any of the faithful. His own career climaxed with a happy ending when he removed the idols at the Ka'ba.

Jesus was realistically aware of prophets' lack of success in their own eras. He spoke of "the blood of all the prophets shed since the foundation of the world, from the blood of Abel to the blood of Zechariah, who was murdered between the altar and the sanctuary."[13] He displayed solidarity with all who had been victimized unjustly; by undergoing torture designed for rebellious slaves, he exposed the sadistic treatment that is often inflicted on the innocent. Jesus found it ironic that after righteous prophets are killed, the responsible religious authorities show delayed appreciation by decorating their tombs.[14]

In his letters Paul observes that Jesus' crucifixion is "a stumbling block to Jews and foolishness to gentiles."[15] According to the Torah, "anyone hung on a tree is under God's curse"[16] because such capital punishment is sanctioned only for criminals. Some Jews would have preferred a Superman in a rabbinic robe. Like Muhammad, most Jews associated fine rewards, not horrible suffering, with devout conduct. Their general view is captured in their proverb: "No harm happens to the righteous, but the wicked have nothing but trouble."[17] Unable to accept both Jesus and his crucifixion, the Jews rejected the former, and the Muslims rejected the latter.

A crude graffito illustrates what Paul wrote about the customary gentile response to the notion of good persons being tortured to death. The oldest extant crucifix was scratched on a Roman wall two centuries after Christianity began. Jesus on the cross is graphically depicted as a human body with an ass's head. Beside that monstrosity is a youth with a hand raised in praise. "Alexamenos worships his God" is sarcastically scribbled beneath.[18] Sharing some of the sentiments of fellow gentiles, Muhammad thought that God would not have permitted one of his best prophets to suffer what Cicero called a punishment too barbaric to describe.[19]

For the first several centuries of the Church, Christians were noted more for their suffering and martyrdom than for their worldly success. As pacifists, they focused on reconciliation rather than on retaliation. After Constantine became emperor, many Christians gained political power and became a part of the ruling structure. From the fourth century onward, Christians have arguably been at least as militant as Muslims and have to a large measure lost a distinctive quality of their religion. When popes held sway over both church and state, or when Muhammad or the caliphs dominated the government and the religious community, the gains in coercive control often came at the expense of social justice.

French philosopher Blaise Pascal offers this telling contrast: "Muhammad chose the way of human success; Jesus Christ that of human defeat."[20] Kenneth Cragg draws this historical parallel: "Muhammad rode into a prostrate Mecca and by that victory clinched the submission of the tribes. Jesus in Jerusalem chose to refuse external patterns of success. . . . He suffered outside its walls."[21] Although self-destruction was not Jesus' aim, he was willing to pay whatever price was demanded to adhere to his principle of love. Antagonism increased throughout his public ministry: he was denied, betrayed, and deserted by his companions; he was tortured, condemned, and executed by his adversaries. Muhammad, in sharp contrast, after a period of loneliness and deprivation, ended life successfully. Further, he lived twice as long as Jesus did.

Hans Kung finds that the last hours of these two prophets reveal well their contrasting styles of life. He makes this somewhat exaggerated comparison:

> Muhammad, after he had thoroughly enjoyed the last years of his life as political ruler of Arabia, died in the midst of his harem in the arms of his favorite wife. Here (in the Gospels) on the other hand we have a young man of thirty, after three years at most of activity, perhaps only a few months. Expelled from society, betrayed and denied by his disciples and supporters, mocked and ridiculed by his opponents, forsaken by men and even by God, he goes through a ritual of death that is one of the most atrocious and enigmatic ever invented by man's ingenious cruelty.[22]

Niccolo Machiavelli, the grand master of power politics, may have had Muhammad and Jesus in mind when he made this famous observation: "Armed prophets conquer and unarmed prophets fail."[23] Within a century of Muhammad's death, those whom he inspired subdued nations from Spain to India, more area than Christian missions gained after many centuries. Military force rapidly established outward control, but it was less effective in transforming the spiritual values of the peoples affected. Neither Machiavelli nor Muhammad grasped the paradox that failing to establish political control might in the long run win greater allegiance.

Max Weber, the stellar sociological theorist, observes regarding Islam: "The most pious adherents of the religion in its first generation became the wealthiest, or more correctly, enriched themselves with military booty."[24] Today, piety and opulence continue to be juxtaposed, but the force of natural resources has largely replaced the force of arms as the means for achieving wealth in the Middle East. Because of the enormous petroleum resources that are largely controlled by Muslims, religion and material success appear to be wedded in Muhammad's homeland.

The rejection of Jesus' crucifixion in the Quran would seem to come from a moral as well as a theological presupposition. Rejecting any value in vicarious suffering, it repeatedly states: "He who finds the right path does so on his own account, and he who goes astray does so at his own peril. No one bears another's burden."[25] This outlook stands in bold contrast to Isaiah's description of the Lord's ideal servant:

> He was wounded for our transgressions,
>   beaten for our iniquities.
> Upon him fell the punishment that reconciled us,
>   and by his bruises we are made whole.[26]

The Quranic rejection of suffering for the good of others subverts the basic Christian doctrine that humans express divine love by enduring undeserved punishment inflicted by unenlightened people. Cragg discusses how the Muslim denial of Jesus' crucifixion vitiates his main purpose in life:

> This final and inclusive encounter Jesus faced, in full loyalty to his own doctrines, not rendering evil for evil, nor countering hatred with guile. . . . A coalition of dark but representative human sins accomplished the death of Christ. There were political and personal sins of convenience and security in Pilate; ecclesiastical sins of prestige and pride in the chief priests; social sins of compromise and brutality in the mob. . . . Here we find a quality of love which makes an end of evil because it freely takes all its consequences upon itself. In

revenge and hatred evil is perpetuated. In pardon and long-suffering it finds its term.[27]

Another reason given for the rejection of Jesus' crucifixion comes from the report in two Gospels that, after he was nailed to a cross, he cried, "My God, why have you forsaken me?"[28] "This is a blatant declaration of disbelief," writes M. T. Al-Hilari; he claims that a true believer could not utter these words.[29] The Quran affirms that Jesus was continuously a true prophet, so an account displaying his loss of faith cannot be accepted.

Christians also acknowledge that there was no lapse in Jesus' devotion to God, but the cry of dereliction is interpreted differently. As pointed out earlier in the discussion of Jesus' use of Hebrew poetry, he was quoting from Psalm 22 of his prayer book. The context of that psalm reveals that it was composed by a person who did not reject trust in God while in dire distress. The psalm concludes with the sufferer's affirmation that God's cause would triumph in the future.

The repeated New Testament claim that Jesus was crucified is also accepted by ancient non-Christian writers and modern scholars. Among the multiple attestations of Jesus' execution are the records kept by Jewish historian Josephus and Roman historian Tacitus.[30] John Crossan, a historical Jesus specialist, treats many of the stories about Jesus from his nativity to his resurrection as fictional mythology but argues convincingly that his crucifixion "is as sure as anything historical can ever be."[31] Using standards of modern historiography, Montgomery Watt, the leading European authority on Muhammad's life, finds Jesus' crucifixion as certain as the fact that Muhammad proclaimed the religion of Islam in Mecca in the early seventh century.[32] The crux of Jesus' life is literally his crucifixion, a fact as firm as any of ancient social history.

It is possible for Muslims to take a position that is both faithful to the Quran's claim that Jesus did not fail and to accept the historical fact of Jesus' crucifixion. Recognizing the dual meaning of "dead" in the Quran might allow them to accept that Jesus was victorious even if he were executed. The literal meaning is expressed in a Quranic verse in which Jesus contemplates "the day I die."[33] Elsewhere, the Quran states that Jesus' enemies did not really kill him, but they thought they did.[34] Could the Quran be treating Jesus as a nonmilitant martyr here? If so, the treatment of the death of martyrs elsewhere in the Quran might be germane to understanding the earthly end of Jesus' life. There are verses in which "dead" refers to ultimate defeat rather than to the cessation of breathing:

"Do not say that those who are killed in the way of God are dead; they are alive even though you are not aware of them";[35] and "Never think of those who are slain in God's cause as dead; rather, they are well supplied by their Lord."[36] Sayyid Qutb comments on the status of martyrs:

> They are with their Lord, well provided, rejoicing in God's grace and bounty, and anticipating with joy the people of faith who are to join them. They watch with interest the happenings in the lives of their brethren. Why should they be mourned when they are alive and in close contact with the living, beside the great bounty and high status which they have attained with God?[37]

The second major theological difference between Muhammad and Jesus pertains to their doctrines of scriptural inspiration. Muhammad's view is set forth in these Quranic words: "This Book is not to be doubted."[38] That opening sentence of the first Quranic chapter following the brief introduction seems to call for a theory of Quranic inerrancy. Those who doubt or scorn the revelation given to Muhammad "will not enter Paradise until a camel passes through the eye of a needle."[39] The Quran does not permit listeners or readers to question what it states because its presumed Author personifies absolute truth. Since God is inerrant, the book that contains His ideas, as channeled through Muhammad, is literally the word of God. Most Muslims believe that the Arabic text prepared by the commission of the third caliph contains exactly the revelation that God gave Muhammad. Understandably, critical inquiry has no place among Muslims who study their scripture in accord with the doctrine of inerrancy. If it is believed that Muhammad proclaimed precisely what God wrote in Arabic on a heavenly tablet and that the oral transmission was recorded without error in the official Uthmanic text, then the task of scholars is simplified. They should memorize as many Quranic verses as possible, learn to chant Arabic eloquently, and apply the teachings of the Quran to particular situations.

Following the logic of Quranic inerrancy, Muslims have traditionally believed that truth in the Torah or Gospels is only what conforms to the Quran. Thus, the canonical Gospels are deficient because they neglect to report that the baby Jesus performed miracles. Also, the entire New Testament errs in stating that Jesus was crucified. There is no truth in the Bible that Muhammad was not to reveal later, so it only confuses the truth seeker to study Jewish or Christian scriptures.

Within both Judaism and Christianity, there are influential groups who have a doctrine of scriptural inerrancy similar to that of Islam. Religious unity has been hindered by those confessional bodies that focus on a particular prophet who supposedly pronounced absolute truth. For example, the Torah does not declare Moses' teaching to be final, but Orthodox Judaism affirms that it is God's last word. According to twelfth-century credal formulator Maimonides, the Law revealed to Moses is immutable.[40]

Beginning early in the twentieth century, a Christian group whose members call themselves "Fundamentalists" have defended five principles, the chief of which is the verbal infallibility of the Bible.[41] For them it is blasphemous to presume that the Bible could contain fallible ideas of mortals as well as God's truth. Fundamentalism is the response of those in search of certainties amid the bewildering new ideas of science and the dilemmas of modern culture. Its simple stance is expressed on this bumpersticker: "God said it, I believe it, and that's that." Slavery, patriarchy, and genocide can all be justified by this approach. Christian fundamentalism probably has stronger support in the United States than in any other nation, but even there its support is declining. A Gallup survey indicates that now about one-third of Americans believe the Bible is "the actual word of God."[42] The text to which Fundamentalists generally appeal is the original Hebrew and Greek autographs, all of which have been lost, but those who are less educated have used the King James version as their ultimate authority.

Fundamentalists' protests notwithstanding, a discerning reader can occasionally find errors in the Holy Writ. For example, the New Testament assertion that only Eve was led astray in the Garden of Eden and sinned is shown to be false by both the Genesis story and another New Testament letter.[43] Also, scribes of all religious traditions have tampered with scriptures. For example, there appears to be an addition to a Hebrew wisdom book by a dissenting copyist who warns readers not to take the skeptical message of that writing seriously.[44] Likewise, some scribe, living a century after the writer of Mark's Gospel, added an ending that misrepresents Jesus as daring his disciples to prove their faith by handling snakes and drinking poison without being hurt.[45]

Human errors by Muhammad may also be the reason for some of the Quran's deviations from the accounts of the Bible. For example, the Arabic name "Miriam" is shared by Mary, the mother of Jesus, and another Israelite who lived more than a millenium earlier; probably because of this, Jesus' mother is confused with the daughter of Amram, the sister of Moses and Aaron.[46]

What should be done about the apparent errors that occasionally can be found in the Quran? If Muslims wish to claim that the *heavenly* Quran is infallible, that presupposition causes no earthly problem. In Semitic religious traditions, God is the source of total truth; the manner in which it is stored in the courts above is independent from its transmission to humans. Muslims accept the maxim "To err is human," and the Quran explicitly states that even Muhammad was not perfect. "God knows the truth," a common saying among Muslims, is used in recognition of human fallibility. Pagan Arabs had developed the language of the Quran, and it has its share of the limitations of human words to express ideas. These factors should convince most reasonable people that any speech or writing by humans cannot be infallible. Even if the Divine Author utters only what is true, human contamination occurs as it comes down to any society. The Quran is as much the book of Muhammad as Deuteronomy is the book of Moses. The early Muslims, who were aware of the process of the final editing of the Quran, seemed to prefer a doctrine of abrogation to a doctrine of inerrancy. Both cannot be logically accepted because the abrogated texts were not all deleted, as demonstrated in earlier chapters.

Both the Bible and the Quran teach that humans should be aware of their shortcomings, especially in the spiritual aspects of their lives. Accordingly, it is befitting humility to say that the Bible and the Quran contain the ideas of humans with all their foibles, as well as some infallible ideas of God. The arduous task of scholarship is to separate what is eternal from what is temporally bound. God speaks only through what has been created, and the difficulty is attempting to distill the Spirit's message out of human and natural happenings.

Jesus belonged to a culture in which the religious writers did not think of themselves as passive instruments through which God dictated. The biblical scribes never claimed that they were reproducing a heavenly record written in Hebrew by God. The writer of Deuteronomy, for example, recorded the oral tradition containing Moses' sermons long after his death. Although Jesus frequently quoted his Bible as authoritative, he also stated views that he recognized as independent of, and even contradictory to, that written record. In the Sermon on the Mount, he repeatedly substituted personal judgment for biblical authority, audaciously countering some laws attributed to God's revelation to Moses with "but I say to you."[47]

Some writers, such as Luke, were not aware that they were recording pages that would in subsequent generations be treasured as Holy Scripture. His two-volume work, which later editors labeled the Gospel of Luke and the Acts of the Apostles, begins with this clarifying opening sentence:

> Since many have undertaken to set down a narrative of the events that have been fulfilled among us, as delivered to us by those who from the beginning were eyewitnesses and ministers of the word, I too decided, after investigating everything carefully from the first, to write an orderly account for you, most excellent Theophilus, so that you may know the reliability of the things about which you have been instructed.[48]

Luke did not sit down and take dictation as the Holy Spirit's secretary, as some Christian art has misrepresented the process. Rather, as any good researcher, he consulted the best written and oral sources he could find and then used his mind to record it as orderly and as accurately as he could.

Far from demeaning God, this fallibility-of-human-authors approach can reveal a more sublime and moral deity. Consider, for example, how this theory helps in interpreting historically those passages examined earlier from the Bible and the Quran that command the extermination of idolaters. Today few Jews, Christians, or Muslims favor the liquidation of polytheistic Hindus who treasure images of their deities. Likewise, this fallibility theory enables the reader of the New Testament to recognize its writers as culturally bound humans who may, for example, express patriarchal prejudices. A broadening of religious understanding comes from recognizing that it is some male chauvinist, not God, who speaks through this text:

> I permit no woman to teach or to have authority over a man; she is to keep silent. For Adam was formed first, then Eve; and Adam was not deceived, but the woman was deceived and became a transgressor. Yet she will be saved through child-bearing.[49]

Devotion to the view that some records made by humans contain God's *ipsissima verba* blocks genuine dialogue between Muslims and non-Muslims, even as it does between fundamentalist and non-

Fundamentalist Jews, Christians, and Muslims. If what is deemed to be scripture is essentially an eternal and infallible document rather than a historical and human document, then the standard approaches of scholarship are invalid. Fundamentalism leads to bibliolatry, the worship of a book, which may be no improvement over other idol adorations. Blind credulity may display more fanaticism than faithfulness to the dictates of the divine.

Paths of Commitment

The Quran declares that "the true faith in God's sight is *islam*"[50] and that Muhammad is "the first of the *muslimun*."[51] The "mu" prefix refers to one who is an adherent to the religion that has "s-l-m" as its basic Arabic consonants. According to the usual English translations, the name of Muhammad's religion means "submission" or "surrender." Today some scholars prefer "commitment," which Thomas Irving uses in his 1985 translation of the Quran. Huston Smith succinctly explains why he prefers this alternate version: "In addition to being exempt from military associations, commitment suggests moving toward rather than giving up."[52] "Submission" and "surrender" have the additional deficiency of suggesting groveling before a superior force that has not captured one's voluntary allegiance.

Also originating in the pregnant "s-l-m" root is *salam*, the common Arabic greeting, meaning "peace." Thus, the basic meaning of "s-l-m" is "peace through commitment." Unexpressed but understood by Muslims is that the commitment is directed toward God and that the peace is a theological by-product. Islam is, therefore, the religion of those who attempt to express Muhammad's full commitment to God as well as who receive the accompanying peace with God from that relationship. In this regard, the Islamic Society of North America provides this summary statement:

> Islam is an Arabic word which means peace, purity, acceptance and commitment. . . . A Muslim is one who freely and willingly accepts the supreme power of God and strives to organize his life in total accord with the teachings of God. He also works for building social institutions which reflect the guidance of God.[53]

The Quran has contributed to interfaith dialogue by giving centrality to the word "Islam." Muhammad declared in the last revelation
given during his final year of life: "I (God) have approved Islam for your
religion."[54] Accordingly, the prophet is the only founder of a great
religion to name his community. Outsiders who are ignorant of the
original names Islam and Muslim have insensitively coined the name
Muhammadanism and Muhammadan. Muslims dislike being called by
names that suggest that they worship Muhammad as Christians worship
Christ.

Had Moses and Jesus taken the opportunity to select names for
their movements, they might also have chosen ones that focus on
religious content rather than ethnic pride. *"Muslimun"* is more adequate
than "Israelite," meaning a descendant of Jacob, and is preferable to
"Judaism," meaning associated with the tribe of Judah that survived the
invaders of Palestine. Judaism is certainly not the worship of a descendant of Abraham. "Muslim" is also arguably more descriptive of church
members than "Christian," which is derived from *"Xristos,"* the Greek
translation of *"Meshicha,"* which is the Aramaic term meaning "anointed
one." That nickname, which may have been coined by opponents of
Jesus' followers, literally means "belonging to the party of the Jewish
Messiah." *"Masihi"* is the Arabic designation for people who in Europe
were called *"Xristianos."* Calling the Jesus movement "Christian" was
probably once as derisive as it originally was to call George Fox's
followers "Quakers."

Muhammad enhanced the legitimacy of his religious community
by an appeal to pristine history. He identified his mission with the
Abraham he had come to know in Arabic tradition. The patriarch had
given up the polytheism of his parents after being overwhelmed by a call
to worship one God.[55] Muhammad also gave up the idolatry engaged in
by his tribe and tried to persuade his people to accept a new commitment.

The pivotal point in the careers of both Abraham and Muhammad
came when those middle-aged men emigrated from their native cities.
The exiles settled in new areas and, after initial hardships, the communities they formed became secure and powerful. Abraham and Ishmael
are said to have constructed a "House of God" at the place where
Muhammad would later assist in its reconstruction. At the initial dedica-
tion of the Meccan sanctuary, Abraham and Ishmael prayed: "Accept
this House from us, Lord. . . . Make us *muslimun* to You and make our

descendants a nation of *muslimun*. . . . Lord, raise up among them a messenger of their own who will declare to them Your revelations."[56] Even as the Bible tells of God promising that Abraham would be a blessing to all people,[57] the Quran proclaims that Muhammad has been sent out to witness to all humanity.[58]

Muhammad was not the first to solicit support from Abraham for establishing the validity of a particular group. Isaiah of Babylonia, eager to restore a sense of dignity to a disheartened Jewish community, recalls the first Hebrews:

> Look to the rock from which you were hewn,
>   and to the quarry from which you were dug.
> Look to Abraham your father
>   and to Sarah who bore you.[59]

Some centuries later, some Jews assumed that they could rely on the faith of Abraham to guarantee approval for all who claimed kinship with him. To those who boasted in that manner, John the Baptist advised: "Bear fruit worthy of repentance. Do not presume to say to yourselves, 'We have Abraham as our ancestor.' "[60]

New Testament writers were bold to call even gentile Christians honorary descendants of Abraham. According to the apostle Paul, Abraham is "the father of all who believe,"[61] whether they are circumcised or uncircumcised. To counter charges of novelty, Paul portrays his gospel as being in line with the best of early Hebrew tradition. In his writings, he argues that Moses and "all who rely on the works of the law"[62] have deviated from the Abrahamic faith. Christians were urged to give priority to God's covenant with Abraham rather than to adhere to a subsequent covenant that emphasized the Law of Moses.[63] Another New Testament writer, after defining faith as a commitment to unseen hopes, commends Abraham, along with Sarah and their offspring, as a spiritual ancestor for Christians:

> By faith he settled as an alien in the promised land . . . because he was looking for the city with solid foundations, designed and built by God. . . . Therefore, since we are surrounded by this large group of witnesses, . . . let us run with determination the race that lies ahead of us, fixing our eyes on Jesus, the leader and completer of faith.[64]

Muhammad agreed with the biblical judgment that some religious leaders after Abraham corrupted the original purity of his primordial monotheism. The Quran repeatedly discusses the involvement of Moses' brother Aaron in the golden-calf idolatry of the Israelites.[65] It also charges Christians with apostasy and claims that only Islam conserves the oldest and the best religious tradition. "Abraham was neither Jew nor Christian,"[66] the Quran points out, but was a "muslimun." In spite of others who have fallen away, Muhammad adhered to Abraham's faith.[67] The Quran places Islam in the direct line of Abrahamic religion, which avoids the aberrant paths of the Israelites and the Christians.

The opening sentence of the New Testament gives prominence to Abraham in reference to Jesus' genealogy. The Gospel of Matthew, which is particularly interested in demonstrating that Jesus is the fulfillment of Israelite prophecy, affirms that Abraham is the first ancestor in Jesus' family tree. Similarly, at the beginning of Muhammad's earliest biography, Ishaq enhances his subject's prestige by tracing his genealogy through Ishmael back to Abraham.[68]

Muhammad was faithful to the facts of history in asserting that Abraham's faith was different from the subsequent religions of Judaism or Christianity. It would be anachronistic to say that Abraham observed the Sabbath or practiced baptism. But he was also far from some of the basic doctrines of Muhammad. For example, in the Genesis saga, Abraham affirms no belief in personal immortality and Paradise. For him and his fellow patriarchs, producing offspring who would survive and carry on the Hebrew culture fulfilled their hopes.

Religions have not followed Abraham without deviation, and this may display ethical and theological improvement. The Quran tells of an occasion when Abraham lied to conceal his destruction of idols in his home town.[69] Also Muhammad retold a biblical story of when the patriarch called his wife his sister.[70] To protect himself, Abraham schemed deceptively to pass Sarah off to Pharaoh's harem.[71] Also, there is no indication that Abraham informed his wife of his plan to sacrifice her only son.[72] Abraham's unquestioning willingness to kill his innocent son in devotion to God displays the outlook of persons who are now called psychopaths.[73] What later prophet would have thought it proper to have Abraham's attitude toward human sacrifice? After criticizing those who had attempted to placate God by sacrificing their children, the prophet Micah proclaimed: "The Lord requires you to act justly, to love loyalty, and to walk humbly with your God."[74] Both Jesus and Muhammad enthusiastically endorsed that higher standard of religious behavior.

Similarities between Muhammad and Jesus can also be found by examining the metaphor for picturing true religion used most frequently in the Quran. Its opening and preeminent chapter conveys the image that true religion is walking a path without going astray. The Quran associates the path with the great prophets, beginning with Noah: "We (God) chose them and guided them to a straight path."[75] This same image is used in the Hebrew Bible: "Noah walked with God."[76] The Quran treats subsequent walkers along the path in this way: "My Lord has guided me along a straight path to a right religion, to the faith of Abraham, who was no idolater."[77] Moses avoided the crooked, repressive way of the Pharaoh and followed God's straight and outward road from Egypt.[78] Jesus' message is given this Quranic summary: "God is my Lord and your Lord; therefore serve Him, for such is the straight path."[79] True prophets recognized that one's walk speaks more loudly than one's talk. Because of the Quranic emphasis on following the path or way (*sunna*) of previous authentic prophets, most Muslims have called themselves Sunnis.

Following the straight path presumes avoiding the alternate way of many who lack rectitude. "You shall not follow a majority in wrongdoing," Moses proclaimed at Sinai.[80] Jesus associated the pursuit of the most popular way with false prophets.[81] As the Quran puts it: "To follow the majority would lead you away from God's path."[82] The metaphor is developed elsewhere in the Quran:

> Have We not brought you where two roads diverge? Yet you have not climbed the steep path. The ascent is freeing the slave, feeding the starving orphaned relative or the poor wretch in misery. . . . Those who do this will stand on the right hand; those who deny Our revelations will stand on the left, with Hell fire close by.[83]

An early name for Jesus' movement was "Those of the *Hodos*," meaning "way" or "road".[84] The name may have resulted from several Gospel associations. John the Baptist envisioned a straight highway with the coming of "one who is more mighty than I."[85] Appropriating a prophecy of Isaiah as his theme, John proclaimed:

> *Prepare the way of the Lord,*
> *make straight his paths. . . .*
> *The crooked shall be made straight,*
> *and the rough ways made smooth.*[86]

Jesus developed the notion, found earlier in his scriptures, of two contrasting paths: "Enter through the narrow gate; for the gate is wide and the road is easy that leads to destruction, and there are many who take it. For the gate is narrow and the path is rough that leads to life, and there are few who find it."[87] What Jesus was planning to accomplish in Jerusalem is related to Moses' out-trekking (ex-hodos) from Egypt.[88] The Fourth Gospel attributes these words to Jesus: "Walk while you have the light, so that the darkness may not overtake you; if you walk in the darkness, you do not know where you are going. . . . I am the way, the truth, and the life."[89]

Followers of Jesus understandably have thought of religion as a difficult way of life. They view their faith not so much as ideas about God but more as the practice of holy, suffering love. "Walk in newness of life,"[90] writes Paul in exhorting Christians to identify themselves with the martyred Jesus. Another New Testament writer tells of Jesus' life and death providing "a new and living way" for his followers.[91] *Pilgrim's Progress* by John Bunyan is one of the more influential books in the course of Christian history. In this allegory, a vision guides a man named Christian while on a treacherous journey. The goal of the venture, the city of God, becomes clearer en route.

Current theologians are renewing the walking metaphor. In Charles Swezey's inaugural address at Union Theological Seminary, he shows that walking the way continues to be the most adequate image for uniting ethics and theology. He concludes: "Through encounters with pitfalls and dangers, the identity of the Christian community is formed and the vision of God gains clarity."[92] Jurgen Moltmann selected *The Way of Jesus Christ* as a book title because it contains a metaphor that is ethical as well as dynamic. He thinks of Christians as being guided along their quest by Jesus the pathfinder.[93] Paul Van Buren has been writing a multivolume treatment of Judeo-Christian-Muslim theology, using "walking in the way" as his lead motif. He asserts: "Faith is not primarily a matter of thinking, but of walking in a certain way."[94]

"The Paths of Those Committed to God" might be a good ecumenical name for religions with the Semitic heritage. "Way Walkers" might be a simple designation for those so committed. With a fuller comprehension of common roots, the past eagerness to supplant the other would be replaced by the determination to supplement one another. The three Semitic religions could at last affirm the common creed the Quran advocates: "We believe in what has been revealed to each of our communities. We are committed (*muslims*) to the one God of all."[95]

Beyond this general orientation, people can walk along their varied roads to the same destination. One route might be more direct, one more scenic, one more of an obstacle course, but all would demand steadfast commitment until the goal is reached. Those who endanger others and themselves by jaywalking or by not honoring any paths would not be respected.

Each tradition contains an ideal embodiment of one who has been the pathfinder *par excellence*. Moses' way, Jesus' way, and Muhammad's way would be appropriate road markers for the questers. Along with other monotheists, I am encouraged by the Quran to include myself among the *muslims*. I can join with Jesus' disciples who are reported to have said: "We are God's helpers! We have faith in God, bearing witness that we are *muslims*."[96]

What are the main vistas that one might expect along Muhammad's and Jesus' paths? In post-Quranic tradition, Muslims defined themselves by five basic pillars.[97] The commitments resemble a desert tent, with one center pole surrounded by four shorter poles. The first pole is the creed, "There is no god but God, and Muhammad is his Apostle."[98] The other supports are daily prayer, generous almsgiving, holy-month fasting, and making a pilgrimage to Mecca. Jesus requested certain commitments from his followers, but there is no classic statement of a given number. They include seeking the just rule of God, forgiving as well as accepting forgiveness, and loving others in accord with the love Jesus exemplified. Those who venture with him are promised joy but no more success than Jesus himself had along the roads of Palestine.

Tolerance of Diversity

Religious intolerance is not a part of the core commitments of either Islam or Christianity. Quranic revelations echo and scorn the smugness that has been characteristic of the Judeo-Christian tradition: "The Jews and the Christians say: 'We are God's children and his favorites' ";[99] and "Scriptural people have said: 'Only Jews and Christians will be admitted to Paradise.' . . . The Jews say, 'There is nothing in the Christian faith,' while the Christians say, 'There is nothing in the Jewish faith.' Both cite the Scripture"[100]; and "If an afterlife with God is for you alone, to the exclusion of all other people, then you should long for death!"[101]

According to the Quran, no religious group can presume that God has elected it irrevocably. The Quran asserts: "Let the scriptural people know that they have no control over the grace of God; that grace is in His hands alone, and that He grants it to whomever He will. God's grace is infinite."[102] According to Fazlur Rahman, the Quran is "absolutely unequivocal" that "*no* community may lay claims to be uniquely guided and elected."[103]

Muhammad used a bold family metaphor to convey his view of the close relationship among prophetic religions: "I am the nearest of kin to Jesus, son of Mary, in this world and the next. The prophets are brothers, sons of one father by co-wives. Their mothers are different but their religion is one."[104] The Quran gives this instruction to Muhammad::

> Say: "We believe in God and the revelation given to us, and to Abraham, Ishmael, Isaac, Israel and the tribes; we believe in what was given to Moses, Jesus, and to all other prophets from the Lord. We make no distinction among them, and we commit ourselves to God."[105]

Other Quranic texts display an even wider openness to other monotheistic faiths. One of them declares: "Believers (Muslims), Jews, Christians, and Sabians—whoever believes in God and the Last Day and does what is right will be rewarded by their Lord; they have nothing to fear."[106] The Sabians were probably followers of John the Baptist and may be identified with the Mandaeans who still live in Iraq.[107] The Zoroastrians are included in the listing of approved faiths elsewhere in the Quran.[108] Another verse is even more inclusive: "All who commit themselves to God and do good, shall be rewarded by their Lord."[109] Muhammad Asad comments that this text shows that salvation "is open to everyone who consciously realizes the oneness of God, surrenders himself to His will and, by living righteously, gives practical effect to this spiritual attitude."[110] These texts illustrate John Hick's comment on covenantal relationships: "Religious pluralism implies that those who are on the other great ways of salvation are no less God's chosen people, although with different vocations."[111]

Muhammad expressed a live-and-let-live outlook even toward idolaters when he addressed the Meccans in an early revelation: "Unbelievers, I do not worship what you worship, nor do you worship what I worship. I will never worship what you worship, nor will you ever worship what I worship. You have your religion and I have mine."[112]

Lamentably, the Quran is not consistent in its tolerance teachings. As David Margoliouth, an Oxford Arabic professor, notes, its utterances vary "from large-minded tolerance to extreme fanaticism."[113] Consider the traditional way Muslim theologians interpret the verse quoted above that expresses openness toward Jews, Christians, and Sabians. That verse was later superseded by this one: "Anyone who chooses a religion other than Islam will not be acceptable and will be one of the lost in the next world."[114] Other verses, such as the following, are more explicit: "Scriptural people who disbelieve, together with idolaters, will abide in the fire of Hell; they are the dregs of all creation."[115] In a Quranic chapter that discusses Jews and Christians, this charge is made:

> They attempt to extinguish the light of God with the words they mouth; but God will perfect His light, no matter how much disbelievers may dislike it. He has sent His Apostle with guidance to make the true religion victorious over all other religions.[116]

In Muslim tradition, Muhammad becomes not merely a prominent prophet but *the* prophet, who is destined to defeat even monotheists whose rituals and ethics are different. Jews and Christians are, at best, merely to be tolerated until the Judgment Day if they pay whatever tax the dominant Muslims levy.[117] Muhammad said: "Do not greet Jews and Christians before they greet you, and when you meet one of them on the road force him to go to the narrowest part of it."[118] Al-Bukhari discusses another record that pertains to Christians who are refused admission to Paradise: "They will say, 'We used to worship Jesus, the Son of God.' It will be said to them, 'You are liars, for God has never taken anyone as a wife or a son.' "[119]

Many participants in the tradition of biblical religion have often disregarded an anti-exclusivism theme. Prophet Amos declared that Israel's covenantal relationship with God does not provide that nation with irrevocable divine protection from heathen invaders.[120] As God's spokesperson, Amos proclaims: "People of Israel, I think as much of the Ethiopians as I do of you. I brought the Philistines from Crete and the Syrians from Kir, even as I brought you out of Egypt."[121] Amos was bold to claim that God's care extended to Africans as well as Asians, and even to the migrations of Israel's enemies.

God's universal sovereignty is also affirmed in a Hebrew poem about an ideal metropolis personified as Mother Zion. Discounting the special election of one people, Psalm 87 envisions the "city of God" as having an international progeny:

> *Of Zion it will be said,*
> *"All nations belong there,"*
> *The God above all gods will strengthen her.*[122]

Among those who know God, the psalmist includes peoples of different pigments, the Ethiopians and the Lebanese. The register of Zion's children encompasses Israel's prominent pagan foes: the Egyptians, Babylonians, and Philistines. Conversion to the psalmist's religion is not a prerequisite to being among the cosmopolitans who sing and dance in Zion.

Psalm 87 inspired the title of the most influential medieval non-biblical book, *The City of God.*[123] Ironically, Bishop Augustine narrowed the family of Mother Zion to include only baptized Catholics who have not lapsed into some heresy or other form of wickedness.[124] Augustine's myopic vision dominated Christian thought for many centuries. Independent of Augustine, modern Zionism has arisen and has been identified more with Jewish exclusivism than with the multiethnic children of Zion that the psalmist imagined.

Even within the era of the Hebrew Bible, a counter-tolerance theme had developed. After the Babylonian exile, the Jewish survivors were led by Nehemiah and Ezra who promoted exclusivism. Nehemiah boasted: "I purified the people from everything foreign."[125] Ezra persuaded the Jews to separate themselves from their foreign wives.[126] Some of those wives, like Ruth, may have adopted the religion of their husbands. In contrast, no divine disapproval was expressed when Judah, Joseph, and Moses had married pagan women earlier.[127]

Jesus emphasized the inclusive motif contained in the Hebrew tradition. When his disciples asked him to denounce a healer who did not belong to their group, Jesus replied: "Do not stop him; . . . for whoever is not against us is for us."[128] As long as people are being helpful to others, Jesus thought that they should be treated with respect.

Historical data does not support the idea that either Jesus or Muhammad thought of himself as God in the flesh or as one who had heavenly preexistence. Despite the Christocentricity of some early Christians, Jesus thought of the rule of God as central. He did not promote himself by saying, "I am the incarnation of God"; rather, he announced that "the kingdom of God is at hand."[129] Both Jesus and

Muhammad were theocentric; they thought of themselves as subordi-nate to God, the Creator and Governor of the world. Geza Vermes comments: "The religion Jesus preached was substantially different from what Christianity has become. Jesus preached a totally God-centered religion, whereas Christianity is Christocentric."[130]

Most of those who have called themselves followers of Jesus for the past two thousand years have neglected his breadth of tolerance and have divided all people into Christians who are "saved"—that is, ac-cepted by God for eternal life—and non-Christians who are damned. C. S. Lewis, the spokesperson for many conservative Christians, asserts: "Where Christianity differs from other religions, Christianity is right and they are wrong."[131] Karl Barth is the most influential twentieth-century Christian representative of the exclusivist position. According to that Swiss theologian, God's revelation is confined to Jesus, and true religion is especially manifested in Protestantism.[132] Lutheran theo-logian Carl Braaten currently defends Barth's monopolistic doctrine at length and asserts that "Jesus Christ is the one and only light that brings life to the world."[133] Braaten has little to say about the Quranic revela-tion other than the untruthful claim that it refers to Jesus' resurrection from the dead.[134]

Other Christians go even further than Lewis, Barth, and Braaten to contend that their particular denomination or sect knows not only the truth about God but exclusively the *whole* truth. They see their confes-sional group as uniquely favored by God. Reflecting on this arrogance and on the New Testament affirmation that "we know only in part,"[135] Reinhold Niebuhr formulates this paradox: "The truth, as it is contained in the Christian revelation, includes the recognition that it is neither possible for man to know the truth fully nor to avoid the error of pretending that he does."[136]

Religious exclusivism is the natural stance of those who have experienced only one culture. Many Jews, Christians, and Muslims never rise to the threshold of discovering perceptions of truth beyond the boundaries of their own tradition. John Bunyan was unusual in being troubled over exclusivism. This seventeenth-century Baptist leader ex-pressed his concerns in the following questions:

How can you tell that the Turks may not have as good scriptures to prove their Muhammad as the Savior as we have to prove our Jesus? Could I think that tens of thousands in many countries and kingdoms should be without the knowl-

edge of the right way to heaven . . . and that we only, who live
in a corner of the earth, should alone be blessed therewith?
Everyone thinks his own religion is right, whether he is a Jew,
or a Muslim, or a polytheist.[137]

The term "pluralism" is increasingly popular among students of
world religions to express an approach that values both tolerance of
other faiths and commitment to their own faith. Pluralists hold to one
faith while entering into dialogue with those adhering to other faiths.
Meaningful dialogue involves both the honest facing of basic differences and a common searching for a truth that no group completely
possesses. The goal of pluralists is not to arrive at a uniform super-
religion, but to improve the faith of participants by understanding the
commitments of others and sometimes adapting beneficent values
proven effective elsewhere.

The logical circles of the following diagram show the conceptual
structure of pluralism *vis-à-vis* religious truth:

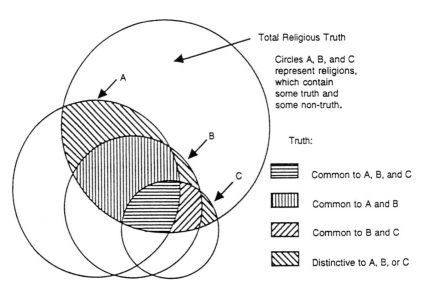

Logical Circles Relating Truth to Religion

The largest circle symbolizes the total religious truth, so everything outside that circle is false. God's truth is frequently referred to in the Hebrew Bible as *emeth*, in the New Testament as *aletheia*, and in the Quran as *haqq*. Judaism, Christianity, and Islam all maintain that God is much greater than humans' ideas of God. This common doctrine nurtures the humility needed for opening doors to greater illumination. Regarding human understanding, the Bible states: "My thoughts are not your thoughts, nor are your ways my ways, says the Lord."[138] The Quran also affirms: "He (God) knows all that is present before humans and everything about them that is yet to be. They comprehend only that part of His knowledge that He wills."[139] In accord with this, there is much agreement in Semitic religions on how to answer the question "Who is God?" All three faiths would probably regard the following traditional catechism answer as an adequate summary: "God is a Spirit, infinite, eternal, and unchangeable, in his being, wisdom, power, holiness, justice, goodness, and truth."[140]

The three smaller circles represent particular religions A, B, and C. The truth portions of A + B + C do not fill up even half of the total religious truth. Many other religions are not represented here, and God's truth may also be partially expressed by non-religious groups. The diagram also shows that what A, B, and C teach is, from a divine perspective, about half false. Those within the groups are unaware of just which parts of their doctrines are ultimately true. Perhaps they become more aware of the amount of God's truth they possessed on the other side of death.

The differing sizes of A, B, and C represent different amounts of truth, but participants are unable to have certain knowledge of where they belong. Given the three options, all religious participants presume that their religion is A, and have more ample means of salvation than the others. Were that not the case and given the choice, the believer would abandon it and adopt the religion that appears to contain more truth. Unless individuals who think of themselves as A circle members are open and positive toward all other circles, they will be deprived of fuller knowledge of religious truth. However, those who claim that all religions are equally true may be more empty-minded than open-minded; various religions do contain some opposing principles that may not be acceptable as mutually true.

Perceptive readers have discerned that I evaluate Jesus as having more of God's truth than Moses and Muhammad do. I like to think of myself as participating in a serious religious debate in which others will examine my outlook, not for the purpose of debunking it, but for advancing their perspectives in a dialectic aimed at obtaining a larger portion of the truth. I have learned much from the scriptures and personal testimonies of those who are convinced that another prophet is in the A circle, and I acknowledge that they indeed may have assimilated more truth about God than Christians have. Some devotees of one prophet are largely ignorant of the life and teachings of other prophets, but some have studied other religions and are still convinced that more truth is revealed by their favorite prophet.

The religious and marital bond can be compared regarding ultimacy. Many spouses genuinely believe that they are individually paired with the best persons that exist, and total affirmation is given to the "one and only" who appears to be the closest approximation of the ideal spouse. A wife may think of her husband as the only man who is just right for her, and a husband may think that their unique relationship has been predestined. But if the spouses had been raised in another environment, they would have somewhat different personalities and thus would be destined for other partners.

Relationships among world religions are also similar to ethnic commitments. Each of us is born into and accepts without choice a particular cultural group. Thus, for example, African-Americans grow up believing that black is beautiful, and Native Americans learn to take pride in their distinctive heritage. This healthy ethnic appreciation does not have to degenerate into a tribalism in which members of one group claim absolute superiority over all others.

We deceive ourselves if we think we can be totally objective. As in all areas of human experience, unavoidable biases are apparent to others even when we believe that subjectivity has been avoided. Like sailboating, the stimulating sport of thrusting first in one direction and then another leads to the destination of fuller truth. Sailing directly into the wind is impossible, and moving toward divine truth without honestly examining the positions of others may also be impossible.

The extensive overlapping of the three particular religions on the logical diagram accurately represent Judaism, Christianity, and Islam. Common elements of all three include accepting Moses as a prophet, praying to one just and merciful God, giving to the needy, and endorsing most of the Ten Commandments. All three advocate honoring parents and forbid polytheism, idolatry, murder, adultery, stealing, lying, and greed. Common elements of two include singing psalms

(Judaism and Christianity), proselytizing people of other cultures (Christianity and Islam), and circumcising for cultic purposes (Judaism and Islam). Distinctions include lamenting during Yom Kippur, making pilgrimages to Mecca, and being baptized.

The diagram is intended to counter the arrogance that causes particular groups to claim finality for their world religion. It does not follow logically to say that if my religion contains a great deal of truth, other religions cannot have as much or more truth than mine. To say, as many others honestly can, that there is more truth and challenge in my religion than I can ever put into practice is not the same as saying that truth is limited to what is expressed in the scriptures and traditions of my religion. People who testify that their religion possesses "the whole truth, and nothing but the truth" display an unbecoming lack of humility.

In an effort to purge exclusive-mindedness from religions, Arnold Toynbee reasons:

> One can be convinced of the essential truth and rightness and value of what one believes to be the fundamental points in one's own religion—and can believe that these tenets have been received by one as a revelation from God—and at the same time not believe that *I, my* church, *my* people, have the sole and unique revelation.[141]

There is a parallel between pluralism in science and in religion. Some astrophysicists are now involved in a cooperative search for the truth about the original state of the universe before the development of the major physical forces and elements that are now known. Teams of scientists in different laboratories pursue different hypotheses and rely more on the quantum theory or more on the wave theory for understanding atomic energy. Similarly, some theologians are pursuing truth that transcends the doctrinal understanding of their particular expressions of faith. While these have some commonalities, there is considerable diversity in both interpretation and method. The competition among the scientific communities is often mutually enriching. Each hopes that its research will provide a step toward the ultimate truth of nature. Isaac Newton, the most brilliant astrophysicist, expressed the spirit needed in both religion and science in this statement: "I seem to have been only like a boy playing on the seashore, and diverting myself

in now and then finding a smoother pebble or a prettier shell than
ordinary, whilst the great ocean of truth lay all undiscovered before
me."[142] This humble genius pursued truth about gravitational force and
about One whom he referred to as omnipotent, omniscient, and omni-
present. Regarding the latter pursuit, Newton said: "As a blind man has
no idea of colors, so have we no idea of the manner by which the all-
wise God perceives and understands all things."[143]

The truth of God is not confined to the historical Jesus or Muhammad, or to the Israelite religion that led up to them. The New Testament
refers to Jesus as the true one and the Quran refers to Muhammad in the
same way.[144] Yet it would go beyond those scriptures to maintain that all
of God's truth was exhaustively contained in what either prophet expressed. The Spirit of God "blows where it chooses"[145] and is not limited
to the synagogue, church, or mosque. In his writings, the apostle Paul
confesses that divine love transcends human understanding.[146] Enthusi-
astic appreciation of one revealer does not demand that other prophets
be denigrated. Indeed, the more secure one is, the more one can be
tolerant of the different commitments of others. Hick uses an astro-
nomical metaphor in his advocacy of pluralism:

> We have to make what might be called a Copernican revolu-
> tion in our theology of religions. . . . We have to realize that
> the universe of faiths centres upon *God*, and not upon Chris-
> tianity or upon any other religion. He is the sun, the origina-
> tive source of light and life, whom all the religions reflect in
> their own different ways.[147]

Wilfred Smith, an eminent comparative-religions scholar, chal-
lenges fellow Christians who "insist that Christ is the center of their
lives . . . (to) rediscover that God is the center of the universe."[148] With
Christocentricity there is the danger of Jesusolatry, the idolizing of the
Nazarene savior. Smith affirms that God's truth is the convergent point
for all religions. He finds this expressed in *Allahu akbar*, the familiar cry of
Muslims, that acknowledges God to be greater than all human theolo-
gizings.

Those accepting the theocentric paradigm no longer measure another's religion by its distance from their own. Pluralistic Muslims and
Christians depend primarily on their particular scriptures, traditions,
community worship, and individual experiences for learning about God,
but they acknowledge that all of God's wisdom is not expressed in these.

While recognizing Muhammad or Jesus as significantly unique, the exhaustive divine truth is not identified with either revealer. Each prophet might best be seen as a shining planet that provides an indirect light from the divine source.

One of the healthiest theological developments of the twentieth century has been the rejection by the world's largest religious denomination of the claims that its church is the sole depository of essential religious truth and that all other religions are false. In 1442, the Ecumenical Council of Florence made this "infallible" pronouncement:

> The holy Roman Church . . . proclaims that outside the Catholic Church no one, neither heathen nor Jew nor unbeliever nor schismatic, will have a share in eternal life, but will, rather, be subject to the everlasting fire which has been prepared for the Devil and his angels, unless he attaches himself to the Catholic Church before his death.[149]

In contrast, the Vatican II Council of the Roman Catholic Church recognized in 1965, as did the early Christians centuries ago, that different religions contain rays of the "true Light that enlightens everyone."[150] The splendor of the divine is enhanced, not diminished, by this variety. Regarding non-Christian religions, the Vatican II Council also stated:

> The Catholic Church rejects nothing which is true and holy in these religions . . . Upon the Muslims, too, the Church looks with esteem. They adore one God. . . . They strive to submit wholeheartedly even to His inscrutable decrees, just as did Abraham, with whom the Islamic faith is pleased to associate itself. Though they do not acknowledge Jesus as God, they revere him as a prophet. . . . They prize the moral life, and give worship to God, especially through prayer, almsgiving, and fasting. Although in the course of the centuries many quarrels and hostilities have arisen between Christians and Muslims . . . let them make common cause of safeguarding and fostering social justice, moral values, peace, and freedom.[151]

Catholic priest Hans Kung, whose writings were one of the causes of the Vatican II Council, articulates well the contemporary spirit of his Church:

The Christian who wishes to engage in dialogue with the Muslim acknowledges from the outset his or her own conviction of faith that for him or her Jesus is the Christ and so is normative and definitive, but he or she also takes very seriously the function of Muhammad as an authentic prophet. . . . Anybody who makes such a basic attitude his or her own, whether as a Christian or not, can combine commitment to faith and readiness to understand, religious loyalty and intellectual honesty. He or she has a critically reflective tie to his or her as well as to the other community of faith not only to interpret something afresh but to change it—with a developing ecumenical community in view.[152]

An evolution in the use of "ecumenical" (literally, "household") parallels changes in religious outlook. Traditionally, the term pertained to councils of the Catholic Church from Nicea onward. It first referred to interfaith dialogues among Protestants in the twentieth century. Subsequently, the term was prominently used to describe cooperative efforts among the Roman Catholics, the Eastern Orthodox, and the Protestants. The "household" term has been used in the past generation to describe the quest for Jewish-Christian unity. As a result of the "trialogue" that is now surfacing, Christians, Jews, and Muslims may eventually feel comfortable residing in Dar-Islam, the household of those committed to God. "Ecumenical" pertains not only to what is inclusive of all Christians or of all biblically oriented people, but also to the wider household of ethical monotheists.

When this unifying effort becomes more apparent, Jews, Christians, and Muslims may mutually appreciate new divine spokespersons. As demonstrated, the New Testament recognizes male and female prophets who lived after Jesus, so Christians should not think that God has been speechless since the time of the Nazarene. Jews and Christians recognize Jeremiah as a true prophet, but they are not likely to so recognize Muhammad. Similarly, the Quran recognizes Moses and Jesus as prophets, but not Jeremiah and Ezekiel. Perhaps the horizons of these three religions could be broadened to accept prophets since Muhammad. Among those who might be ranked as authentic spokespersons for God are Al-Ghazali (died 1111), Joan of Arc (martyred 1431), Baruch Spinoza (died 1677), Sarah Grimké (died 1873), Baha'u'llah (died 1892), Martin Luther King (martyred 1968), and Archbishop Oscar Romero (martyred 1980).

Christians and Muslims have both been given the imperative to propagate their faith. In this regard, a text from the Quran has inspired action: "It is He who has sent forth His Apostle with guidance and the true faith to make it triumphant over all religions."[153] Correspondingly, many Christians have been profoundly influenced by Jesus' command that initiating baptisms be performed and that his teachings be transmitted so as to "make disciples of all nations."[154] Recognizing the benefit of any religion engaging in missionary activity, Jacques Jomier asks: "Is it not a deeply human reaction to want to share with others that which gives one's own existence all its meaning and appears as the height of what human beings can have in this world: faith in the God who loves them and whom they love?"[155]

According to the Quran, God addresses Jews, Christians, and Muslims, suggesting that there is virtue in competing communities:

> We have revealed to you the Book with truth, confirming the
> Scriptures which came before it. . . . For each of you We have
> ordained a Law and a Way. Had God pleased, He could have
> made all of you a single community. However it is His will to
> test you by the revelation given you, so compete in goodness.
> To God you will all return and He will resolve your dis-
> putes.[156]

In religious competitions, only poor sports compare one's ideals with another's practices. For example, some Christians enjoy contrasting Jesus' acceptance of other ethnics with military conquests by early Muslim leaders. In return, some Muslims contrast their ideal of a common humanity with the holy wars of Christians. But fairness demands on-the-level comparisons. If ideals were compared with ideals and practices with practices, invidious comparisons would diminish.

Jesus advocated the good-works test of prophetic movements: "By their fruits you shall know them."[157] Children of Abraham should get beyond asserting that Moses, Jesus, or Muhammad is the greatest, and let the impact of their messages be the standard for evaluation. Independent of Moses' personal lifestyle, some of the commandments that he proclaimed have had a positive influence on civilization. The same might be said for later prophets in the Judeo-Christian-Muslim tradition.

Gotthold Lessing, a philosopher during the German Enlightenment period of the eighteenth century, wrote an intriguing play about a dying sultan who loved each of his three sons equally. He could not decide who should be willed his opal ring, the potent symbol of his authority. Consequently, he had two duplicate rings made so that each son would inherit an opal ring. In appearance, the three rings could not be distinguished from one another. After their father's death, the sons went to a wise man to ascertain who possessed the authentic ring. This advice was offered: "Let each think his own is the true ring. Possibly the father wished to tolerate no longer in his house the tyranny of just one ring."[158] The sage encouraged each son to emulate his father's "unprejudiced affection" with "gentleness, a heart-felt peacefulness, good works, and deep submission to God's will."[159] In essence, then, each son should aim at genuine piety and high morality, without disparaging the striving of the others. In a future age, the "powers of the stones" would reveal which is authentic by the quality of the descendants.[160]

Lessing provided a parable of pluralism. The story does not convey relativism, however, because all rings are not of equal worth. In the end, the family of one offspring may be universally recognized as the best expression of the will of God. The determination will not come by the pronouncement of some authority after the development of a new scientific test to distinguish replicas from the original. Rather, recognition will come pragmatically by people discerning a different quality in the lives of their neighbors and judging that some live more in accord with the character of the One bestowing the gift than others do. In real life, both Muslims and Christians highly respected a prophet who once offered this test: "Anyone who resolves to do the will of God will know whether the teaching is from God."[161]

NOTES

CHAPTER 1: *Introduction*

1. *Quran* (henceforth cited as "Q") 2:253.
2. Genesis 11:10–32.
3. Q 19:31, 29:30.
4. Q 2:87, 4:171.
5. Rendel Harris, "Sayings of Jesus from Moslem Sources," *The Expositor* 16 (1918): 151–60.
6. Q 3:45; *Washington Post* (December 16, 1990): K1.
7. W. Montgomery Watt, *Muhammad at Mecca* (Oxford: Clarendon Press, 1953), p. 52.
8. Genesis 25:6.
9. *Sanhedrin* 91a.
10. *Esther Rabbah* 1, 17.
11. Galatians 4:29–30; Genesis 21:10.
12. Sozomen, *Church History* 6, 38.
13. Seyyed Nasr, "Islamic Conception of Intellectual Life," *Dictionary of the History of Ideas* (New York: Scribner's, 1973).
14. John of Damascus, *The Fount of Knowledge* 2, 101, in Daniel Sahas, *John of Damascus on Islam* (London: Brill, 1972), p. 133.
15. Harry Turtledove, *The Chronicle of Theophanes* (Philadelphia: University of Pennsylvania Press, 1982), p. 35.
16. *Song of Roland* part 1, poem 71, in Charles Eliot, ed., *Harvard Classics* 49 (New York: Collier, 1910), p. 127.
17. *Song of Roland* part 1, poems 143, 223 in Eliot, pp. 159, 197.
18. James Kritzeck, *Peter the Venerable and Islam* (Princeton: Princeton University Press, 1964), p. 132.
19. James Waltz, "Muhammad and the Muslims in St. Thomas Aquinas," *The Muslim World* 66 (4/76): 88–89.
20. Aquinas, *Summa contra Gentiles* 1, 6.
21. Aquinas, *Summa contra Gentiles* 1, 6.
22. Dante Alighieri, *Divine Comedy: Inferno* 28.
23. Miguel Asin, *Islam and the Divine Comedy* (New York: Dutton, 1926).

24. Marie-Rose Seguy, *The Miraculous Journey of Mahomet* (New York: Braziller, 1977), p. 19.

25. Revelation 9:13–19; Theodore Bachmann, ed., *Luther's Works* 35 (Philadelphia: Muhlenberg Press, 1960), p. 404.

26. Jaroslav Pelikan, ed., *Luther's Works* 15 (St. Louis: Concordia, 1966), p. 340.

27. Robert Schultz, ed., *Luther's Works* 46 (Philadelphia: Fortress, 1967), p. 179.

28. Gustav Wienche, ed., *Luther's Works* 43 (Philadelphia: Fortress, 1968), p. 238.

29. Jaroslav Pelikan, ed., *Luther's Works* 8 (St. Louis: Concordia, 1966), p. 187.

30. *D. Martin Luthers Werke* 53 (Weimar, 1920), pp. 395–96.

31. Paul Lunde, "The Lure of Mecca," *Aramco World Magazine* 25, 6 (1974): 14–15.

32. Norman Daniel, *Islam and the West* (Edinburgh: University of Edinburgh Press, 1960), p. 32.

33. William Shakespeare, *I Henry VI* 1, 2, 140–41.

34. Francis Bacon, "Of Boldness."

35. Voltaire, *Mahomet the Prophet, or Fanaticism* (1742) 5, 4.

36. Voltaire, "Mahometans," *Dictionaire Philosophique*, in Ben Redman, ed., *The Portable Voltaire* (New York: Penguin, 1977), p. 163.

37. Redman, p. 164.

38. Sigismund Koelle, *Mohammed and Mohammedism* (London: Rivington, 1889), pp. 468–69.

39. Samuel Zwemer, *Islam* (New York: Layman's Missionary Movement, 1909), p. 44.

40. Duncan Macdonald, *Aspects of Islam* (New York: Macmillan, 1911), pp. 72, 74.

41. Marius Baar, *The Unholy War* (Nashville: Nelson, 1980), pp. 71, 155.

42. *The Intermountain* (January 12, 1981).

43. *The Intermountain* (January 12, 1981).

44. Salman Rushdie, *The Satanic Verses* (New York: Viking, 1989).

45. Robert Burns, "The De'il's Awa."

46. W. Young, *Patriarch, Shah, and Caliph* (Rawalpindi: Christian Study Centre, 1974), p. 203.

47. George Sale, *The Koran* (New York: Warne, 1891), p. xii.

48. Sale, p. vii.

49. Sale, p. x.

50. Edward Gibbon, *The Decline and Fall of the Roman Empire* (1788), chapter 50.

51. Gibbon, chapter 50, note 159.

52. Thomas Carlyle, *On Heroes, Hero-Worship, and the Heroic in History* (1840), lecture 2.

53. Thomas Carlyle, *On Heroes* (London: Oxford University Press, 1968), p. 57.

54. Carlyle, *On Heroes*, p. 57.

55. Carlyle, *On Heroes*, p. 85.

56. Johann Doellinger, *Muhammed's Religion* (1838), p. 3, in *The Moslem World* 34 (1944): 96.

57. Kenneth Cragg, *The Call of the Minaret* (New York: Oxford University Press, 1964), pp. 94–95.

58. Guilio Basetti-Sani, *The Koran in the Light of Christ* (Chicago: Franciscan Herald Press, 1977), p. 186.

59. Genesis 17:20.

60. Alfred Guillaume, *Islam* (Baltimore: Penguin Books, 1954), p. 53.

61. Will Durant, *The Age of Faith* (New York: Simon & Schuster, 1950), p. 174.

62. Michael Hart, *The 100: A Ranking of the Most Influential Persons in History* (New York: Hart, 1978), p. 33.

63. Hart, p. 33.

64. Religion demographer David Barrett estimates that there are 1,833 million Christians, or 33 percent of the world population, and 971 million Muslims, or 18 percent of the world population; in "Religious Statistics," Daphne Daume, ed., *Britannica Book of the Year* (Chicago: Encyclopaedia Britannica, 1993).

65. Francis Peters, "The Quest of the Historical Muhammad," *International Journal of Middle East Studies* 23 (1991): 291–307.

66. A. Roy Eckardt, *Reclaiming the Jesus of History* (Minneapolis: Fortress, 1992), pp. 6–8; E. P. Sanders, *Jesus and Judaism* (Philadelphia: Fortress, 1985), p. 2.

67. Ahmed Ali, *Al-Qur'an* (Princeton: Princeton University Press, 1988); Arthur Arberry, *The Koran Interpreted* (London: Oxford University Press, 1982); Kenneth Cragg, *Readings in the Quran* (London: Collins, 1988); N. J. Dawood, *The Koran* (New York: Penguin, 1991); Thomas Irving, *The Qur'an* (Brattleboro, VT: Amana, 1985); Mohammed Pickthall, *The Meaning of the Glorious Koran* (New York: Mentor, 1953); Hanna Kassis, *A Concordance of the Quran* (Berkeley: University of California Press, 1983).

68. Alfred Guillaume, *The Life of Muhammad: A Translation of Ibn Ishaq's Sirat Rasul Allah* (Lahore: Oxford University Press, 1955); Muhammad Khan, trans., *Sahih al-Bukhari* (Chicago: Kazi Publishers, 1979), 9 vols.; James Robson, trans., *Mishkat Al-Masabih* (Lahore: Muhammad Ashraf Publishers, 1973), 2 vols.; Martin Lings, *Muhammad: His Life Based on the Earliest Sources* (New York: Inner Traditions International, 1983).

69. Fazlur Rahman, *Islam* (Chicago: University of Chicago Press, 1979); Hans Kung and Jurgen Moltman, *Christianity Among World Religions* (Edinburgh: Clark, 1986).

70. Karen Armstrong, *Muhammad* (San Francisco: Harper, 1991); Marcus Borg, *Jesus: A New Vision* (San Francisco: Harper, 1987).

71. Maulana Ali, *Muhammad and Christ* (Madras: SPCK, 1921).

72. Claus Schedl, *Muhammad und Jesus* (Wien: Herder, 1978).
73. Maxime Rodinson, *Mohammed* (New York: Vintage, 1974), p. 313.
74. William Phipps, *The Wisdom and Wit of Rabbi Jesus* (Louisville: Westminster/ John Knox, 1993), pp. 117–24.
75. Dagobert Runes, ed., *Dictionary of Philosophy* (Ames, IA: Littlefield, Adams, 1958).
76. The Westminster Shorter Catechism (London, 1647), question 1.
77. John Calvin, *Institutes of the Christian Religion* (1559) 2, 2, 15.
78. Johann Goethe, *Kunst und Altertum* (1832).
79. Mark 10:11–12.
80. Paul Knitter, *No Other Name?* (Maryknoll, NY: Orbis, 1985), p. 225.

CHAPTER 2: *Antecedents*

1. Numbers 13:27.
2. Josephus, *Antiquities* 17, 295.
3. Genesis 37:25.
4. 1 Kings 10:14–15.
5. 1 Kings 9:26–27.
6. Ezekiel 27:22.
7. DeLacy O'Leary, *Arabia Before Muhammad* (London: Kegan Paul, 1927), pp. 182–88.
8. Procopius, *History of the Wars* 1, 20, 9.
9. Ilse Kohler-Rollefson, "Camels and Camel Pastoralism in Arabia," *Biblical Archaeologist* 56 (December 1993): 183–84.
10. Judges 6:2–6, 11; 8:24.
11. 2 Chronicles 21:17.
12. Ammianus Marcellinus, *History* 14, 3-4.
13. Irfan Shahid, "Pre-Islamic Arabia" in P. M. Holt, ed., *The Cambridge History of Islam* (New York: Cambridge University Press, 1970), vol. 1, p. 24.
14. Q 2:183; Ishaq, *Sirat Rasul Allah*, p. 105 of Guillaume's translation (henceforth cited as "I").
15. I, p. 9.
16. Mircea Eliade, *Patterns in Comparative Religion* (New York: Sheed & Ward, 1958), pp. 227–28.
17. Maxime Rodinson, *Mohammed* (New York: Vintage, 1974), pp. 39–40.
18. I, p. 35.
19. Joseph Henninger, "Pre-Islamic Bedouin Religion," in Merlin Swartz, ed., *Studies on Islam* (Oxford: Oxford University Press, 1981), p. 13.
20. I, p. 9.
21. Chaim Bermant and Michael Weitzman, *Ebla* (New York: Times Books, 1979), p. 165.

22. William Phipps, *Genesis and Gender* (New York: Praeger, 1989), p. 2.

23. Walther Eichrodt, *Theology of the Old Testament* (Philadelphia: Westminster, 1961), p. 185.

24. Arthur Arberry, *Aspects of Islamic Civilization* (Ann Arbor: University of Michigan Press, 1967), p. 23.

25. Fazlur Rahman, *Islam* (Chicago: University of Chicago Press, 1979), p. 34.

26. 2 Kings 13:23.

27. Q 11:61.

28. Q 11:62.

29. Q 29:61–63.

30. Q 29:65, 31:32.

31. Wilhelm Schmidt, *The Origin and Growth of Religion* (London: Methuen, 1935), p. 193.

32. Herodotus, *History* 3, 8.

33. "Al-Lat," in *The Encyclopaedia of Islam* (London: Brill, 1986).

34. John Lawlor, *The Nabataeans in Historical Perspective* (Grand Rapids: Baker, 1974), p. 121.

35. Lawlor, p. 121.

36. Epiphanius, *Pararion* 51 in John Trimingham, *Christianity Among the Arabs in Pre-Islamic Times* (London: Longman, 1979), p. 80.

37. Jack Finegan, *The Archeology of World Religions* (Princeton: Princeton University Press, 1952), p. 483.

38. Exodus 3:6; Mark 12:26.

39. I, p. 84.

40. Morris Seale, *Quran and Bible* (London: Croom Helm, 1978), p. 16.

41. John Glubb, *The Life and Times of Muhammad* (New York: Stein & Day, 1970), p. 243.

42. William Albright, *The Biblical Period from Abraham to Ezra* (New York: Harper, 1963), p. 5.

43. Genesis 16:1–17:20.

44. Genesis 17:25.

45. Genesis 21:9–21.

46. Genesis 25:12–18.

47. Trimingham, pp. 10–11, 313.

48. Louis Ginzberg, *Legends of the Bible* (New York: Simon & Schuster, 1956), p. 124.

49. Gordon Newby, *A History of the Jews of Arabia* (Columbia: University of South Carolina Press, 1988), pp. 18–19, 33–34.

50. Sozomen, *Church History* 6, 38.

51. Josephus, *Antiquities* 1, 214 and 221.

52. Acts 2:11.

53. Philostorgius, *Church History* 3, 5.

54. Hartwig Hirschfeld, *Jewish Quarterly Review* 1 (1910): 447.

55. Newby, *A History of the Jews of Arabia*, p. 75.

56. Newby, *A History of the Jews of Arabia*, pp. 48–49, 75.

57. Heinrich Graetz, *History of the Jews* (Philadelphia: The Jewish Publication Society, 1902), vol. 3, pp. 53–54, 60.

58. "Bible: Arabic," *Encyclopaedia Judaica* (Jerusalem: Keter, 1971).

59. Gordon Newby, *The Making of the Last Prophet* (Columbia: University of South Carolina Press, 1989), p. 12.

60. Rodinson, p. 64.

61. I, p. 99.

62. I, p. 100.

63. Rodinson, pp. 15–16.

64. I, p. 66–68.

65. "*Dahr*", *The Encyclopaedia of Islam* (London: Brill, 1965).

66. Rodinson, *Mohammed*, p. 18.

67. Tarafa, *Mu'allaq*, in Trimingham, p. 244, and in Seale, p. 15.

68. Theodor Noeldeke, "Arabs (Ancient)," James Hastings, ed., *Encyclopaedia of Religion and Ethics* (New York: Scribner's, 1928).

69. Q 44:35.

70. Job 7:9, 14:12.

71. Morris Seale in Arnold Toynbee, ed., *Life after Death* (New York: McGraw-Hill, 1976), p. 123; Emil Homerin, "Echoes of a Thirsty Owl: Death and Afterlife in Pre-Islamic Arabic Poetry," *Journal of Near Eastern Studies* 44 (1985): 165–184.

72. Noeldeke, "Arabs (Ancient)."

73. Toshihiko Izutsu, *Ethio-Religious Concepts in the Quran* (Montreal: McGill University, 1966), p. 86.

74. Izutsu, pp. 51–52, 75–104.

75. Dwight Donaldson, *Studies in Muslim Ethics* (London: SPCK, 1953), p. 7.

76. E. g., Matthew 9:13, cp. Hosea 6:6; Mark 4:12, cp. Isaiah 6:9–10; Luke 7:22, cp. Isaiah 35:5–6.

77. Matthew 21:16; Psalm 8:2.

78. Mark 14:26.

79. Mark 15:34, cp. Psalm 22:1; Luke 23:46, cp. Psalm 31:5.

80. William Phipps, *Assertive Biblical Women* (Westport, CT: Greenwood, 1992), pp. 3–5.

81. *Sirach* 25:24, 42:13–14.

82. *Aboth* 2:7.

83. Josephus, *Life* 10; *Against Apion* 200.

84. *Shabbat* 2, 5b.

85. *Mekilta Exodus* 21, 7 and 20, cp. Exodus 21:7.

86. *Berakoth* 3:3.

87. Josephus, *Against Apion* 2, 103.

88. *Sotah* 3:4.

89. *Nedarim* 4:3.

90. Judith Wegner, *Chattel or Person* (New York: Oxford, 1988), p. 162.

91. Wegner, p. 198.

92. Leviticus 15:19

93. *Niddah* 4:7.

94. *Niddah* 7:1.

95. *Mikwaoth* 8:5.

96. Numbers 5:11–28.

97. *Sotah* 1:5–6.

98. *Sotah* 3:4.

99. Elise Boulding, *The Underside of History* (Boulder, CO: Westview, 1976), pp. 286–96.

100. Nabia Abbott, "Pre-Islamic Arab Queens," *American Journal of Semitic Languages and Literatures* 58 (1941): 1–22.

101. Nabia Abbott, "Women and the State on the Eve of Islam," *American Journal of Semitic Languages and Literatures* 58 (1941): p. 259.

102. Abbott, pp. 261–262.

103. Stanley Lane-Poole, *The Speeches and Table-Talk of the Prophet Mohammad* (New York: Macmillan, 1905), p. xv; the poetry was translated by C. J. Lyall and published in *Journal of the Asiatic Society of Bengal* (1877).

104. Lane-Poole, p. xvi.

105. William Smith, *Kinship and Marriage in Early Arabia* (London: Black, 1903), pp. 96, 104–105.

106. Genesis 34:12.

107. Deuteronomy 25:5–10.

108. Leila Ahmed, "Women and the Advent of Islam," *Signs* 11 (1986): p. 680.

109. Geoffrey Parrinder, *Sex in the World's Religions* (New York: Oxford, 1980), p. 158.

110. Smith, pp. 82–86, 147–79; Ira Lapidus, *A History of Islamic Societies* (Cambridge: Cambridge University Press, 1988), p. 29.

111. Ammianus Marcellinus, *History* 14, 4.

112. Ilse Lichtenstadter, *Women in the Aiyam Al-Arab* (London: Royal Asiatic Society, 1935), p. 86.

113. Gustave von Grunebaum, *Classical Islam* (London: Unwin, 1970), pp. 24–26.

114. Reuven Firestone, *Journeys in Holy Lands* (Albany: State University of New York Press, 1990), pp. 158–89.

CHAPTER 3: *Early Life*

1. 1 Corinthians 15:3–8.

2. In Tor Andrae, *Mohammed* (New York: Harper, 1960), p. 34.

3. I, pp. 58, 73, 79–81.
4. Quoted in Alfred Guillaume, *Islam* (Baltimore: Penguin, 1954), p. 26.
5. Guillaume, p. 26.
6. I, pp. 82, 792.
7. Ehsan Yar-Shater, ed., *The History of al-Tabari* (Albany: State University of New York Press, 1988), vol. 6, p. 49.
8. I, p. 83.
9. Q 93:8.
10. Alfred Guillaume, *New Light on the Life of Muhammad* (Manchester: University of Manchester Press, 1960), p. 27.
11. I, p. 84–86.
12. I, p. 102, 105.
13. Q 97:1.
14. Q 53:7–10.
15. Q 96:1.
16. Q 96:1–5.
17. Jeremiah 1:4–6.
18. Jeremiah 20:7–9.
19. Q 28:86.
20. I, p. 106.
21. I, p. 106.
22. I, p. 107.
23. I, p. 107.
24. Q 10:94.
25. Q 53:36–37.
26. Fatima Mernissi, *The Veil and the Male Elite* (New York: Addison-Wesley, 1991), p. 103.
27. I, p. 155.
28. I, p. 121.
29. Luke 3:2–9; Acts 2:14–24.
30. Q 106:3–5.
31. Q 8:35, 37.
32. Q 10:15–16.
33. I, p. 119.
34. I, p. 119.
35. Q 68:51.
36. Q 8:30, 34.
37. Q 34:43.
38. I, p. 131.
39. I, p. 131.
40. I, p. 131.
41. I, p. 131.
42. I, p. 131.

43. I, p. 133.
44. I, p. 134.
45. Q 21:5.
46. Q 17:90.
47. Q 10:5–6.
48. Al-Bukhari, Sahih 18, 1; Mishkat 4, 51.
49. Q 25:8.
50. Q 6:7.
51. Q 29:50.
52. Q 29:51.
53. Huston Smith, *The World's Religions* (San Francisco: Harper, 1991), p. 227.
54. I, pp. 143–45, 159–60.
55. I, pp. 114–15.
56. I 155–58.
57. *Mishkat* 21, 4.
58. *Mishkat* 22, 1.
59. I, p. 151.
60. I, p. 152.
61. I, p. 167.
62. I 161.
63. Q 111:1–4.
64. Q 9:23.
65. Q 9:24.
66. I, p. 192.
67. I, p. 193.
68. I, p. 193.
69. Gordon Newby, *A History of the Jews of Arabia* (Columbia: University of South Carolina Press, 1988), pp. 40, 47.
70. I, p. 198.
71. I, pp. 201–08.
72. I, p. 94.
73. I, p. 259.
74. I, pp. 221–27.
75. Matthew 2:13–14, 19–21.
76. Josephus, *Antiquities* 17, 305–11; 18, 117; Mark 6:17–29.
77. *Kiddushin* 76b.
78. Genesis 17:12; Luke 2:21.
79. Leviticus 12:8; Luke 2:22–24.
80. Letter of Aristeas 184–86.
81. Matthew 1:16; 13:55; Luke 2:33; 4:22.
82. Matthew 1:19.
83. Luke 1:51–53.
84. George Moore, *Judaism* (New York: Schocken, 1971), vol. 1, pp. 303–4, 316–18.

85. Zechariah 2:12.
86. Ezekiel 5:5; William Phipps, "Cultural Commitments and World Maps," *Focus* 41 (1991): 7–8.
87. Luke 11:31.
88. Deuteronomy 16:16.
89. Leviticus 15.
90. Psalm 26:6.
91. Acts 21:24.
92. Psalm 122:1–6.
93. Luke 2:52.
94. *Aboth* 5:15
95. *Aboth* 5:15
96. William Phipps, *Was Jesus Married?* (New York: Harper, 1970), pp. 34–70.
97. Genesis 1:28, 2:24.
98. *Kiddushin* 4, 13.
99. Matthew 3:9–10.
100. Luke 13:3–9.
101. Isaiah 6:1–5.
102. 1 Kings 22:19–22; Isaiah 6:8–13; Ezekiel 1–3.
103. Mark 1:10–11.
104. Deuteronomy 8:3; Luke 4:3.
105. Psalm 91:5–8.
106. Psalm 91:11–12.
107. Q 8:9–13.
108. Mark 1:7.
109. 2 Kings 21:1–23:29.
110. Josephus, *Antiquities* 18, 190–92.
111. Deuteronomy 6:16.
112. Exodus 17:2–7.
113. Matthew 13:52.
114. Mark 2:22.
115. Hosea 6:6; Matthew 12:7.
116. Isaiah 40:9, 42:1–4, 49:6, 53:3–5.
117. Isaiah 53:3–5.
118. Mark 2:16–17.
119. Mark 1:15.
120. Mark 1:34, 3:2, 6:5.
121. Mark 5:34, 10:52.
122. Mark 6:5–6.
123. "Leprosy," George Buttrick, ed., *The Interpreter's Dictionary of the Bible* (Nashville: Abingdon, 1962).
124. Leviticus 13–14.
125. Mark 1:40–41.

126. Mark 14:3.
127. Luke 4:43.
128. Mark 1:21–22.
129. George Bernard Shaw, *Complete Plays with Prefaces* 5 (New York: Dodd, Mead, 1962): 345–46.
130. Mark 8:29–33; 14:29–31, 66–72.
131. Matthew 16:18.
132. Acts 5:29.
133. Luke 14:28–30.
134. *Gospel of Thomas* 82.
135. Luke 9:57–58.
136. Matthew 10:36; Micah 7:6.
137. Mark 3:21–35.
138. Luke 3:17.
139. Luke 7:19.
140. Luke 7:21–22; Isaiah 35:5–6.
141. Luke 4:18–19; Isaiah 61:1–2.
142. 1 Kings 16:31, 17:8–24.
143. 2 Kings 5:1–14.
144. Luke 4:22–28.
145. Luke 4:28–30.
146. Luke 4:24; Mark 6:4.

CHAPTER 4: *Later Life*

1. I, p. 228.
2. Q 24:58; Al-Bukhari, *Sahih* 3, 7.
3. Q 62:9.
4. Al-Bukhari, *Sahih* 11, 30.
5. Al-Bukhari, *Sahih* 11, 1.
6. *Mishkat* 4, 5.
7. I, p. 232.
8. I, p. 232.
9. I, pp. 231–33.
10. Q 88:21–22; 42:47.
11. Q 26:108.
12. W. Montgomery Watt, *Muhammad* (London: Oxford, 1964), p. 85.
13. I, p. 255.
14. Q 2:125, 142; I, p. 259.
15. Watt, p. 114.
16. Q 2:217.
17. Q 8:1, 41.
18. I, pp. 299, 304.

19. I, p. 300.

20. I, p. 300.

21. I, p. 308.

22. Ehsan Yar-Shater, ed., *The History of al-Tabari* 9 (Albany: State University of New York Press, 1990): 154; "Dhu'l Fakar," *Encyclopaedia of Islam* (London: Brill, 1965).

23. Q 62:5.

24. I, p. 363.

25. I, p. 363.

26. Q 3:12–13.

27. I, p. 751.

28. Watt, pp. 130–31.

29. I, p. 361.

30. I, pp. 437–38.

31. Q 59:3–4.

32. I, p. 369.

33. I, pp. 381–83, 389.

34. I, p. 385.

35. I, p. 386.

36. I, p. 386.

37. Q 3:152–53.

38. I, p. 450.

39. I, p. 452.

40. I, p. 454.

41. Ali Dashti, *Twenty-Three Years* (London: Allen & Unwin, 1985), p. 107.

42. I, p. 462.

43. I, p. 464.

44. I, p. 466.

45. Q 33:26–7.

46. Maxime Rodinson, *Mohammed* (New York: Vintage, 1974), p. 214.

47. Q 6:92, 42:7.

48. I, p. 502.

49. I, p. 504.

50. I, p. 507.

51. I, p. 438.

52. Al-Bukhari, *Sahih* 53, 26.

53. I, pp. 515–17.

54. I, p. 531.

55. I, pp. 546–52.

56. I, p. 530.

57. Genesis 28:18–19.

58. Joshua 24:26.

59. I, pp. 552–53.

60. Q 110:1–2; I, p. 628.
61. Q 49:14.
62. Dashti, p. 197.
63. Rodinson, pp. 268–69.
64. Fazlur Rahman, *Islam* (Chicago: Chicago University Press, 1979) pp. 24–25.
65. I, p. 605.
66. I, p. 607.
67. Q 9:38, 42.
68. I, pp. 659–60.
69. I, pp. 678–79.
70. Q 3:97.
71. *Mishkat* 11, 3.
72. Q 2:158.
73. Q 2:198.
74. I, p. 651.
75. Q 22:36, 37:107.
76. Q 2:196–97, 203.
77. I, pp. 678–82.
78. I, p. 689.
79. Al-Bukhari, *Sahih* 8, 55.
80. *Mishkat* 21, 5.
81. *Mishkat* 5, 6.
82. *Mishkat* 25, 3.
83. I, p. 682.
84. I, p. 683.
85. Q 3:144.
86. I, p. 688.
87. Robert Ellwood, *Many Peoples, Many Faiths* (Englewood Cliffs, NJ: Prentice-Hall, 1976), pp. 320–21.
88. Mark 2:1, 3:19.
89. Luke 3:19–20; Leviticus 20:21.
90. Josephus, *Antiquities* 18, 119.
91. Mark 6:17–28.
92. Josephus, *Antiquities* 18, 109–17.
93. Mark 6:15.
94. Luke 7:16.
95. Mark 6:14–16.
96. Luke 13:31.
97. Mark 3:6.
98. Mark 6:7–13.
99. Mark 8:34–36.
100. Josephus, *Antiquities* 17, 295.

101. Luke 9:23.
102. Luke 13:33.
103. Psalm 118:25, 27.
104. Mark 11:10.
105. Psalm of Solomon 17:23–27.
106. Mark 10:37.
107. Acts 12:2.
108. Mark 10:42–45.
109. Psalm 2:9.
110. Joel 3:10–16.
112. Isaiah 2:4, 9:6.
113. Jeremiah 27:2–13.
114. Jeremiah 38:4.
115. Luke 21:20–21.
116. Luke 13:34.
117. Jeremiah 22:5; Matthew 23:38.
118. Matthew 21:1–11.
119. Zechariah 9:9–10.
120. Zechariah 14:21.
121. Luke 19:41–44.
122. Jeremiah 26:12–13.
123. Marcus Borg, *Jesus: A New Vision* (San Francisco: Harper, 1987), p. 174.
124. Jeremiah 7:11–14; Mark 11:17, 13:1–2.
125. Isaiah 56:6–7; Mark 11:17.
126. Mark 11:27–12:12.
127. Mark 12:14.
128. Mark 12:17.
129. Mark 13:2.
130. Howard Kee and Franklin Young, *Understanding the New Testament* (Englewood Cliffs, NJ: Prentice-Hall, 1957), p. 159.
131. Mark 11:18; 14:1–2, 10.
132. John Crossan, *Jesus* (San Francisco: Harper, 1994), pp. 132–33, 196.
133. Jeremiah 31:27–34; 1 Corinthians 11:12.
134. Mark 14:22.
135. Mark 14:24.
136. Isaiah 53:12.
137. Mark 14:43–48.
138. Mark 14:61.
139. Mark 14:65.
140. Mark 14:53–65.
140. Jeremiah 26:11, 37:15.
141. John 18:31.
142. Mark 15:2.

143. Mark 15:10–15.
144. Claude Montefiore, *The Synoptic Gospels* (New York: Ktav, 1968), vol. 1, p. 352.
145. Raymond Brown, *The Death of the Messiah* (New York: Doubleday, 1994), vol. 1, pp. 515–47.
146. Mark 15:16–26.
147. Robert Funk, *The Five Gospels* (New York: Macmillan, 1993), p. 549.
148. David Flusser, *Jesus* (New York: Herder & Herder, 1969), p. 70.
149. Matthew 5:10, 6:33.
150. Mark 15:31.
151. Mark 14:50, 15:40–47.
152. John 19:40.
153. 1 Corinthians 15:3–5.
154. Psalm 118:22.
155. Mark 12:10–11; Ephesians 2:19–22; 1 Peter 2:4–7.
156. Psalm 118:23.

CHAPTER 5: *Scriptures*

1. John 1:14.
2. Rifiq Zakaria, *Muhammad and the Quran* (New York: Penguin, 1991), pp. 19, 24.
3. John Calvin, *Institutes of the Christian Religion* (1559), 1, 13, 11.
4. Q 43:4.
5. Q 85:21–22.
6. Q 56:78.
7. Q 46:12.
8. Q 39:28.
9. Q 10:37.
10. Q 42:51.
11. Q 2:97.
12. Zakaria, p. 3.
13. Al-Bukhari, *Sahih* 1, 2.
14. *Mishkat* 1, 6.
15. Cyril Glasse, "Koran," in *The Concise Encyclopedia of Islam* (San Francisco: Harper, 1989).
16. Q 42:15; 2:213.
17. Q 5:68.
18. Q 3:3–4.
19. Reuven Firestone, *Journeys in Holy Lands* (Albany: State University of New York Press, 1990), p. 156.
20. Q 6:84–87.
21. H. Freedman, ed., *Midrash Rabbah* (London: Soncino, 1939), vol. 1, pp. 310–11.

22. Q 21:65–71.
23. Genesis 1:26, 3:22, 11:7; Isaiah 6:8.
24. Genesis 21:14–15.
25. I, p. 45.
26. Q 3:96.
27. Psalm 84:6.
28. I, p. 62.
29. Q 2:124-133.
30. Al-Bukhari, *Sahih* 55, 9.
31. Q 22:26–28.
32. Firestone, pp. 135–51, 170–78; Isaac is named as the intended victim in *Mishkat* 14, 3; Ishmael is named by Ishaq in Gordon Newby, *The Making of the Last Prophet* (Columbia: University of South Carolina Press, 1969), p. 76.
33. Q 37:101–06.
34. Francis Peters, *Children of Abraham* (Princeton: Princeton University Press, 1982), pp. 197–98.
35. W. Montgomery Watt, *Muhammad* (London: Oxford, 1964), pp. 117–18.
36. Q 12:3.
37. Robert Bellah, *Beyond Belief* (New York: Harper, 1970), p. 150.
38. Q 20:11–13.
39. Exodus 3:5.
40. Exodus 34:29–35.
41. Q 73:1; 74:1.
42. Exodus 8:1.
43. Q 10:108.
44. Q 61:5.
45. Guilio Basetti-Sani, *The Koran in the Light of Christ* (Chicago: Franciscan Herald Press, 1977), p. 205.
46. Q 17:23.
47. Q 17:23–39.
48. Q 6:154.
49. Q 4:160.
50. Leviticus 11:4.
51. Q 16:123–24.
52. Exodus 17:9; Q 5:21–24.
53. Richard Bell, *The Origin of Islam in Its Christian Environment* (London: Cass, 1968), p. 160.
54. Q 33:25–27.
55. Martin Lings, *Muhammad: His Life Based on the Earliest Sources* (New York: Inner Traditions International, 1983), p. 232.
56. Deuteronomy 20:12–14.
57. Glasse, "Qurayzah."
58. Q 2:251.

59. Q 3:13.
60. Q 2:249; cp. Judges 7, 1 Samuel 17.
61. Q 28:38; cp. Esther 3:1, Genesis 11:1–9.
62. I, p. 552.
63. Q 66:12.
64. Q 3:47.
65. Q 32:7–9.
66. Q 3:59.
67. Q 3:37.
68. Newby, p. 207.
69. Q 19:23.
70. Q 19:24–26.
71. Q 19:30–32.
72. Q 3:49.
73. Q 5:112–113.
74. Q 5:114.
75. Q 5:115.
76. Al-Bukhari, *Sahih* 92, 25.
77. John Kelsay, *Islam and War* (Louisville: Westminster/John Knox, 1993), p. 24.
78. Q 3:45.
79. Q 4:171.
80. Q 2:87, 253.
81. Mark 1:7.
82. John 3:30.
83. Q 61:6.
84. John 16:7.
85. I, p. 104.
86. Newby, pp. 209–10.
87. Newby, p. 210.
88. Newby, p. 150.
89. Q 2:173.
90. Q 22:36.
91. *Mishkat* 1, 6.
92. Q 13:39.
93. Q 16:101.
94. Muhammad Asad, *The Message of the Quran* (London: Brill, 1980), p. 23; Ahmed Ali, *Al-Qur'an*, in Q 2:106.
95. Daniel 6:10; Q 2:142–45.
96. Q 7:157.
97. Q 3:20, 75; Ahmed Ali, *Al-Qur'an* (Princeton: Princeton University Press, 1988), p. 153.
98. I, pp. 231, 656.

99. Q 25:4–5.

100. Q 16:103.

101. Maxime Rodinson, *Mohammed* (New York: Vintage, 1974), p. 61.

102. *Mishkat* 26, 5; David Halperin, "The Ibn Sayyad Traditions," *Journal of the American Oriental Society* 96 (1976): 213–25.

103. David McKain, ed., *Christianity: Some Non-Christian Appraisals* (New York: McGraw-Hill, 1964), p. 244.

104. Q 33:40.

105. *Mishkat* 21, 2.

106. John 6:27.

107. W. Montgomery Watt, *Islam and Christianity Today* (London: Routledge and Kegan Paul, 1983), p. 38.

108. I, p. 649.

109. I, p. 649.

110. I, p. 377; Watt, *Muhammad*, p. 225.

111. John Trimingham, *Christianity Among the Arabs in Pre-Islamic Times* (London: Longman, 1979), p. 142.

112. Mani, *Shabuhragan* in Francis Burkitt, *The Religion of the Manichees* (Cambridge, England: Cambridge University Press, 1925), p. 37.

113. Al-Bukhari, *Sahih* 61, 23.

114. Al-Bukhari, *Sahih* 61, 3.

115. Charles Adams, "Quran," in Mircea Eliade, ed., *The Encyclopedia of Religion* (New York: Macmillan, 1987).

116. Peters, pp. 39–40.

117. Nadeem Khan, *The Bulletin of Christian Institutes of Islamic Studies* 4 (1981): 159.

118. Khan, p. 158.

119. Mark 4:11–12.

120. Luke 15:11–32.

121. Mark 12:30.

122. Luke 11:9.

123. Matthew 16:15.

124. Matthew 16:16.

125. Matthew 16:17.

126. Psalms 8:3, 19:1.

127. Luke 12:22–27.

128. Q 16:68–69.

129. Q 2:20.

130. Luke 4:18–19.

131. Leviticus 25:10.

132. Mark 10:42–45.

133. Q 28:4–6.

134. Mark 12:26.

135. Mark 2:25–26, 7:6–7.

136. Luke 7:26–28.
137. E.g., Genesis 32:26–30; Exodus 3:3–6; Isaiah 6.
138. E.g., Genesis 6:13; 1 Samuel 15:10; Jeremiah 1:4–5.
139. Mark 1:10–11.
140. Millar Burrows, *An Outline of Biblical Theology* (Philadelphia: Westminster, 1946), p. 32.
141. Matthew 13:17.
142. Matthew 5:21–22.
143. Exodus 20:1, 21:24.
144. Matthew 5:21–38.
145. John Meier, *The Vision of Matthew* (New York: Crossroad, 1991) pp. 64, 133.
146. Deuteronomy 6:1, 23:1.
147. Isaiah 56:4–5.
148. Philip Sigal, *The Halakhah of Jesus of Nazareth According to the Gospel of Matthew* (Lanham, MD: University Press of America, 1987), p. 16.
149. Q 3:50.
150. Mark 7:18–22.
151. Mark 13:32.
152. Mark 13:33–37.
153. Q 7:187.
154. Matthew 7:15.
155. *Mishkat* 25, 6.
156. Deuteronomy 18:15.
157. Acts 3:22, 7:37.
158. I, p. 160.
159. Matthew 10:19–20.
160. John 16:13.
161. Acts 21:9; 1 Corinthians 11:5.
162. 1 Corinthians 12:28.
163. 1 Timothy 4:14; Justin, *Dialogue with Trypho* 82; Eusebius, *Church History* 5, 17.
164. Numbers 27:1–11; Deuteronomy 21:15–17.
165. Q 4:11–12.
166. Luke 12:13–21.
167. Luke 5:39.
168. Q 5:104.
169. Luke 6:39.
170. Luke 11:52.
171. Luke 11:47–48.
172. Luke 11:42, 46.
173. *Shabbat* 7:2.
174. 1 Samuel 21:1–6.
175. Leviticus 24:5–9.

176. Mark 2:27.
177. Acts 8:14, 11:1–2.
178. *Aboth* 2:8.
179. Gospel of Thomas 108.
180. Q 3:36.
181. Al-Bukhari, *Sahih* 60, 54.
182. Q 3:42.
183. Edward Gibbon, *The Decline and Fall of the Roman Empire* (1776), chapter 50.
184. Quoted in Mahmoud Ayoub, *The Qur'an and Its Interpreters* (Albany: State University of New York Press, 1992), vol. 2, p. 191.
185. Ayoub, vol. 2, p. 191.
186. Q 5:82–83.
187. I, p. 271.
188. William Hone, ed., *The Lost Books of the Bible* (New York: Bell, 1979), p. 38.
189. Hone, p. 53.
190. Mark 3:31–35; John 2:2–4.

CHAPTER 6: *Personal Conduct*

1. Q 73:20, 76:26.
2. Q 62:9.
3. Q 6:121.
4. Al-Bukhari, *Sahih* 19, 12.
5. Q 5:6.
6. I, p. 112.
7. Q 48:29.
8. Wisdom of Solomon 16:28; Psalm 88:13.
9. Qumran Community Rule 11:10.
10. Mark 1:35.
11. Mark 6:46.
12. Mark 11:25, 14:35; Luke 22:41.
13. Mark 6:41, 14:22.
14. Luke 5:33.
15. Mark 14:36.
16. Q 18:23–24.
17. Matthew 6:5.
18. Mark 7:6–7; Isaiah 29:13.
19. Q 4:142.
20. Q 4:43.
21. Al-Bukhari, *Sahih* 9, 13.
22. Q 48:29.
23. Q 14:24–26.
24. Luke 8:8–15, 13:18–19.

25. Q 1:1–7.
26. Luke 11:1–4.
27. Psalm 103:13.
28. Ignaz Goldziher, *Muslim Studies* (Albany: State University of New York Press, 1971), p. 350.
29. Matthew 6:12.
30. Matthew 5:23–24.
31. Matthew 18:21–22.
32. Luke 23:34.
33. Q 24:22.
34. *Mishkat* 12, 9.
35. *Mishkat* 16, 1.
36. *Mishkat* 13, 18.
37. Frithjof Schuon, *Dimensions of Islam* (London: Allen and Unwin, 1970), pp. 13–29; William Phipps, *Wisdom and Wit of Rabbi Jesus* (Louisville: Westminster/John Knox, 1993), pp. 90–93, 197.
38. Q 28:16; cp. Exodus 2:11–12.
39. Q 7:151; cp. Exodus 32:32.
40. Q 48:2.
41. *Mishkat* 10, 3.
42. Q 47:19.
43. Q 3:16.
44. Q 60:4.
45. Q 60:8.
46. I, p. 308.
47. I, p. 676.
48. I, p. 676.
49. I, p. 676.
50. I, p. 676.
51. I, p. 676; William Muir, *The Life of Mahomet* (London: Smith, Elder, 1894), p. 232.
52. W. Montgomery Watt, *Muhammad* (London: Oxford Press, 1964), p. 123.
53. I, p. 551.
54. Q 18:110, 41:6.
55. Q 17:93.
56. Q 46:9.
57. Q 31:18–19.
58. Q 17:37.
59. *Mishkat* 24, 13.
60. Q 80:1–6.
61. I, p. 167.
62. Annemarie Schimmel, *And Muhammad Is His Messenger* (Chapel Hill: University of North Carolina Press, 1985), p. 47.

63. Schimmel, p. 47.

64. Al-Bukhari, *Sahih* 4, 60.

65. *Mishkat* 25, 1 and 2.

66. Edward Gibbon, *The Decline and Fall of the Roman Empire* (1776), chapter 50.

67. Luke 12:27–28.

68. Mark 12:38–39.

69. Luke 14:8–11.

70. Mark 9:35–37.

71. Luke 22:27.

72. Mark 10:45.

73. John 13:5.

74. 1 Samuel 25:41.

75. Q 4:172.

76. Matthew 11:28–29.

77. Celsus, *On the True Doctrine* (New York: Oxford, 1987), p. 73.

78. Luke 14:12–14.

79. Albert Nolan, *Jesus Before Christianity* (Maryknoll, NY: Orbis, 1978), p. 58.

80. Bernard Shaw, *Complete Plays* (New York: Dodd, Mead, 1962), vol. 5, p. 422.

81. Charles H. Dodd, *The Founder of Christianity* (New York: Macmillan, 1970), pp. 110–12.

82. Psalm 8:4.

83. Psalm 8:5.

84. James Charlesworth, ed., *Jesus' Jewishness* (New York: Crossroad, 1991), p. 100.

85. John Crossan, *The Historical Jesus* (San Francisco: Harper, 1991), p. 243.

86. John Crossan, *Jesus* (San Francisco: Harper, 1994), p. 51.

87. 2 Corinthians 5:21; 1 John 3:5; 1 Peter 2:21–24; Hebrews 4:15.

88. Mark 10:18.

89. Mark 1:4.

90. Matthew 6:1–18; Luke 18:9–14.

91. Matthew 25:37–39.

92. W. Montgomery Watt, *Muhammad in Medina* (Oxford: Clarendon, 1956), pp. 322–23.

93. *Mishkat* 4, 20.

94. Al-Bukhari, *Al Adab* 18.

95. I, p. 535.

96. Al-Bukhari, *Sahih* 72, 25.

97. Q 93:9–11.

98. Q 2:233.

99. Mark 10:14.

100. Exodus 21:15, 17; Leviticus 20:9.

101. Deuteronomy 21:18–21.

102. Matthew 18:6, 10.

103. Matthew 18:3.
104. Matthew 11:17.
105. Mark 6:3.
106. Matthew 21:15–16.
107. Mark 2:22.
108. Isaiah 40:9, 42:9.
109. Mark 10:24; John 21:5.
110. Luke 3:23.
111. Mark 14:36.
112. Luke 23:46.
113. Psalm 31:5.
114. Luke 10:21.
115. Q 91:8–10.
116. Q 2:30.
117. Q 15:28–43.
118. Q 29:2.
119. Q 6:112.
120. Q 22:52.
121. Q 7:200.
122. *Mishkat* 13, 15.
123. Q 17:73–74.
124. Rafiq Zakaria, *Muhammad and the Quran* (New York: Penguin Books, 1991), p. 12.
125. Ehsan Yar-Shater, ed., *The History of al-Tabari* (Albany: State University of New York Press, 1988), vol. 6, p. 109.
126. Q 53:19–23; I, p. 166.
127. Q 22:52.
128. Genesis 6:5; *Berakoth* 9:5.
129. Jeffrey Russell, *Satan* (Ithaca: Cornell University Press, 1981), pp. 219–30.
130. Sirach 21:27.
131. Mark 7:21.
132. Matthew 16:17.
133. Matthew 16:23.
134. Mark 14:38.
135. Q 7:179.
136. Q 8:21–22.
137. Q 17:36.
138. Q 16:125.
139. Luke 2:46.
140. Luke 8:15.
141. Luke 8:8.
142. Q 16:67.
143. Q 2:219.

144. Q 5:90.
145. Fazlur Rahman, *Islam* (Chicago: University of Chicago Press, 1979), p. 38.
146. Q 2:183.
147. Deuteronomy 9:9; Leviticus 16:29.
148. Matthew 4:2.
149. Q 73:2–6, 20.
150. Q 2:184–87.
151. David Knowles, *Christian Monasticism* (New York: McGraw-Hill, 1969), pp. 124–34.
152. Basil, *Ascetic Works*, The Long Rules, 17.
153. Q 24:32.
154. Q 7:32–33.
155. Q 57:27.
156. Matthew 6:25.
157. Luke 7:33–34, 21:34.
158. Mark 2:18–19.
159. Matthew 6:16–17.
160. Matthew 5:29.
161. Goldziher, pp. 359–60.
162. Al-Bukhari, *Sahih* 62, 2.
163. I, p. 675.
164. Goldziher, p. 358.
165. Q 104:1–3.
166. Q 102:1–6.
167. Q 3:180.
168. Al-Bukhari, *Sahih* 60, 66.
169. Watt, *Muhammad*, pp. 51–52.
170. Q 3:130.
171. I, p. 650.
172. Maxime Rodinson, *Islam and Capitalism* (London: Penguin, 1974), p. 14.
173. Q 38:21–25; 2 Samuel 12:1–7.
174. Q 107.
175. Q 25:67.
176. Q 17:26, 28.
177. Q 57:7.
178. Q 63:10–11.
179. Arthur Jeffery, ed., *A Reader on Islam* (The Hague: Mouton, 1962), pp. 83–84.
180. Q 2:184; I, pp. 235–36.
181. Q 2:264–65.
182. Q 2:264, 271.
183. Q 57:18.
184. Q 30:46.

185. Q 6:118.
186. Q 2:263.
187. *Mishkat* 12, 17.
188. Q 10:60.
189. Q 36:32–35.
190. Q 17:67.
191. Q 16:78, 83.
192. Q 10:58.
193. Mark 6:41, 14:22–23.
194. Luke 17:12–19.
195. Mark 12:41–44.
196. James 1:27.
197. Justin, *Apology* 1, 67.
198. Luke 8:3.
199. Ernest Renan, *The Life of Jesus* (London: Dent, 1927), p. 103.
200. Luke 18:24.
201. Luke 19:9; *soteria*, now commonly translated as "salvation," meant restoration to wholeness and was translated as "health" by Wycliffe and Tyndale.
202. Genesis 13:2.
203. Luke 16:22–30.
204. Acts 20:35.
205. Luke 7:38.
206. Luke 7:40–47.
207. Mark 14:3–6.
208. Luke 12:42–44; Matthew 20:8.
209. Luke 16:8.
210. Matthew 25:14–25.
211. Luke 15:31.
212. Matthew 10:8.
213. Luke 12:15.
214. Luke 12:16–19.
215. Q 18:33–43.
216. Luke 12:25.
217. Luke 12:24.
218. Luke 12:22–31.
219. Luke 12:32–34.
220. *Mishkat* 25, 1.
221. Proverbs 19:17.
222. Luke 16:13.
223. Luke 11:39.
224. Luke 11:41.
225. Matthew 6:1.
226. Matthew 12:7.

227. Q 22:37.
228. Matthew 5:42.
229. Matthew 7:6.
230. *Didache* 1:5–6.

CHAPTER 7: *Social Teachings*

1. Elisabeth Fiorenza, *In Memory of Her* (New York: Crossroad, 1983), pp. 140–54; Leonard Swidler, *Biblical Affirmations of Woman* (Philadelphia: Westminster Press, 1979), pp. 163–328, 352–56; Rosemary Ruether, *Religion and Sexism* (New York: Simon & Schuster, 1974), pp. 137–42.
2. Luke 10:38–42.
3. Luke 8:1–3; Mark 15:40–41.
4. John 20:17–18; Romans 16:1–7.
5. Luke 11:31.
6. John 8:4.
7. Leviticus 20:10; Deuteronomy 22:23–24.
8. John 8:7.
9. John 8:2–11.
10. Luke 13:16.
11. Luke 8:2.
12. Mark 8:31–33, 9:30–32, 10:32–37.
13. Mark 14:9.
14. John Crossan, *Jesus* (San Francisco: Harper, 1994), p. 192.
15. Leviticus 15:19.
16. Leviticus 15:25–27.
17. Mark 5:25–34.
18. Claude Montefiore, *The Synoptic Gospels* (New York: Ktav, 1968), vol. 1, p. 389.
19. Matthew 25:1–3; Luke 13:21, 18:1–5.
20. Mark 12:40.
21. Deuteronomy 24:1.
22. *Yebamoth* 14:1.
23. Matthew 19:3.
24. *Gettin* 9:10.
25. *Gettin* 9:10.
26. *Ketuboth* 7:6.
27. Genesis 2:18.
28. Mark 10:8.
29. Mark 10:5–12.
30. Genesis 24.
31. *Mishkat* 13, 3.
32. Q 30:21.

33. Q 4:129.
34. Q 2:223.
35. Isma'il Faruqi, *The Great Asian Religions* (New York: Macmillan, 1969), p. 314.
36. *Mishkat* 13, 6.
37. *Mishkat* 13, 4.
38. Leila Ahmed, *Women and Gender in Islam* (New Haven: Yale University Press, 1992), pp. 44–45.
39. Q 4:3.
40. Q 4:129.
41. Q 33:4.
42. Syed Ali, *The Spirit of Islam* (London: Chatto and Windus, 1964), p. 246.
43. Fazlur Rahman, *Islam* (Chicago: University of Chicago Press, 1979), p. 29.
44. Ahmed Ali, *Al-Qur'an* (Princeton: Princeton University Press, 1988), p. 73.
45. Karen Armstrong, *Muhammad* (San Francisco: Harper, 1992), p. 191.
46. Q 4:15.
47. Q 24:6–8.
48. Q 24:2.
49. *Mishkat* 26, 1.
50. I, p. 267.
51. I, p. 267.
52. Q 4:128.
53. Q 4:34.
54. I, p. 651.
55. I, p. 651.
56. Al-Bukhari, *Sahih* 62, 132.
57. Q 4:35.
58. Q 60:10.
59. Q 65:4.
60. Q 2:228–29, 4:11.
61. Q 64:14.
62. Al-Bukhari, *Sahih*, 55, 1; 62, 80.
63. I, pp. 493–94.
64. Q 24:11–20.
65. Arthur Jeffery, ed., *A Reader on Islam* (The Hague: Mouton, 1962), p. 332; *Mishkat* 26, 20.
66. Ahmed, pp. 52–53.
67. Q 5:5.
68. Q 66:3.
69. Nabia Abbott, *Aishah* (Chicago: University of Chicago Press, 1942), pp. 38, 45, 67.
70. Quoted in Charles Eaton, *Islam and the Destiny of Man* (Albany: State University of New York Press, 1985), p. 123.
71. Abbott, pp. 61–66.

72. Al-Bukhari, *Sahih* 73, 20.

73. Q 33:50.

74. Q 33:51.

75. Fatima Mernissi, *The Veil and the Male Elite* (New York: Addison-Wesley, 1991), p. 174.

76. Q 2:240.

77. I, p. 99.

78. *Mishkat* 13, 3; Ehsan Yar-Shater, ed., *The History of al-Tabari* (Albany: State University of New York Press, 1990), vol. 9, p. 131.

79. I 493.

80. I 515, 517.

81. Al-Bukhari, *Sahih* 62, 16.

82. Q 33:53.

83. Q 24:60, 33:59.

84. Q 24:31.

85. Abbott, p. vii.

86. Al-Bukhari, *Sahih* 5, 13.

87. Q 2:222.

88. *Mishkat* 3:13; Al-Bukhari, *Sahih* 6, 7.

89. Mernissi, p. 104.

90. W. Montgomery Watt, *Muhammad* (London: Oxford Press, 1964), pp. 156–57.

91. William Smith, *Kinship and Marriage in Early Arabia* (London: Black, 1903), p. 52.

92. Watt, p. 158.

93. Q 33:37.

94. Q 33:53.

95. Al-Bukhari, *Sahih* 60, 241.

96. *Mishkat* 13:1.

97. *Mishkat* 13:1.

98. *Mishkat* 13:1.

99. *Mishkat* 13:1.

100. Q 74:13.

101. Q 33:53.

102. Abbott, *Aishah*, p. 66.

103. Edwin Burtt, *Man Seeks the Divine* (New York: Harper, 1970), p. 411.

104. Armstrong, p. 191.

105. Armstrong, p. 191.

106. Q 4:11-12.

107. *Mishkat* 12, 20.

108. Rahman, p. 38.

109. Maulana Ali, *Muhammad the Prophet* (Lahore: Ahmadiyya Press, 1924), p. 28.

110. Q 2:228; see the translations by Ahmed Ali and N. J. Dawood.

111. Q 17:31.
112. Sarah Pomeroy, *Goddesses, Whores, Wives and Slaves* (New York: Schocken Books, 1975), pp. 140, 228.
113. *Oxyrhynchus Papyri* 4:744.
114. Q 16:58–59.
115. Q 81:8–9.
116. Q 24:33.
117. Q 16:57.
118. Q 43:18–19.
119. Q 33:35.
120. Q 49:10–11.
121. Q 4:19.
122. Q 4:4, 20.
123. *Mishkat* 13, 8.
124. Q 4:124, 40:40.
125. Al-Bukhari, *Sahih* 76, 51.
126. Jane Smith and Yvonne Haddad, "Women in the Afterlife," *Journal of the American Academy of Religion*, 43 (1975): 44–45.
127. Genesis 9:21–25.
128. Q 66:10.
129. 1 Kings 10:1–13.
130. Q 27:22–44.
131. *Mishkat* 17, 1.
132. Nabia Abbott, "Women and the State in Early Islam," *Journal of Near Eastern Studies* 1 (1942): 107.
133. Tor Andrae, *Mohammed* (New York: Harper and Row, 1960), pp. 78–79.
134. Ilse Lichtenstadter, *Women in the Aiyam Al-Arab* (London: Royal Asiatic Society, 1935), p. 81.
135. Al-Bukhari, *Sahih* 62, 37.
136. Ahmed, pp. 42, 53, 62.
137. Leila Ahmed, "Women and the Advent of Islam," *Signs* 11 (1986): 668–91.
138. *Mishkat* 25, 1.
139. Matthew 5:43.
140. Leviticus 19:18.
141. Deuteronomy 23:3–6.
142. 1 Kings 8:41–45.
143. Howard Kee, *The New Testament in Context* (Englewood Cliffs, NJ: Prentice-Hall, 1984), p. 203.
144. Norman Perrin, *Rediscovering the Teaching of Jesus* (New York: Harper, 1967), p. 94.
145. *Tohoroth* 7:6.
146. *Abodah Zarah* 2:1.
147. Luke 2:52.

148. Isaiah 49:3–6.
149. Isaiah 42:4.
150. Matthew 12:15–21; Luke 2:32.
151. Mark 5:1–20.
152. Mark 7:24–30; cp. Matthew 15:21–28.
153. *Aboth* 1:5.
154. Matthew 15:24.
155. Matthew 15:26.
156. Matthew 10:5.
157. Matthew 28:19.
158. Luke 7:1–10.
159. Luke 10:29–37, 17:11–19.
160. Luke 10:13–15, 11:29–32, 12:48.
161. Luke 3:38.
162. Luke 9:54.
163. *Mishkat* 20, 2.
164. Ernest Renan, *The Life of Jesus* (London: Dent, 1927), p. 70.
165. Q 49:13.
166. Muhammad Asad, *The Message of the Quran* (London: Brill, 1980), p. 794.
167. Q 7:172–73.
168. Q 5:51.
169. Q 3:110.
170. Q 9:28.
171. Jacques Jomier, *How to Understand Islam* (New York: Crossroad, 1989), p. 15.
172. Michael Cook, *Muhammad* (Oxford: Oxford University Press, 1983), p. 56.
173. Q 16:71, 75.
174. Q 24:33, 90:10–16.
175. *Mishkat* 16, 1.
176. I, p. 678.
177. *Mishkat* 13, 18.
178. Luke 7:2–9.
179. Luke 12:37, 43.
180. Mark 10:43–44.
181. Mark 7:1–5.
182. Luke 5:29–30, 15:2.
183. John 7:49.
184. Jacob Neusner, *From Politics to Piety* (Englewood Cliffs, NJ: Prentice-Hall, 1973), p. 80.
185. Cp. Exodus 20:3 with 17:16.
186. Numbers 31:18.
187. Joshua 6:17–21.
188. James Pritchard, ed., *Ancient Near Eastern Texts* (Princeton: Princeton University Press, 1955), pp. 175–78; Deuteronomy 19:21.

189. Genesis 50:15–21; Proverbs 20:22; 25:21–22; Romans 12:17–21.
190. Isaiah 1:21–23, 2:4.
191. Acts 10:36.
192. Matthew 5:9.
193. Matthew 26:51–52.
194. Tertullian, *On Idolatry* 19.
195. Tertullian, *On Idolatry* 19.
196. Roland Bainton, *Christian Attitudes Toward War and Peace* (Nashville: Abingdon, 1960) p. 66.
197. Arnold Toynbee, *Christianity Among the Religions of the World* (New York: Scribner's, 1957), p. 68.
198. Eusebius, *Life of Constantine* 1, 28.
199. Eusebius, *Life of Constantine* 1, 28.
200. William Phipps, *Death: Confronting the Reality* (Atlanta: John Knox, 1987), pp. 106–08.
201. In Hans Kung and Jurgen Moltmann, eds., *Christianity Among World Religions* (Edinburgh: Clark, 1986), p. 7.
202. Stephen Neill, *A History of Christian Missions* (New York: Penguin, 1990), p. 96.
203. Q 22:77–78.
204. Q 49:15.
205. Cyril Glasse, "Sword of Islam," *The Concise Encyclopedia of Islam* (San Francisco: Harper, 1989); I have been unable to find this greater *jihad* saying in the *hadith*.
206. *Mishkat* 17, 1.
207. Q 41:34–35.
208. Q 42:41.
209. Q 16:126.
210. I, p. 213.
211. Q 2:106.
212. Q 2:190–91.
213. Q 5:33.
214. Q 5:33.
215. Q 22:40.
216. Q 8:67–70, 47:4.
217. *Mishkat* 5, 5.
218. John Kelsay, *Islam and War* (Louisville: Westminster/John Knox Press, 1993), p. 62.
219. Q 8:17.
220. Q 47:4, 6.
221. Q 8:65.
222. Q 9:5.
223. Those Muslim interpreters are named in "Quran," Thomas Hughes, ed., *A Dictionary of Islam* (Clifton, NJ: Reference Books Publishers, 1965).

224. Q 28:54, 23:96.

225. Faruq Sherif, *A Guide to the Contents of the Qur'an* (London: Ithaca Press, 1985), p. 39.

226. Sherif, pp. 95, 113–114.

227. Q 8:60; *The Washington Post* 5/15/94, p. A12.

228. Q 2:256.

229. Mahmoud Ayoub, *The Qur'an and Its Interpreters* (Albany: State University of New York Press, 1984), vol. 1, p. 253.

230. Josef van Ess in Hans Kung, *Christianity and the World Religions* (Garden City, NY: Doubleday, 1986), p. 105.

231. Q 9:29.

232. Gustave von Grunebaum, *Classical Islam* (London: Unwin, 1970), p. 48.

233. Q 9:21, 73.

234. David Margoliouth, *The Early Development of Mohammedanism* (London: Williams and Norgate, 1914), p. 2.

235. Al-Bukhari, *Sahih* 90, 1.

236. Al-Bukhari, *Sahih* 23, 71.

237. Axel Molberg, ed., *The Book of the Himyarites* (Lund: Gleerup, 1924), p. 9.

238. Molberg, p. 9.

239. John Trimingham, *Christianity Among the Arabs in Pre-Islamic Times* (London: Longman, 1979), pp. 298–99.

240. Q 85:3–8.

241. Glasse, "*Jihad.*"

242. Q 48:16–17.

243. Q 9:81.

244. Daniel 8:5–8.

245. Q 18:84–90.

246. Gordon Newby, *The Making of the Last Prophet* (Columbia: University of South Carolina Press, 1989), pp. 193–95.

247. Kenneth Cragg, *The Call of the Minaret* (New York: Oxford, 1964), p. 91.

248. John Trimingham, *Christianity Among the Arabs in Pre-Islamic Times* (London: Longman, 1979), p. 307.

249. Francis Peters, *Children of Abraham* (Princeton: Princeton University Press, 1982), p. 64.

250. Watt, p. 236.

251. Watt, p. 237.

CHAPTER 8: *Sanctions*

1. Q 2:115.

2. Q 65:12.

3. Q 2:255.

4. Q 25:61.

5. Q 41:37.
6. Q 45:24.
7. Fazlur Rahman, *Major Themes of the Qur'an* (Chicago: Bibliotheca Islamica, 1980), p. 12.
8. Rahman, p. 12.
9. Q 3:145.
10. Q 6:74–79.
11. Q 57:22.
12. Rahman, p. 15.
13. Q 13:11.
14. Q 10:108.
15. Q 23:12–14.
16. Q 25:47.
17. Q 16:40.
18. Q 19:66–67.
19. Q 16:80–81.
20. Q 9:40.
21. Q 9:40.
22. Q 29:60.
23. Q 6:59.
24. Q 58:7.
25. Q 50:16.
26. Q 24:35.
27. Q 42:11.
28. *Mishkat* 15, 3.
29. Q 15:29; cp. Genesis 2:7–8.
30. Q 4:164; 7:145; cp. Exodus 3:4; 34:1.
31. Q 13:33, 4:81, 8:17; cp. Psalm 2.
32. Max Muller, ed., *Sacred Books of the East* (Oxford: Clarendon, 1895), vol. 6, p. 26; cp. Deuteronomy 32:6.
33. Q 7:54; cp. Genesis 1; Isaiah 6:1–5.
34. Daniel 7:9.
35. Josef van Ess, "The Youthful God: Anthropomorphism in Early Islam," *Annual Lecture in Religion* (Arizona State University, 1988), p. 10.
36. Betty Kelen, *Muhammad* (Nashville: Nelson, 1975), p. 106.
37. Q 11:90.
38. E.g., Q 19:18, 26, 58, 61, 75, 87, 91, 92, 93, 96.
39. I, p. 231.
40. Q 3:76.
41. Q 49:9.
42. Q 3:146.
43. Q 3:146.

44. William Graham, *Divine Word and Prophetic Word in Early Islam* (The Hague: Mouton, 1977), p. 142.

45. Q 3:32.

46. Q 5:54.

47. Jacques Jomier, *How to Understand Islam* (New York: Crossroad, 1989), p. 93.

48. Q 28:77.

49. Q 24:22.

50. Q 93:6–10.

51. Q 92:19–20.

52. Q 76:8.

53. Matthew 5:35; Q 59:23.

54. Q 7:180.

55. *Mishkat* 10, 1.

56. Mark 5:19; Luke 6:35, 11:49.

57. Mark 14:62; Luke 6:48, 15:18.

58. John 4:20–24.

59. Luke 17:21.

60. Alfred, Lord Tennyson, *The Higher Pantheism* (1869), stanza 6.

61. Matthew 11:25.

62. Psalm 103:13; Isaiah 64:8; Malachi 2:10.

63. John 17:11.

64. Mark 12:29; Deuteronomy 6:5.

65. Mark 12:31; Leviticus 19:18.

66. Luke 10:29–37.

67. Matthew 5:44–45.

68. Matthew 5:48.

69. Luke 15:7.

70. Luke 12:6–7.

71. Psalm 50:11.

72. Luke 6:36.

73. Luke 15:13.

74. Luke 15:13.

75. Luke 15:20.

76. Luke 15:25–32.

77. Frederick Sontag, "Moon, Mohammad and Jesus," *Asia Journal of Theology* 3 (1989): 425, 427.

78. Q 105.

79. Q 30:1–5.

80. Q 33:36.

81. *Mishkat* 17, 1.

82. E.g., Q 4:59.

83. *Mishkat* 17, 1.

84. Q 4:135.

85. Q 5:8.
86. John Glubb, *The Life and Times of Muhammad* (New York: Stein & Day, 1970), p. 194.
87. I, pp. 312–13.
88. Matthew 10:34.
89. Q 21:105; Psalm 37:29.
90. Q 62:10.
91. Q 35:29–30.
92. Karen Armstrong, *Muhammad* (San Francisco: Harper, 1992), pp. 250, 264.
93. *Mishkat* 25, 5.
94. Q 34:16–17.
95. Matthew 5:45, 7:25.
96. Q 32:21.
97. Q 5:38.
98. Q 5:39.
99. Al-Bukhari, *Sahih* 81, 14.
100. *Mishkat* 16, 2.
101. Q 4:92.
102. Q 17:33.
103. Q 2:178.
104. *Mishkat* 15, 2.
105. Q 5:45.
106. *Mishkat* 15, 1.
107. Genesis 19; Q 7:80–84, 11:78–83, 15:67–77, 26:165–173, 27:54–58, 29:28–31, 54:33–38; see Khalid Duran, "Homosexuality and Islam" in Arlene Swidler, ed., *Homosexuality and World Religions* (Valley Forge: Trinity, 1993), pp. 181–184.
108. *Mishkat* 16, 1.
109. *Mishkat* 16, 1.
110. Jude 7; 2 Peter 2:6–7; 2 Esdras 2:8.
111. Luke 10:13–15.
112. Matthew 18:23–25.
113. Matthew 5:6–9.
114. J. Hamilton-Patterson and C. Andrews, *Mummies* (New York: Viking, 1979), p. 65.
115. William Phipps, *Death* (Atlanta: John Knox, 1987), pp. 163–66.
116. Daniel 12:2.
117. Q 3:169–70.
118. Q 10:45.
119. I, p. 678.
120. Al-Bukhari, *Sahih* 23, 85.
121. *Mishkat* 1, 5.
122. Al-Bukhari, *Sahih* 23, 87.

123. I, p. 306.
124. I, p. 306.
125. *Mishkat* 1, 5.
126. Q 23:100.
127. *Mishkat* 5, 6; 14, 5.
128. *Mishkat* 5, 4.
129. *Mishkat* 5, 5–6.
130. Q 20:55.
131. Cyril Glasse, "Tombs," *The Concise Encyclopedia of Islam* (San Francisco: Harper, 1989).
132. Q 36:50.
133. *Mishkat* 26, 18.
134. *Mishkat* 26, 10.
135. Q 7:8.
136. Q 101:6–11.
137. Q 57:20.
138. Jane Smith and Yvonne Haddad, *The Islamic Understanding of Death and Resurrection* (Albany: State University of New York Press, 1981), p. 84.
139. Smith and Haddad, p. 84.
140. *Mishkat* 26, 20.
141. Augustine, *City of God* 22, 15; *Mishkat* 26, 13.
142. George Moore, *Judaism in the First Centuries of the Christian Era* (New York: Schocken, 1971), vol. 2, p. 385.
143. Ezekiel 37:1–14.
144. Benjamin Mazar, ed., *Views of the Biblical World* (Jerusalem: International Publishing, 1960), vol. 3, p. 195.
145. Q 75:3–4.
146. Q 2:259.
147. Al-Bukhari, *Sahih* 60, 332.
148. Q 45:25.
149. I, p. 165.
150. I, p. 94.
151. I, p. 94.
152. Q 82:10–12.
153. Q 69:19–25.
154. Q 45:29–34.
155. Daniel 7:10.
156. Revelation 20:12.
157. 1 Corinthians 15:52.
158. E.g., Ephesians 1:20–21; Acts 7:55; Hebrews 12:2.
159. Luke 12:8; Romans 8:34.
160. Q 17:14.
161. Huston Smith, *The World's Religions* (San Francisco: Harper, 1991), p. 242.

162. Q 41:20–21.
163. Q 34:33.
164. Rahman, p. 120.
165. Q 34:28.
166. Q 75:22–23.
167. Al-Bukhari, *Sahih* 60, 80.
168. *Mishkat* 26, 14.
169. *Mishkat* 26, 13.
170. Gospel of Thomas 17.
171. *Mishkat* 5, 1.
172. William Phipps, "The Origin of Hospices/Hospitals," *Death Studies* 12 (1988): 94.
173. Matthew 25:37–40.
174. Q 4:93; Smith and Haddad, *The Islamic Understanding of Death and Resurrection*, p. 86.
175. *Mishkat* 24, 10.
176. *Mishkat* 1, 4.
177. *Mishkat* 1, 4.
178. Q 89:24.
179. Q 7:50, 53.
180. Q 39:59.
181. Luke 16:19–31.
182. Q 47:15.
183. Al-Bukhari, *Sahih* 76, 51.
184. *Mishkat* 26, 13.
185. *Mishkat* 20, 4.
186. *Mishkat* 16, 7.
187. Q 83:25.
188. Q 4:124, 33:73.
189. Q 43:70–71.
190. Q 44:54, 52:20, 55:72–76, 56:34–37, 78:33.
191. Jane Smith and Yvonne Haddad, "Women in the Afterlife," *Journal of the American Academy of Religion* 43 (1975): 49.
192. Ronald Bodley, *The Messenger* (New York: Greenwood, 1946), p. 96.
193. Q 56:35–36; *Mishkat* 24, 12.
194. Q 13:23, 40:8.
195. Smith and Haddad, *The Islamic Understanding of Death and Resurrection*, p. 165.
196. Cited in Fatima Mernissi, *Beyond the Veil* (Cambridge, MA: Schenkman, 1975), pp. 2–3.
197. John Glubb, *A Short History of the Arab Peoples* (New York: Stein & Day, 1969), p. 34.
198. Ephraim, *Hymns of Paradise* 3.
199. Tor Andrae, *Mohammed* (New York: Harper, 1960), pp. 87–88.

200. Q 9:34–35.
201. Q 46:20.
202. Jeremiah 32:35.
203. Jeremiah 7:32–33; Isaiah 66:24.
204. Q 4:56.
205. Q 2:80.
206. Q 11:106–7.
207. Luke 23:43.
208. Mark 1:14–15.
209. Genesis 3:19, 22.
210. Mark 8:36; John 3:16.
211. William Phipps, *The Wisdom and Wit of Rabbi Jesus* (Louisville: Westminster/ John Knox, 1993), pp. 128–31.
212. Matthew 7:9–11.
213. *Aboth* 5:22.
214. Matthew 10:28.
215. Romans 6:23; William Phipps, *Paul Against Supernaturalism* (New York: Philosophical Library, 1987), pp. 74–83.
216. Albert Nolan, *Jesus Before Christianity* (Maryknoll, NY: Orbis, 1978), p. 89.
217. Mark 12:18–23.
218. *Tobit* 3:8.
219. Deuteronomy 25:5.
220. Josephus, *Antiquities* 18, 16.
221. E.g., *Apocalypse of Baruch* 50:2.
222. Mark 12:24.
223. Mark 12:26.
224. Exodus 3:6.
225. Mark 12:27.
226. Luke 20:35.
227. Exodus 3:14–15.
228. Luke 20:35.
229. Luke 20:36.
230. Mark 12:25.
231. Mark 3:21, 31–35.
232. For an expansion of this exposition, see William Phipps, "Jesus on Marriage and the Afterlife," *The Christian Century* 102 (1985): 327–28.
233. Luke 16:20–22.
234. Matthew 8:11.

CHAPTER 9: *Enlargements*

1. Q 49:2–3.
2. Q 3:31.

3. Q 4:80.
4. Q 33:21.
5. Hans Kung, *Christianity and the World Religions* (Garden City, NY: Doubleday, 1986), p. 18.
6. I, p. 503.
7. Annemarie Schimmel, *And Muhammad Is His Messenger* (Chapel Hill: University of North Carolina Press, 1985), p. 32.
8. Maxime Rodinson, *Mohammed* (New York: Vintage, 1974), p. 308.
9. Al-Ghazali, *Ihya Ulum al-Din*, book 20, trans. James Robson in *The Muslim World* 45 (1955): 327.
10. Al-Busiri, *Burdah* 34, 38, 42–43 in Arthur Jeffery, ed., *A Reader on Islam* (The Hague: Mouton, 1962), pp. 609–10.
11. Kamal al-Din, *Ideal Prophet* (Woking, England: Muslim Mission and Literary Trust, 1956), p. 155.
12. Karen Armstrong, *Muhammad* (San Francisco: Harper, 1992), p. 262.
13. Armstrong, p. 263.
14. Qassim Jairazbhoy, *Muhammad "A Mercy to All the Nations"* (London: Luzac, 1937), p. 344.
15. Robert Gulick, *Muhammad the Educator* (Lahore: Institute of Islamic Culture, 1961), p. 95.
16. Ahmed Ali, *Al-Qur'an* (Princeton: Princeton University Press, 1988), pp. 96, 239, 311.
17. Lamin Sanneh, "Muhammad, Prophet of Islam, and Jesus Christ, Image of God: a Personal Testimony," *International Bulletin of Missionary Research* (October 1984): 170.
18. Sanneh, p. 170.
19. Hamilton Gibb, *Mohammedanism* (London: Oxford, 1949).
20. Rafiq Zakaria, *Muhammad and the Quran* (New York: Penguin Books, 1991), p. 7.
21. Wilfred Smith, *Modern Islam in India* (Lahore, 1947), p. 24.
22. Ninian Smart, *The World's Religions* (Englewood Cliffs, NJ: Prentice-Hall, 1989), p. 279.
23. C. L. Geddes, *Guide to Reference Books for Islamic Studies* (Denver: American Institute for Islamic Studies, 1985), p. 102.
24. Rodinson, p. 299.
25. Rodinson, p. 308.
26. Chrysostom, *Homilies* 31.
27. Francis Robinson, *Atlas of the Islamic World* (New York: Facts on File, 1982), p. 191.
28. Cyril Glasse, "Mawlid an-Nabi," *The Concise Encyclopedia of Islam* (San Francisco: Harper, 1989).
29. Rodinson, pp. 310–11.
30. Exodus 4:3; Q 7:107.

31. Q 27:22–44.
32. Ali Dashti, *Twenty-Three Years* (London: Allen & Unwin, 1985), pp. 1, 26.
33. Q 54:1.
34. Glasse, "Moon."
35. Al-Bukhari, *Sahih* 60, 287.
36. I, p. 178.
37. Ehsan Yar-Shater, ed., *The History of al-Tabari* (Albany: State University of New York Press, 1988), vol. 6, p. 67.
38. I, p. 246.
39. I, pp. 451–52.
40. Exodus 17:5–6; Numbers 20:11.
41. I, p. 605.
42. Al-Bukhari, *Sahih* 17, 13.
43. Al-Bukhari, *Sahih* 17, 13.
44. Q 70:3–4; Genesis 28:12.
45. Q 17:92–93.
46. I, p. 135.
47. I, p. 135.
48. I, p. 183.
49. *Mishkat* 26, 23.
50. Celsus, *On the True Doctrine* (New York: Oxford, 1987), p. 95.
51. I, pp. 185–186.
52. Yar-Shater, vol. 6, p. 79.
53. Al-Bukhari, *Sahih* 55, 43.
54. I, pp. 182–86.
55. Q 17:1.
56. Q 23:86.
57. The paintings are published in Marie-Rose Seguy, *The Miraculous Journey of Mahomet* (New York: Braziller, 1977).
58. Arthur Jeffery, ed., *Islam: Muhammad and His Religion* (New York: Bobbs-Merrill, 1958), p. 45.
59. Luke 9:32.
60. Matthew 17:9.
61. See, for example, John Calvin, *Commentary on a Harmony of the Evangelists* (Grand Rapids: Eerdmans, 1949), vol. 2, pp. 310–11.
62. Aquinas, *Summa contra Gentiles* 1, 6.
63. Mohamed al-Nowaihi, "Toward a Re-evaluation of Muhammad," *The Muslim World* 60 (1970): 300–1.
64. I, p. 69.
65. Glasse, "Nur Muhammadi."
66. Luke 1:35.
67. Luke 2:25–32; Isaiah 49:6.
68. Q 94:1–3.

69. I, p. 72.
70. I, p. 81.
71. I, p. 80.
72. Acts 3:13, 26; 4:27; 1 Peter 2:13–25.
73. Mark 12:35–37.
74. Thomas Sheehan, *The First Coming* (New York: Random House, 1986), p. 5.
75. Luke 1:33.
76. Matthew 2:2.
77. Michael Grant, *Jesus* (New York: Scribner's, 1977), p. 72; John Meier, *A Marginal Jew* (New York: Doubleday, 1991), p. 407; Sheehan, p. 52.
78. Mark 6:1; John 4:44.
79. John 1:46.
80. John 7:41–42.
81. Micah 5:2.
82. Luke 2:1, 11; 23:25; Acts 25:26; George Buttrick, ed., *The Interpreter's Dictionary of the Bible* (Nashville: Abingdon, 1962), vol. 4, p. 177.
83. 1 Corinthians 1:22.
84. William Phipps, *Paul Against Supernaturalism* (New York: Philosophical Library, 1987), pp. 21–22.
85. Mark 15:32; Luke 23:8.
86. 1 Corinthians 1:18–24.
87. Phipps, pp. 23–35.
88. Mark 5:22–23; Matthew 9:18.
89. 1 Kings 17:8–24; Luke 7:11–16, 8:49–56, 9:14–16.
90. Infancy Gospel of Thomas 4, 13.
91. The Gospel of Pseudo-Matthew 22.
92. The Gospel of Pseudo-Matthew 22.
93. C. Milo Connick, *Jesus, the Man, the Mission, and the Message* (Englewood Cliffs, NJ: Prentice-Hall, 1963), p. 281.
94. Irenaeus, *Against Heresies* 1, 24, 4.
95. Mark 15:21.
96. "Apostles' Creed," in John Leith, ed., *Creeds of the Churches* (New York: Doubleday, 1963), p. 24.
97. Francis Burkitt, *The Religion of the Manichees*, (Cambridge, England: Cambridge University Press, 1925), p. 41.
98. Kenneth Latourette, *A History of Christianity* (London: Eyre and Spottiswoode, 1954), pp. 282–83, 319–22.
99. John Trimingham, *Christianity Among the Arabs in Pre-Islamic Times* (London: Longman, 1979), p. 85.
100. Q 4:157.
101. I, p. 271.
102. Q 19:21.
103. Mark 12:29–30; Deuteronomy 6:4–5.

104. Exodus 20:3.
105. Latourette, pp. 43, 122–89.
106. Mark 12:9.
107. Mark 13:35.
108. Matthew 21:30.
109. E.g., Genesis 24:9, 43:20.
110. Mark 12:36–37.
111. Psalm 110:1.
112. Mark 11:3.
113. Hosea 11:9.
114. 2 Samuel 7:34.
115. Psalm 2:7.
116. Psalm 89:26.
117. Hans Kung, *On Being a Christian* (Garden City, NY: Doubleday, 1976) p. 390.
118. E.g., Mark 8:31, 9:31, 10:33–34; Matthew 8:20.
119. Mark 10:45; Luke 22:27; John 13:14–16.
120. Cp. Mark 14:61–62 with Matthew 26:64 and Luke 22:70.
121. Luke 16:8; John 12:36.
122. Romans 8:16–23.
123. Q 5:116.
124. Leith, p. 30.
125. Glasse, "*Adhan.*"
126. Deuteronomy 6:5.
127. Epiphanius, *Against Heresies* 62, 1; quoted in Henry Bettenson, *Documents of the Christian Church* (Oxford: Oxford University Press, 1947), p. 54.
128. John 8:12.
129. Latourette, pp. 152–64.
130. Augustine, *On Faith and the Creed* 9, 17.
131. Q 5:73, 116.
132. Q 5:117.
133. *Mishkat* 1, 1.
134. Q 17:110.
135. Epiphanius, *Panarion* 79.
136. Epiphanius, *Panarion* 79.
137. Nestorius, *Bazaar of Heracleides* 1, 3.
138. Walter Abbott, ed., *The Documents of Vatican II* (New York: Association Press, 1966), p. 94.
139. Hans Kung, *On Being a Christian*, p. 461.
140. Jeremiah 44:19.
141. James Hastings, ed., "Abyssinia," *Encyclopedia of Religion and Ethics* (New York: Scribner's, 1928).
142. Q 37:152–54.

143. Q 53:21.
144. David McKain, ed., *Christianity: Some Non-Christian Appraisals* New York: McGraw-Hill, 1964), p. 244.
145. James Ross and Mary McLaughlin, eds., *The Portable Medieval Reader* (New York: Viking, 1949), p. 451.
146. Q 23:13–14.
147. Muhammad Asad, *The Message of the Quran* (London: Brill, 1980), p. 262.
148. E.g., Q 4:116, 6:14–15, 10:66–70.
149. Q 9:30–31.
150. Gordon Newby, *A History of the Jews of Arabia* (Columbia: University of South Carolina Press, 1988), p. 61.
151. John 17:11.
152. Mark 10:8.
153. *Mishkat* 26, 19.
154. E. R. Dodds, *Pagan and Christian in an Age of Anxiety* (New York: Norton, 1970, pp. 124–46.
155. Morris Jastrow, *The Religion of Babylonia and Assyria* (Boston: Ginn, 1898), pp. 356–73.
156. Deuteronomy 4:19, 18:10.

CHAPTER 10:   *Conclusion*

1. Seyyed Nasr, *Islamic Life and Thought* (Albany: State University of New York Press, 1981), p. 209.
2. John Leith, ed., *Creeds of the Churches* (New York: Doubleday, 1963), p. 24.
3. Q 4:159.
4. *Mishkat* 26, 6.
5. *Mishkat* 26, 6.
6. Maulvie Ali, *Muhammad and Christ* (Madras: SPCK, 1921), p. 140.
7. Q 3:112.
8. Mark 15:15–20; Luke 23:34.
9. *Mishkat* 25, 5.
10. Fazlur Rahman, *Major Themes of the Qur'an* (Minneapolis: Bibliotheca Islamica, 1980), pp. 86–87; Cyril Glasse, "Isa," *Concise Encyclopaedia of Islam* (San Francisco: Harper, 1989).
11. Q 37:116.
12. Q 19:15.
13. Luke 11:50–51.
14. Luke 11:47.
15. 1 Corinthians 1:23.
16. Deuteronomy 21:23.
17. Proverbs 12:21.

18. Tim Dowley, ed., *The History of Christianity* (Grand Rapids: Eerdmans, 1977), p. 57.

19. Cicero, *Against Verres* 66.

20. Blaise Pascal, *Pensées* 598.

21. Kenneth Cragg, *The Call of the Minaret* (New York: Oxford, 1964), p. 302.

22. Hans Kung, *On Being a Christian*, p. 335.

23. Niccolo Machiavelli, *The Prince* 6.

24. Max Weber, *The Sociology of Religion* (Boston: Beacon, 1922), p. 262.

25. Q 17:15, 6:164, 53:38.

26. Isaiah 53:5.

27. Cragg, pp. 298–99.

28. Mark 15:34; Matthew 27:46.

29. M. T. Al-Hilari, "Biblical Evidence of Jesus Being a Servant of God," in Muhammad Khan, ed., *Sahih Al-Bukhari* (Chicago: Kazi, 1979), vol. 1, pp. lxi–lxiv.

30. Josephus, *Antiquities* 18:63; Tacitus, *Annals* 15:44.

31. John Crossan, *Jesus* (San Francisco: Harper, 1994), p. 145.

32. W. Montgomery Watt, *Islam and Christianity Today* (London: Routledge and Kegan Paul, 1983), p. 144.

33. Q 19:33.

34. Q 4:157.

35. Q 2:154.

36. Q 3:169.

37. Quoted in Mahmoud Ayoub, *The Qur'an and Its Interpreters* (Albany: State University of New York Press, 1992), vol. 2, p. 379.

38. Q 2:2.

39. Q 7:40.

40. "Thirteen Principles of Faith," Cecil Roth, ed., *The New Standard Jewish Encyclopedia* (New York: Doubleday, 1970).

41. William Sweet, *The Story of Religion in America* (New York: Harper, 1950), p. 407.

42. George Gallup, "Americans and the Bible," *Bible Review* (June 1990): 37.

43. 1 Timothy 2:14; Genesis 3:17; Romans 5:12.

44. Ecclesiastes 12:11–14; Robert Gordis, *The Wisdom of Koheleth* (London: East and West Library, 1950), p. 30.

45. Mark 16:18; Bruce Metzger, *A Textual Commentary on the Greek New Testament* (New York: United Bible Societies, 1971), pp. 122–26; Vincent Taylor, *The Gospel According to St. Mark* (London: Macmillan, 1963), p. 160.

46. Cp. Q 3:35, 19:28–34 with Numbers 26:59.

47. Matthew 5:21–48.

48. Luke 1:1–4.

49. 1 Timothy 2:11–15.

50. Q 3:19.
51. Q 6:163.
52. Huston Smith, *The World's Religions* (San Francisco: Harper, 1991), p. 240.
53. "Islam at a Glance," (Plainfield, IN: Islamic Teaching Center).
54. Q 5:3.
55. Q 21:51–71.
56. Q 2:127–29.
57. Genesis 12:3.
58. Q 34:28.
59. Isaiah 51:1–2.
60. Matthew 3:8–9.
61. Romans 4:11.
62. Galatians 3:10.
63. Galatians 3:7–18.
64. Hebrews 11:9–10, 12:1–2.
65. Q 4:153, 7:150, 20:88–94.
66. Q 3:67.
67. Q 3:68.
68. I, p. 3.
69. Q 21:55–64.
70. Al-Bukhari, *Sahih* 55, 9.
71. Genesis 12:10–20.
72. Genesis 22:1–14.
73. William Phipps, *Assertive Biblical Women* (New York: Greenwood, 1992), pp. 9–17.
74. Micah 6:8.
75. Q 6:87.
76. Genesis 6:9.
77. Q 6:161.
78. Q 10:89–90.
79. Q 19:36.
80. Exodus 23:2.
81. Luke 6:26.
82. Q 6:116.
83. Q 90:8–20.
84. Acts 9:2.
85. Luke 3:16.
86. Isaiah 40:3–4; Luke 3:4–5.
87. Matthew 7:13–14; cp. Proverbs 14:2.
88. Luke 9:31.
89. John 12:35, 14:6.
90. Romans 6:4.

91. Hebrews 10:20.
92. Charles Swezey, "Christian Ethics as Walking the Way," *Affirmation* (Fall 1991): 80.
93. Jurgen Moltmann, *The Way of Jesus Christ* (London: Student Christian Movement, 1990), pp. xiii–xiv.
94. Paul Van Buren, *Discerning the Way* (New York: Seabury, 1980), pp. 3, 20.
95. Q 29:46.
96. Q 3:52.
97. Al-Bukhari, *Sahih* 2, 1.
98. Cyril Glasse, "*Adhan*," *The Concise Encyclopedia of Islam* (San Francisco: Harper, 1989).
99. Q 5:18.
100. Q 2:111, 113.
101. Q 2:94.
102. Q 57:29.
103. Rahman, p. 165.
104. *Mishkat* 26, 17.
105. Q 2:136.
106. Q 2:62.
107. Muhammad Asad, *The Message of the Qur'an* (London: Brill, 1980), p. 14.
108. Q 22:17.
109. Q 2:112.
110. Asad, p. 24.
111. Leroy Rouner, ed., *Religious Pluralism* (Notre Dame: University of Notre Dame Press, 1984), p. 195.
112. Q 109.
113. James Hastings, ed., "Muhammad," *Encyclopaedia of Religion and Ethics* (New York: Scribner's, 1928).
114. Q 3:85; Ayoub, vol. 2, p. 241.
115. Q 98:6.
116. Q 61:8–9.
117. Q 9:29.
118. *Mishkat* 24, 1.
119. Al-Bukhari, *Sahih* 60, 80.
120. Amos 3:2.
121. Amos 9:7.
122. Psalm 87:5.
123. Augustine, *The City of God* 17, 16.
124. Augustine, *The City of God* 21, 20–21; *Sermons on the Psalms* 87, 1.
125. Nehemiah 13:30.
126. Ezra 10:10–12.
127. Genesis 38:2, 41:45; Exodus 2:21.
128. Mark 9:39–40.

129. Mark 1:15.
130. *Bible Review* 10 (June 1994): 34.
131. Clive Lewis, *Mere Christianity* (New York: Macmillan, 1955), p. 29.
132. Karl Barth, *Church Dogmatics* (Edinburgh: Clark, 1956), vol. 1, part 2, pp. 326, 343–44.
133. Carl Braaten, *No Other Gospel!* (Minneapolis: Fortress, 1992), p. 57.
134. Braaten, p. 100.
135. 1 Corinthians 13:9.
136. Reinhold Niebuhr, *The Nature and Destiny of Man* (New York: Scribner's, 1949), part 2, p. 217.
137. John Bunyan, *Grace Abounding* (rewritten in modern English) paragraph 97.
138. Isaiah 55:8.
139. Q 2:255.
140. The Westminster Shorter Catechism (London, 1647), question 4.
141. Arnold Toynbee, *Christianity Among the Religions of the World* (New York: Scribner's, 1957), p. 96.
142. David Brewster, *Memoirs of Newton*, (1855), vol. 2, ch. 27.
143. Isaac Newton, *Principia Mathematica* (1686), Bk. 3, General Scholium.
144. Revelation 3:7; Q 3:86.
145. John 3:8.
146. 1 Corinthians 13:12–13.
147. John Hick and Brian Hebblethwaite, eds., *Christianity and Other Religions* (Philadelphia: Fortress, 1981), pp. 180–81.
148. Wilfred Smith, *Toward a World Theology* (Philadelphia: Westminster, 1981), p. 177.
149. Quoted in Hans Kung, *Christianity and the World Religions* (Garden City, NY: Doubleday, 1986), p. 23.
150. John 1:9; Justin Martyr, *Apology* 2, 13.
151. *Nostra Aetate*, Walter Abbott, ed., *The Documents of Vatican II* (New York: Association Press, 1966), pp. 662–63.
152. Hans Kung and Jurgen Moltman, *Christianity Among World Religions* (Edinburgh: Clark, 1986), p. 124.
153. Q 9:33.
154. Matthew 28:19.
155. Jacques Jomier, *How to Understand Islam* (New York: Crossroad, 1989), p. 133.
156. Q 5:48.
157. Matthew 7:20.
158. Gotthold Lessing, *Nathan Der Weise* act 3, scene 7.
159. Lessing, act 3, scene 7.
160. Lessing, act 3, scene 7.
161. John 7:17.

INDEXES

SCRIPTURAL TEXTS

The Bible